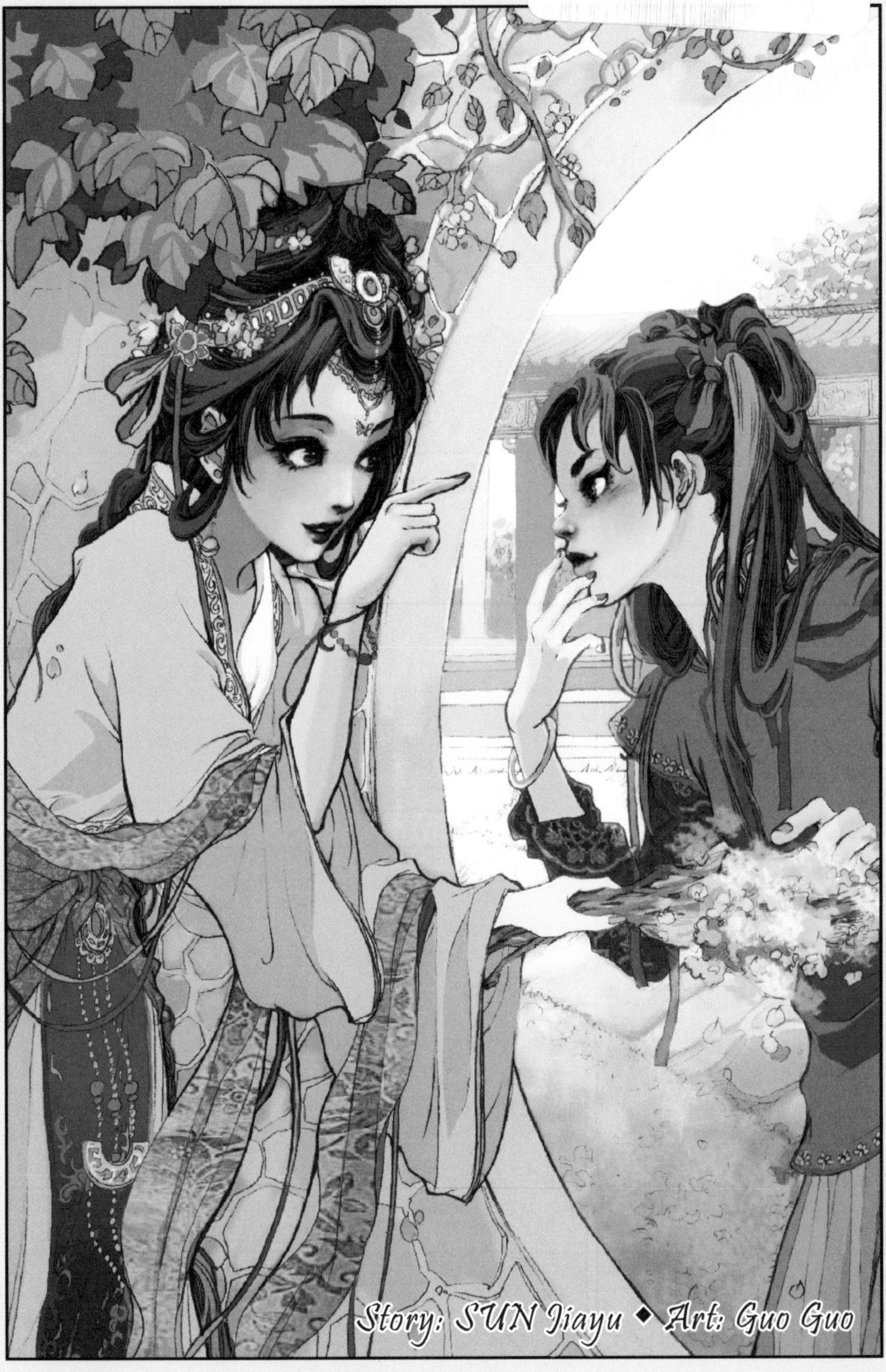
Story: SUN Jiayu ◆ Art: Guo Guo

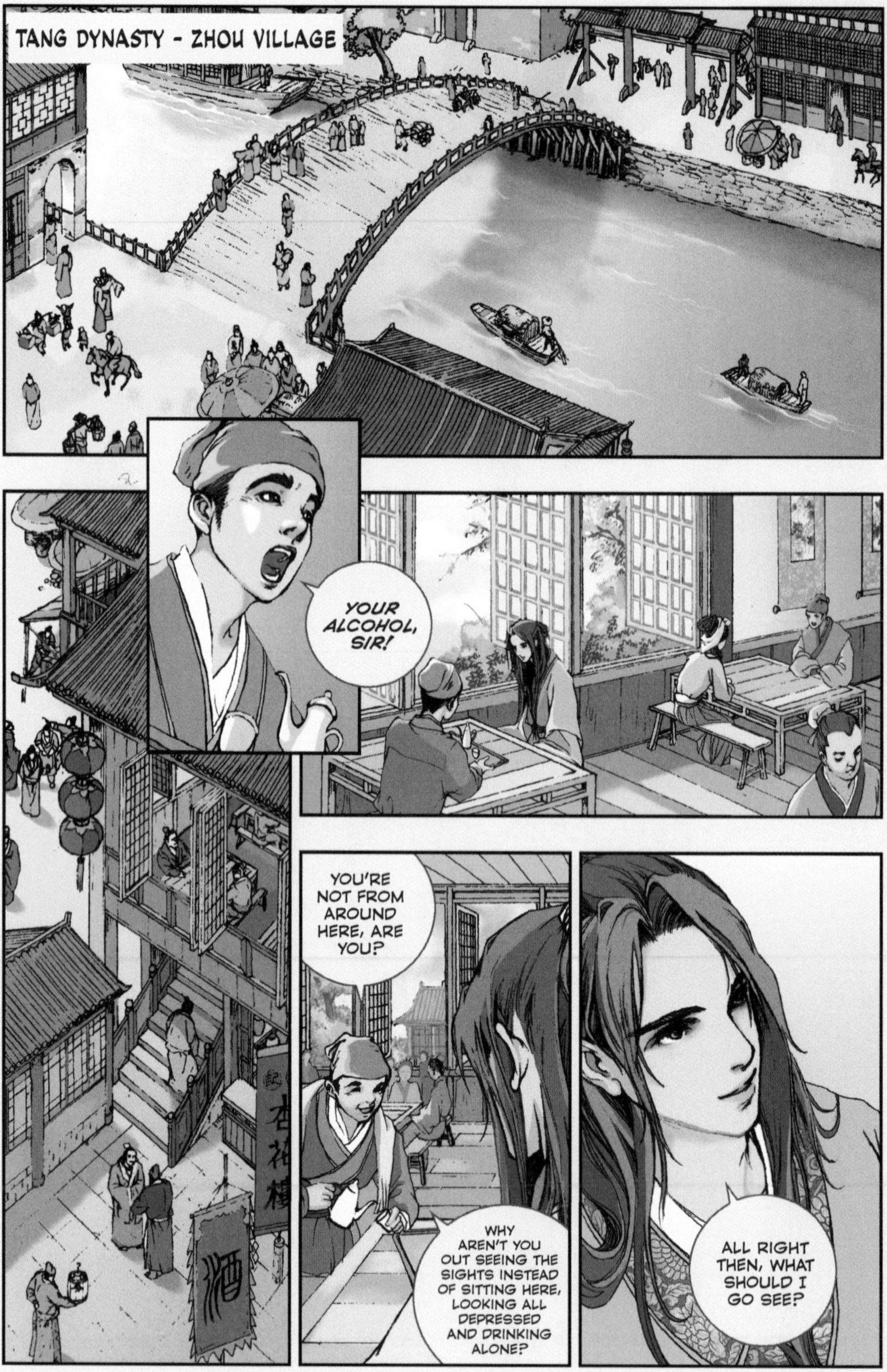
TANG DYNASTY - ZHOU VILLAGE
YOUR ALCOHOL, SIR!
酒
YOU'RE NOT FROM AROUND HERE, ARE YOU?
WHY AREN'T YOU OUT SEEING THE SIGHTS INSTEAD OF SITTING HERE, LOOKING ALL DEPRESSED AND DRINKING ALONE?
ALL RIGHT THEN, WHAT SHOULD I GO SEE?

西厢记

the History of the West Wing

西 Xi: West 厢 Xiang: Wing 记 Ji: History

Xixiang Ji can be translated literally as "The History of the West Wing."

If there exists anywhere a singular example of classical Chinese theater in the *zaju** style, this is it.
At least in part, the play was written by WANG Shifu, a playwright from the Yuan Mongol period (A.D. 1279-1638). It seems that he, in turn, was influenced by *Yingying Zhuan*, a fable by YUAN Zhen (779-831). In this tale, the author relates the various romantic setbacks of the beautiful Yingying, who gives herself to a somewhat frivolous student before they are married. WANG Shifu's adaptation is much more wholesome and constitutes one of the most beautiful traditional love stories ever written. It has become a central work in China and has been translated into English by Stephen H. West (published as *The Story of the Western Wing* by University of California Press).

The "west wing" in the title is where the mother and daughter of the tale reside as guests of the temple's head monk, who was a friend of their late husband and father respectively. The daughter is accompanied by a young servant, HONG Niang, who has served the daughter since childhood. She becomes the link between the two lovers, helping them to fulfill their mutual desire for happiness. She has become so famous that, in China today, *hongnianging* means "playing the matchmaker."

Though SUN Jiayu's graphic novel is heavily influenced by WANG Shifu's play, the names of the main characters have been slightly altered (for example, Yingying has become YE Pianpian, which means "beautiful and elegant woman"). And the story takes place during the Tang Dynasty (618-907) in the village of Pu Zhou (nowadays known as Yong Ji), which is in the province of Shan Xi.

Here, then, we proudly present a true treasure (*zhen bao*) of classical Chinese literature further elevated by the artistic talent of the young Guo Guo . . .

---

*Zaju: a form of Chinese drama in four acts that alternates between singing and dialogue.

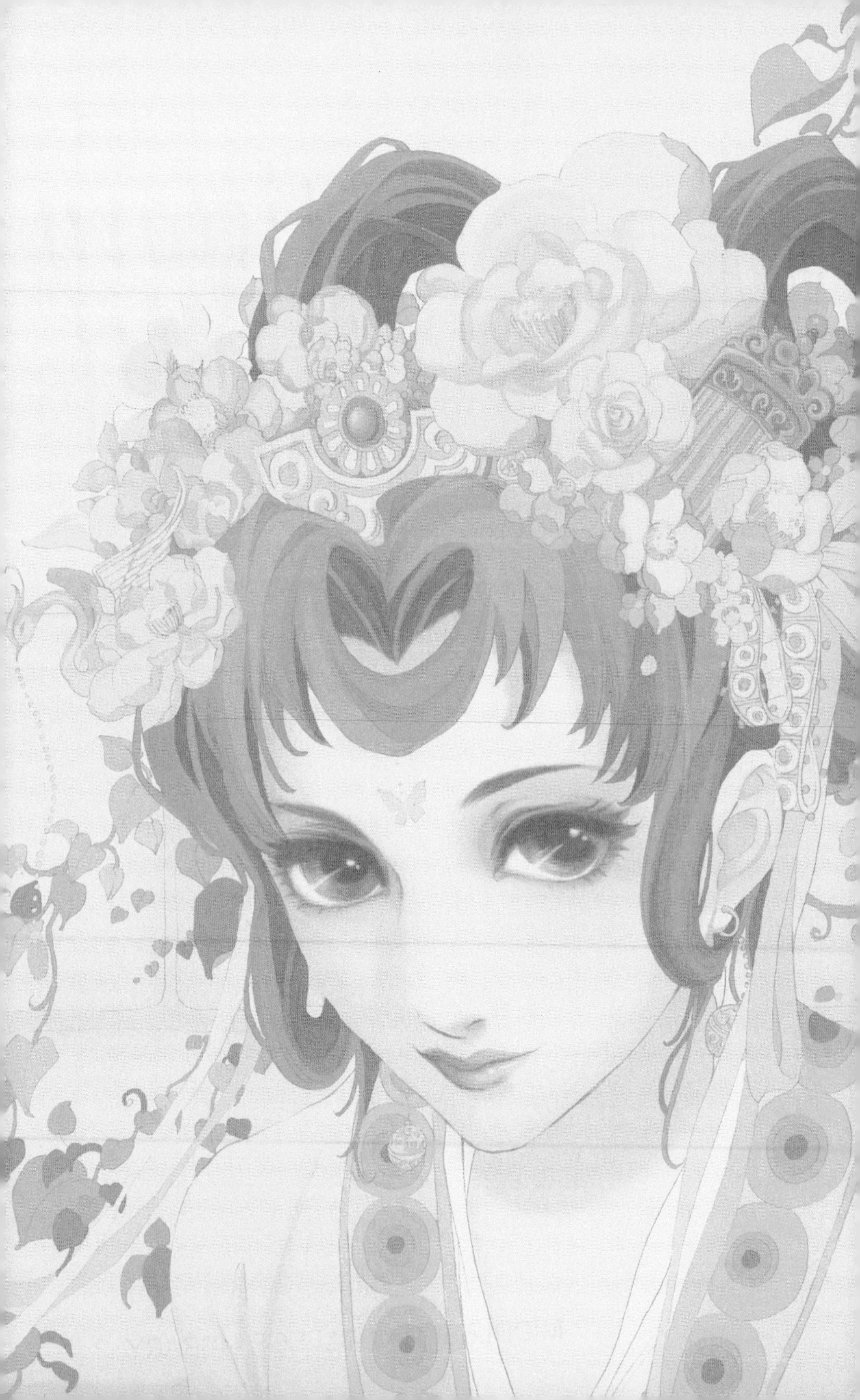

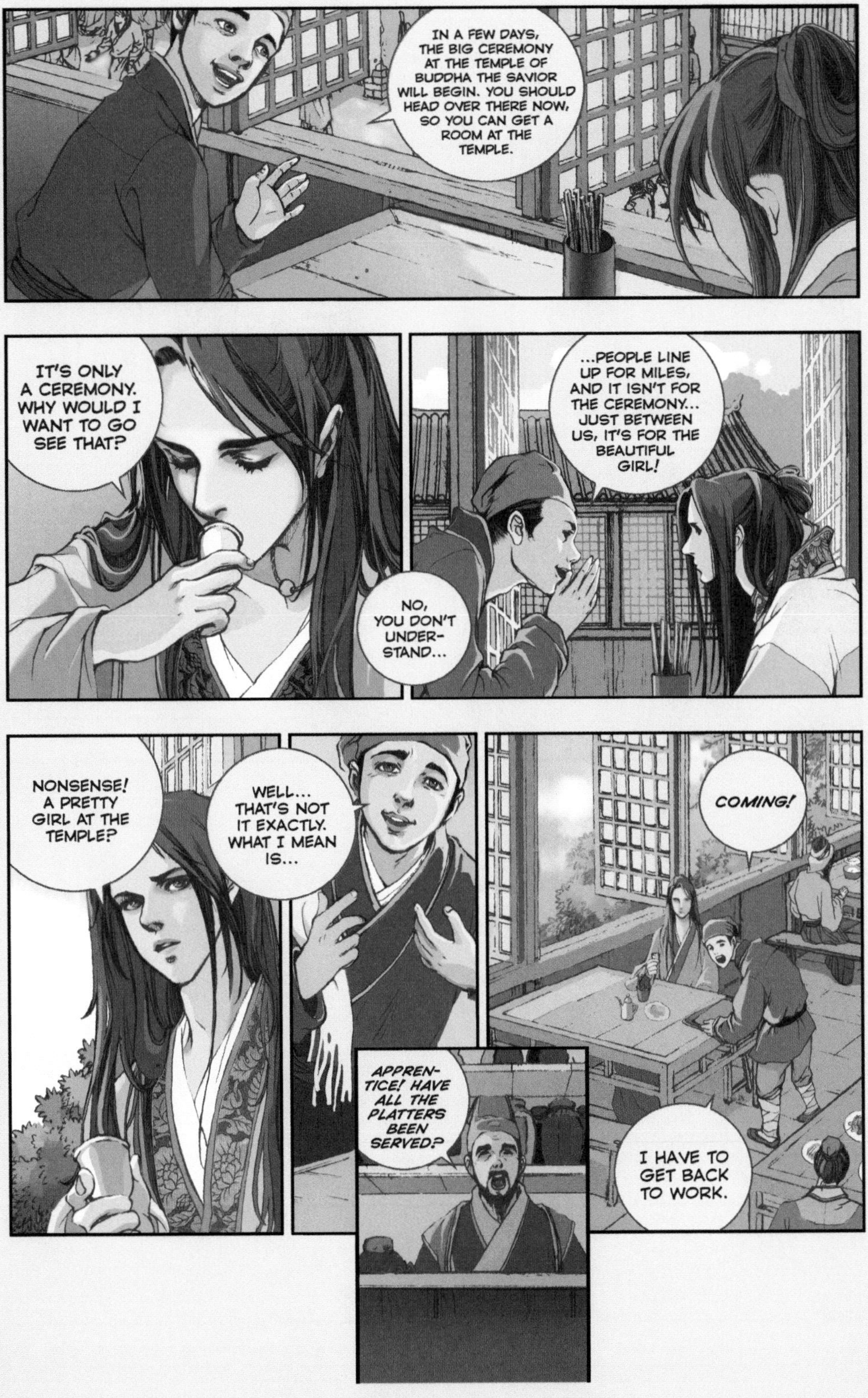
IN A FEW DAYS, THE BIG CEREMONY AT THE TEMPLE OF BUDDHA THE SAVIOR WILL BEGIN. YOU SHOULD HEAD OVER THERE NOW, SO YOU CAN GET A ROOM AT THE TEMPLE.
IT'S ONLY A CEREMONY. WHY WOULD I WANT TO GO SEE THAT?
...PEOPLE LINE UP FOR MILES, AND IT ISN'T FOR THE CEREMONY... JUST BETWEEN US, IT'S FOR THE BEAUTIFUL GIRL!
NO, YOU DON'T UNDER-STAND...
NONSENSE! A PRETTY GIRL AT THE TEMPLE?
WELL... THAT'S NOT IT EXACTLY. WHAT I MEAN IS...
COMING!
I HAVE TO GET BACK TO WORK.
APPREN-TICE! HAVE ALL THE PLATTERS BEEN SERVED?

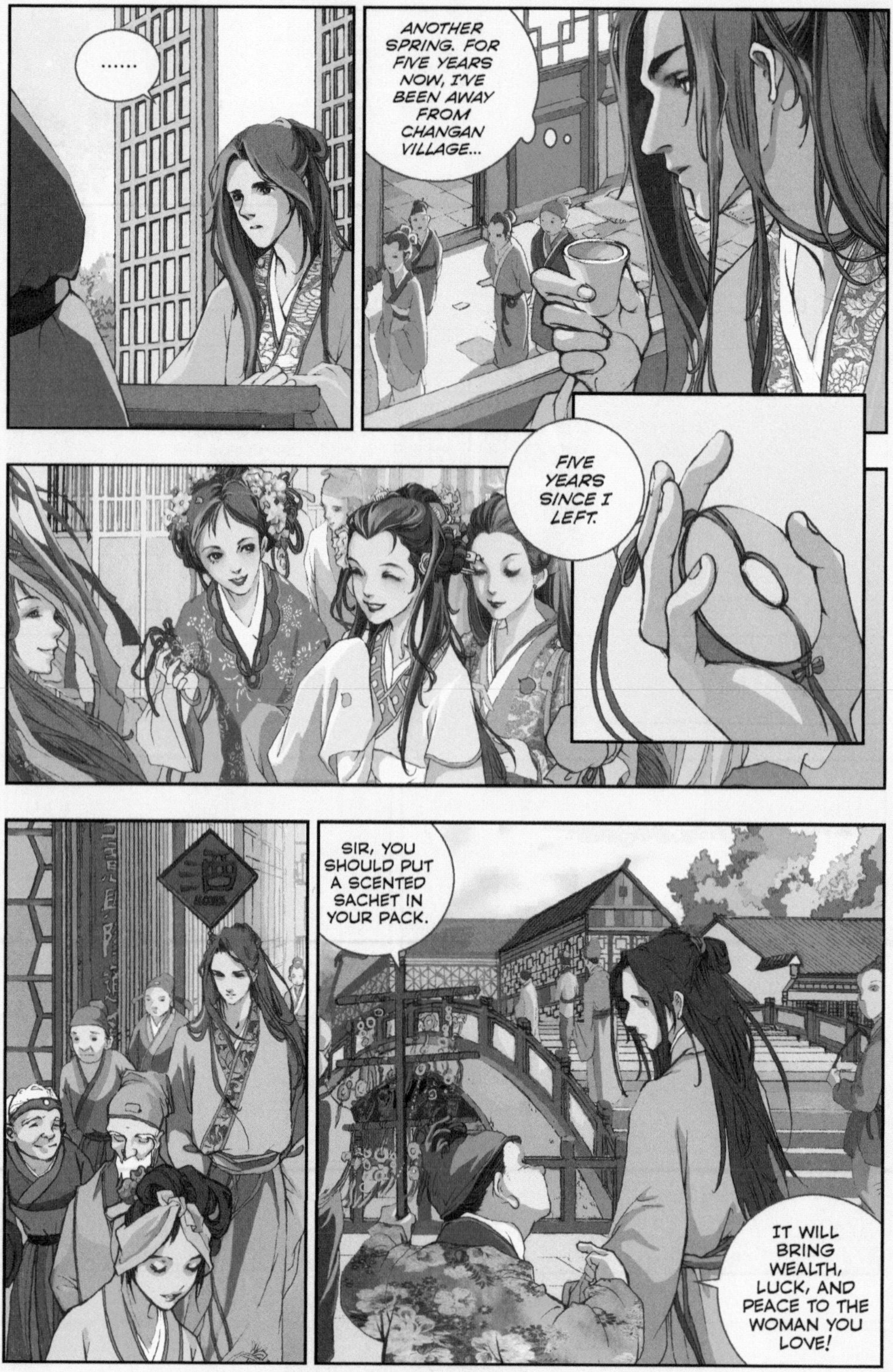
......
ANOTHER SPRING. FOR FIVE YEARS NOW, I'VE BEEN AWAY FROM CHANGAN VILLAGE...
FIVE YEARS SINCE I LEFT.
SIR, YOU SHOULD PUT A SCENTED SACHET IN YOUR PACK.
IT WILL BRING WEALTH, LUCK, AND PEACE TO THE WOMAN YOU LOVE!

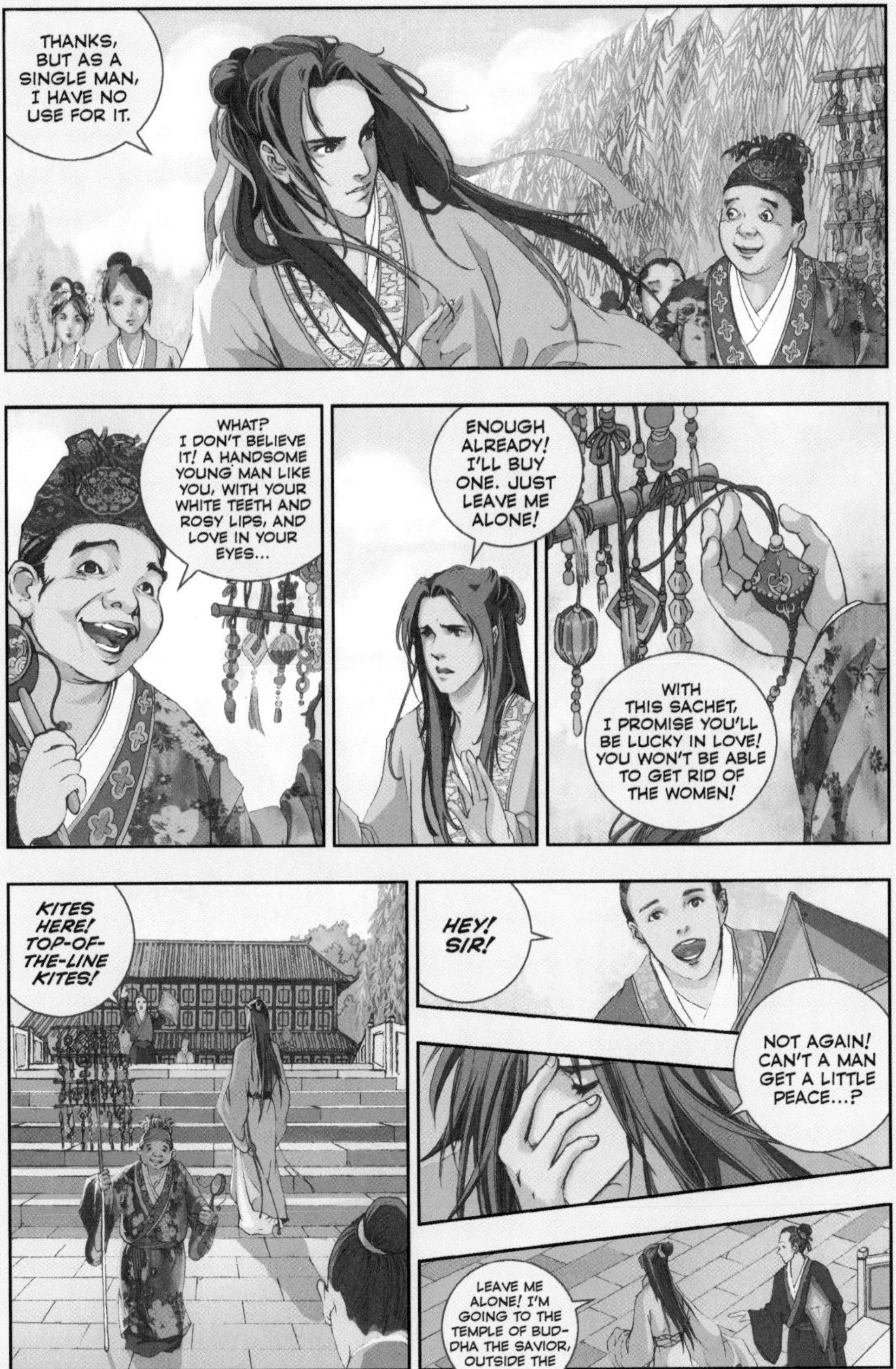
THANKS, BUT AS A SINGLE MAN, I HAVE NO USE FOR IT.
WHAT? I DON'T BELIEVE IT! A HANDSOME YOUNG MAN LIKE YOU, WITH YOUR WHITE TEETH AND ROSY LIPS, AND LOVE IN YOUR EYES...
ENOUGH ALREADY! I'LL BUY ONE. JUST LEAVE ME ALONE!
WITH THIS SACHET, I PROMISE YOU'LL BE LUCKY IN LOVE! YOU WON'T BE ABLE TO GET RID OF THE WOMEN!
KITES HERE! TOP-OF-THE-LINE KITES!
HEY! SIR!
NOT AGAIN! CAN'T A MAN GET A LITTLE PEACE...?
LEAVE ME ALONE! I'M GOING TO THE TEMPLE OF BUD-DHA THE SAVIOR, OUTSIDE THE WALLS.

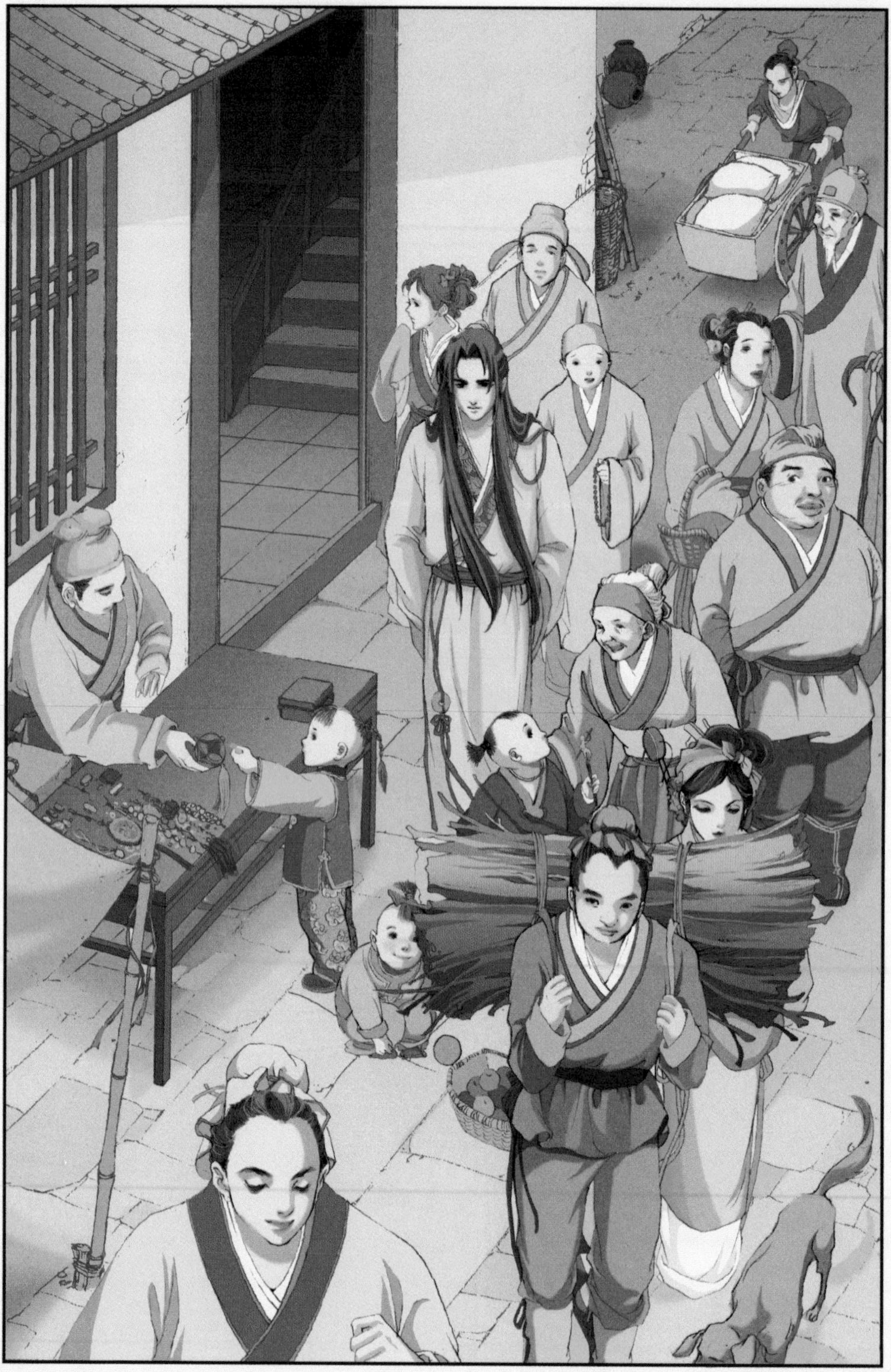

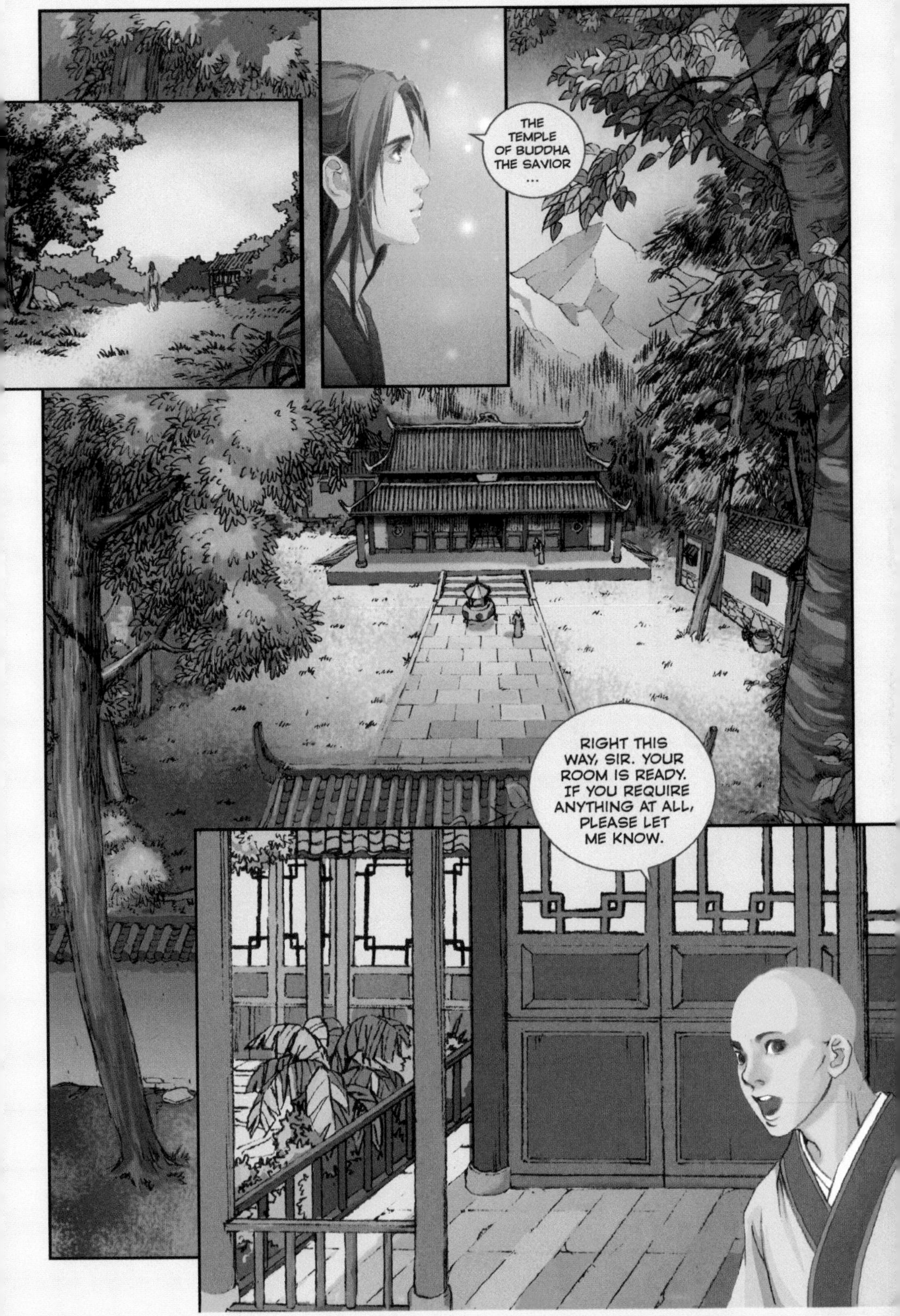
THE TEMPLE OF BUDDHA THE SAVIOR ...
RIGHT THIS WAY, SIR. YOUR ROOM IS READY. IF YOU REQUIRE ANYTHING AT ALL, PLEASE LET ME KNOW.

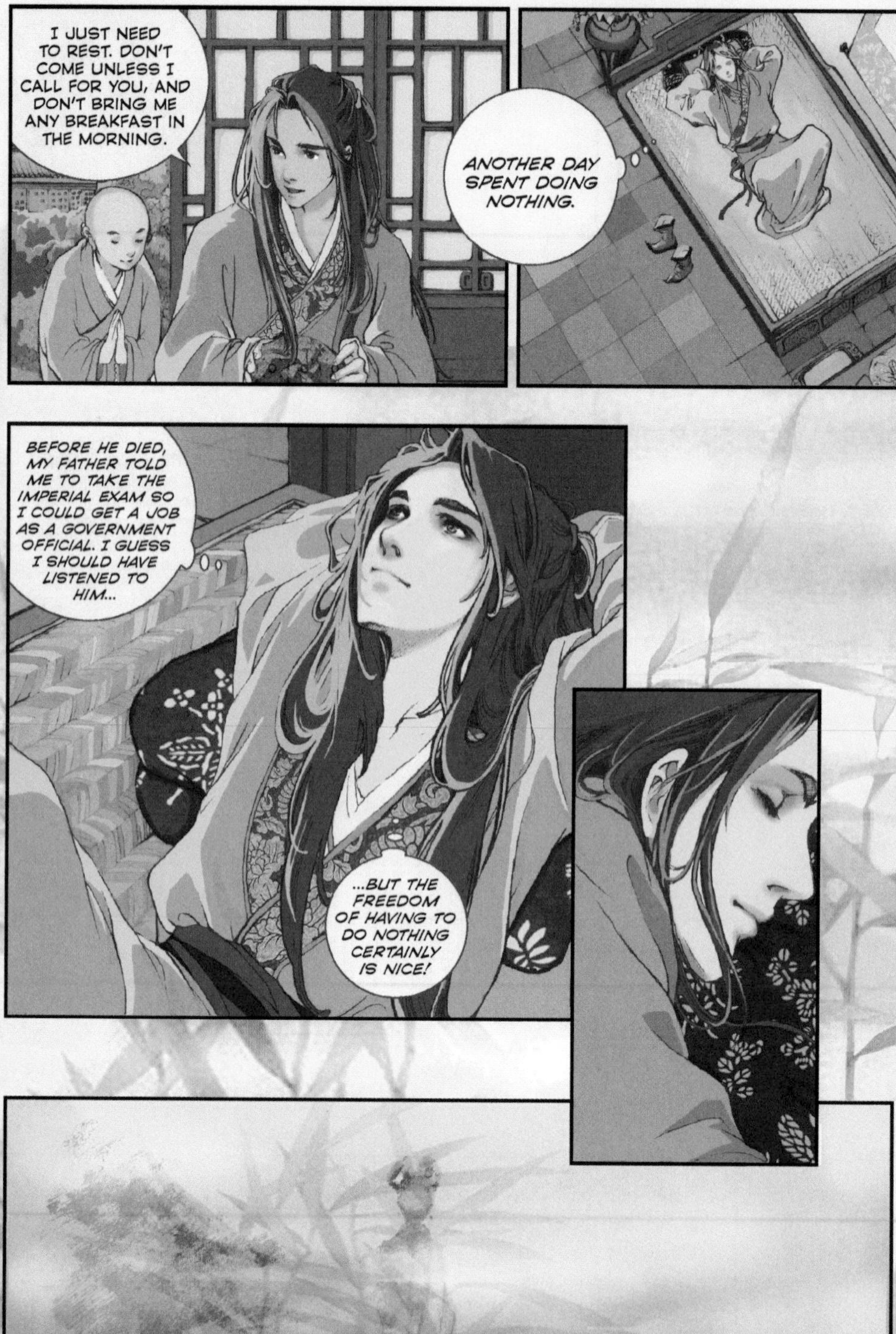
I JUST NEED TO REST. DON'T COME UNLESS I CALL FOR YOU, AND DON'T BRING ME ANY BREAKFAST IN THE MORNING.
ANOTHER DAY SPENT DOING NOTHING.
BEFORE HE DIED, MY FATHER TOLD ME TO TAKE THE IMPERIAL EXAM SO I COULD GET A JOB AS A GOVERNMENT OFFICIAL. I GUESS I SHOULD HAVE LISTENED TO HIM...
...BUT THE FREEDOM OF HAVING TO DO NOTHING CERTAINLY IS NICE!

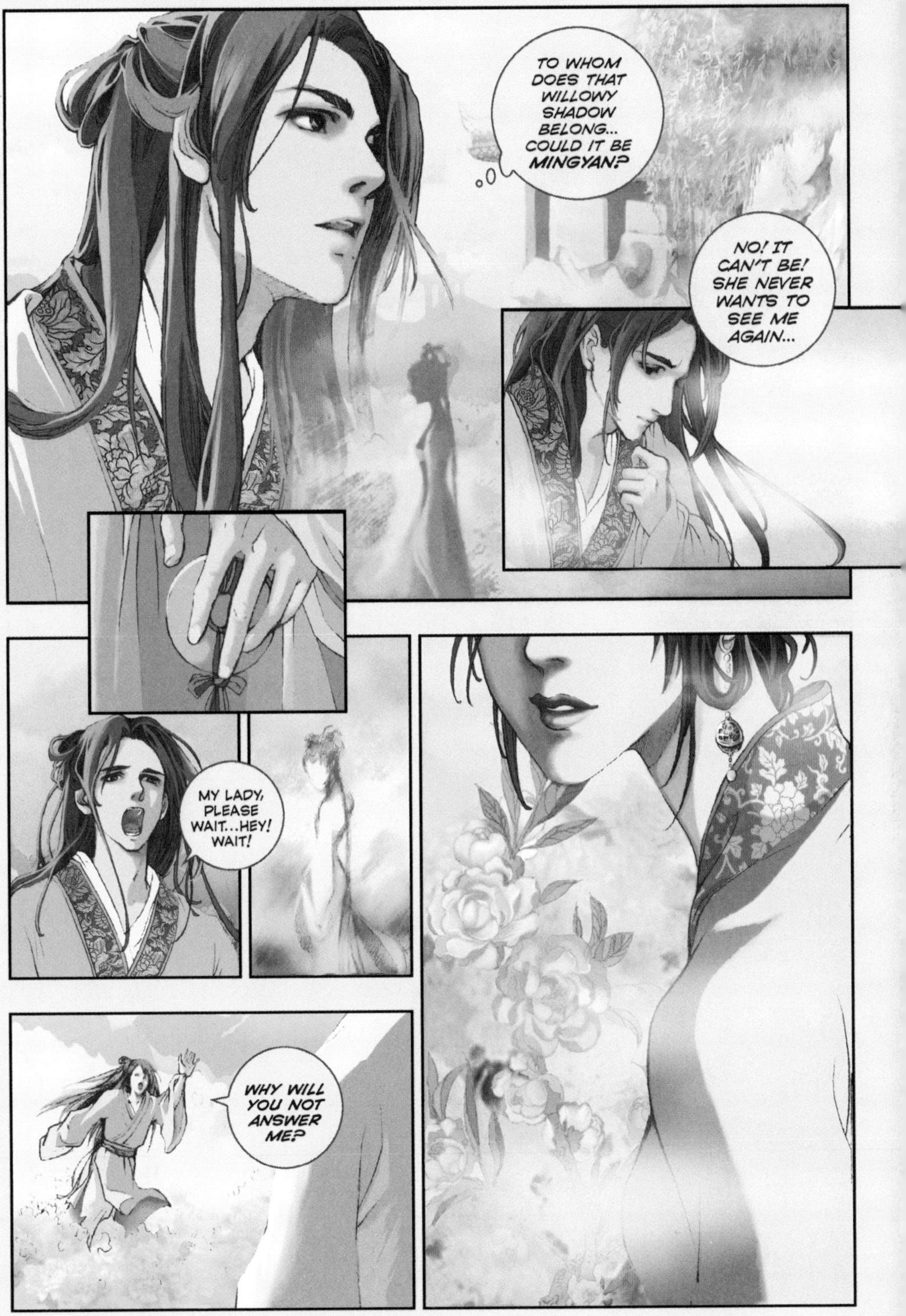
TO WHOM DOES THAT WILLOWY SHADOW BELONG... COULD IT BE MINGYAN?
NO! IT CAN'T BE! SHE NEVER WANTS TO SEE ME AGAIN...
MY LADY, PLEASE WAIT...HEY! WAIT!
WHY WILL YOU NOT ANSWER ME?

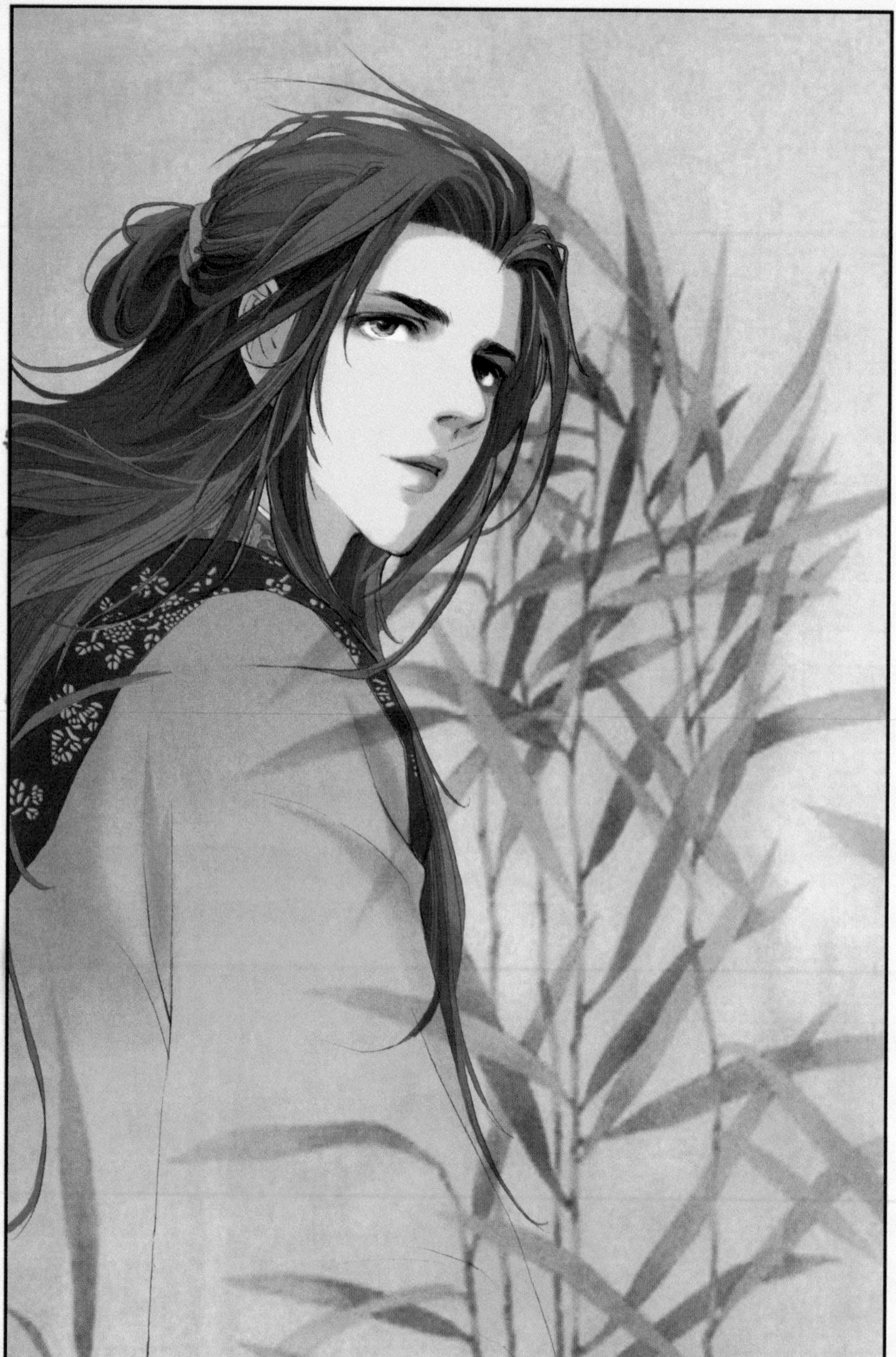

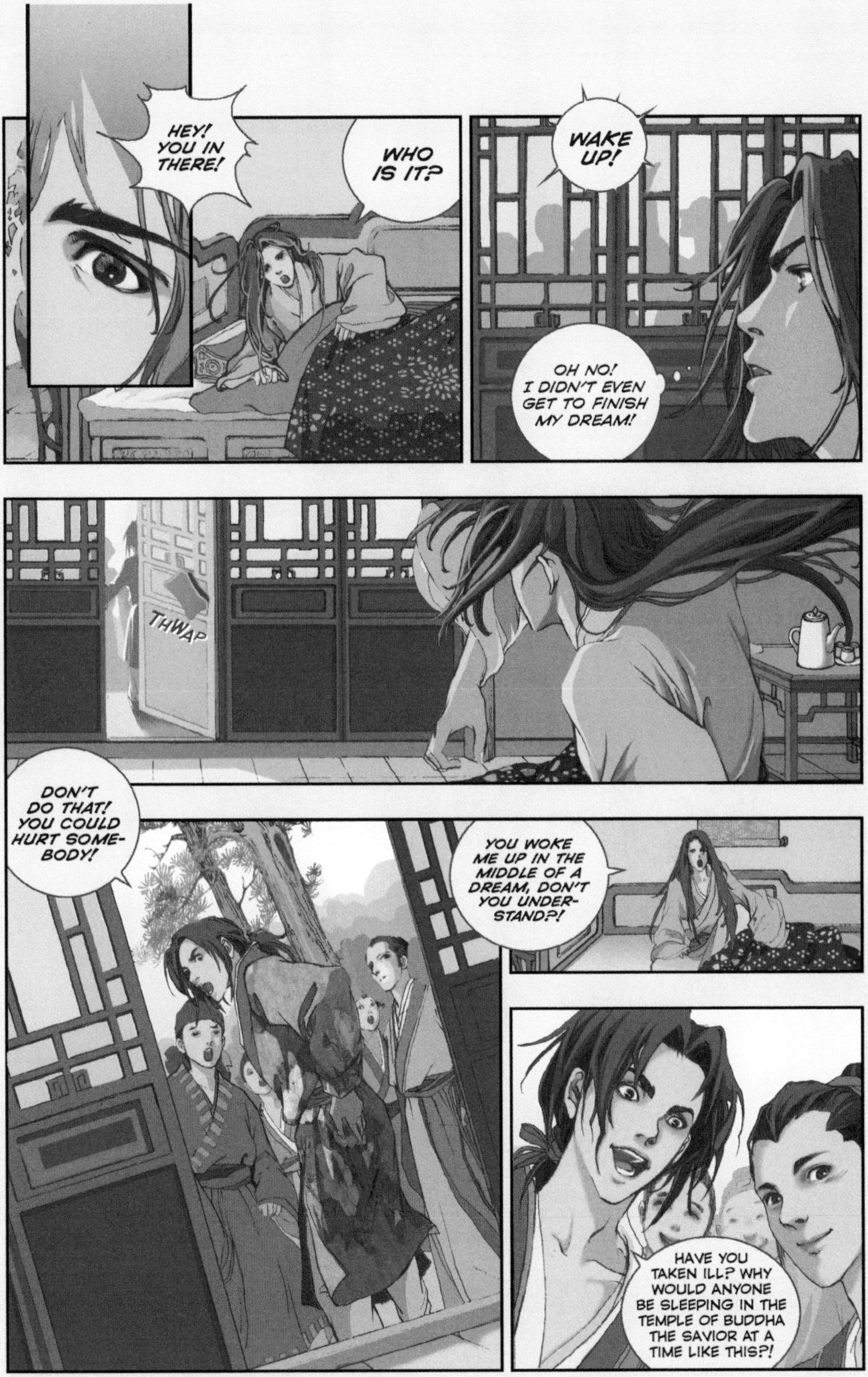
HEY! YOU IN THERE!
WHO IS IT?
WAKE UP!
OH NO! I DIDN'T EVEN GET TO FINISH MY DREAM!
THWAP
DON'T DO THAT! YOU COULD HURT SOME-BODY!
YOU WOKE ME UP IN THE MIDDLE OF A DREAM, DON'T YOU UNDER-STAND?!
HAVE YOU TAKEN ILL? WHY WOULD ANYONE BE SLEEPING IN THE TEMPLE OF BUDDHA THE SAVIOR AT A TIME LIKE THIS?!

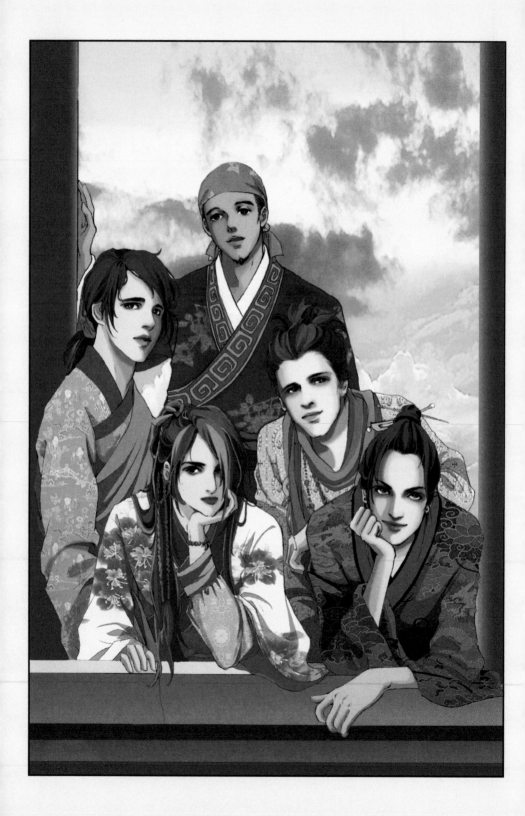

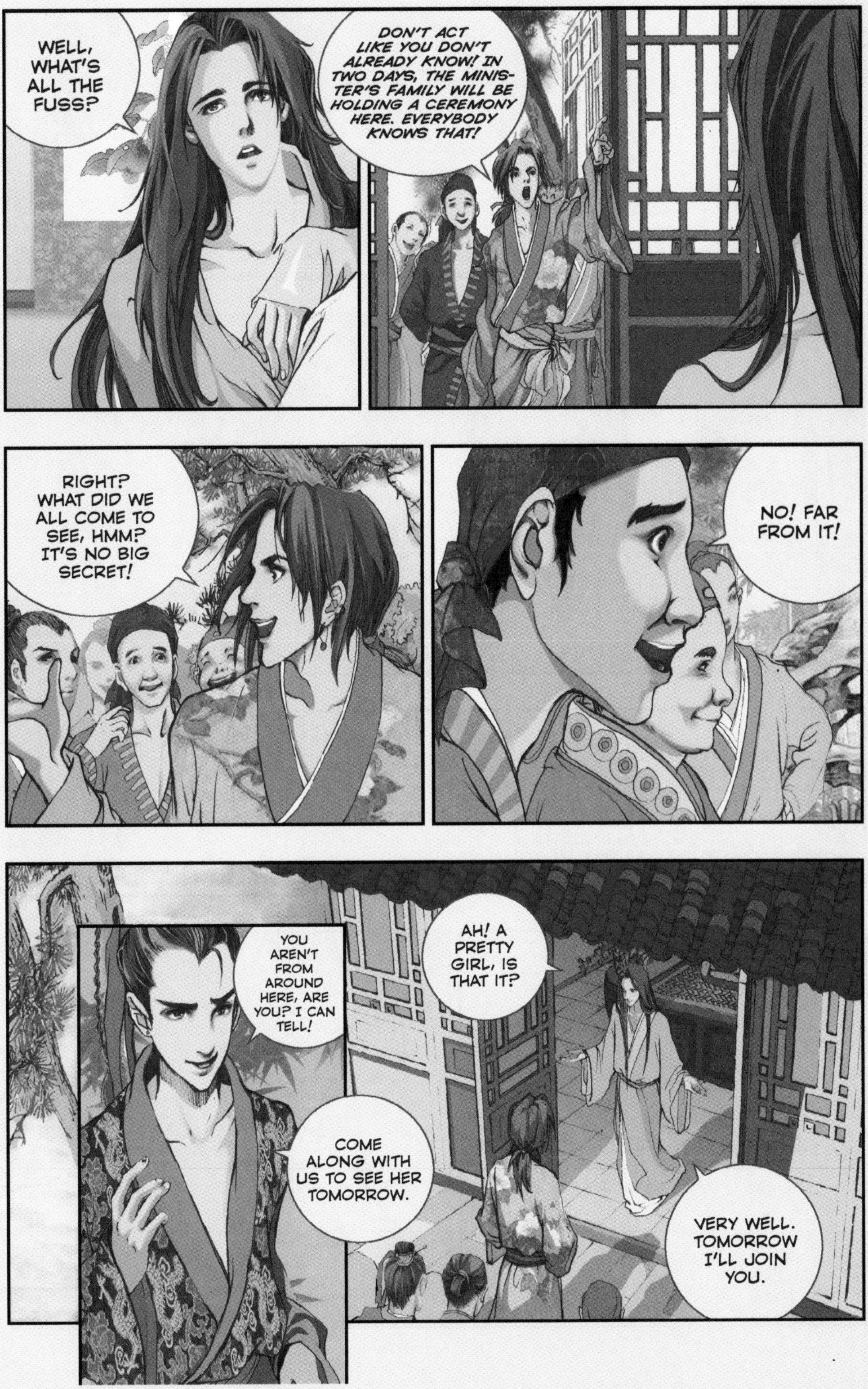
WELL, WHAT'S ALL THE FUSS?
DON'T ACT LIKE YOU DON'T ALREADY KNOW! IN TWO DAYS, THE MINISTER'S FAMILY WILL BE HOLDING A CEREMONY HERE. EVERYBODY KNOWS THAT!
RIGHT? WHAT DID WE ALL COME TO SEE, HMM? IT'S NO BIG SECRET!
NO! FAR FROM IT!
YOU AREN'T FROM AROUND HERE, ARE YOU? I CAN TELL!
COME ALONG WITH US TO SEE HER TOMORROW.
AH! A PRETTY GIRL, IS THAT IT?
VERY WELL. TOMORROW I'LL JOIN YOU.

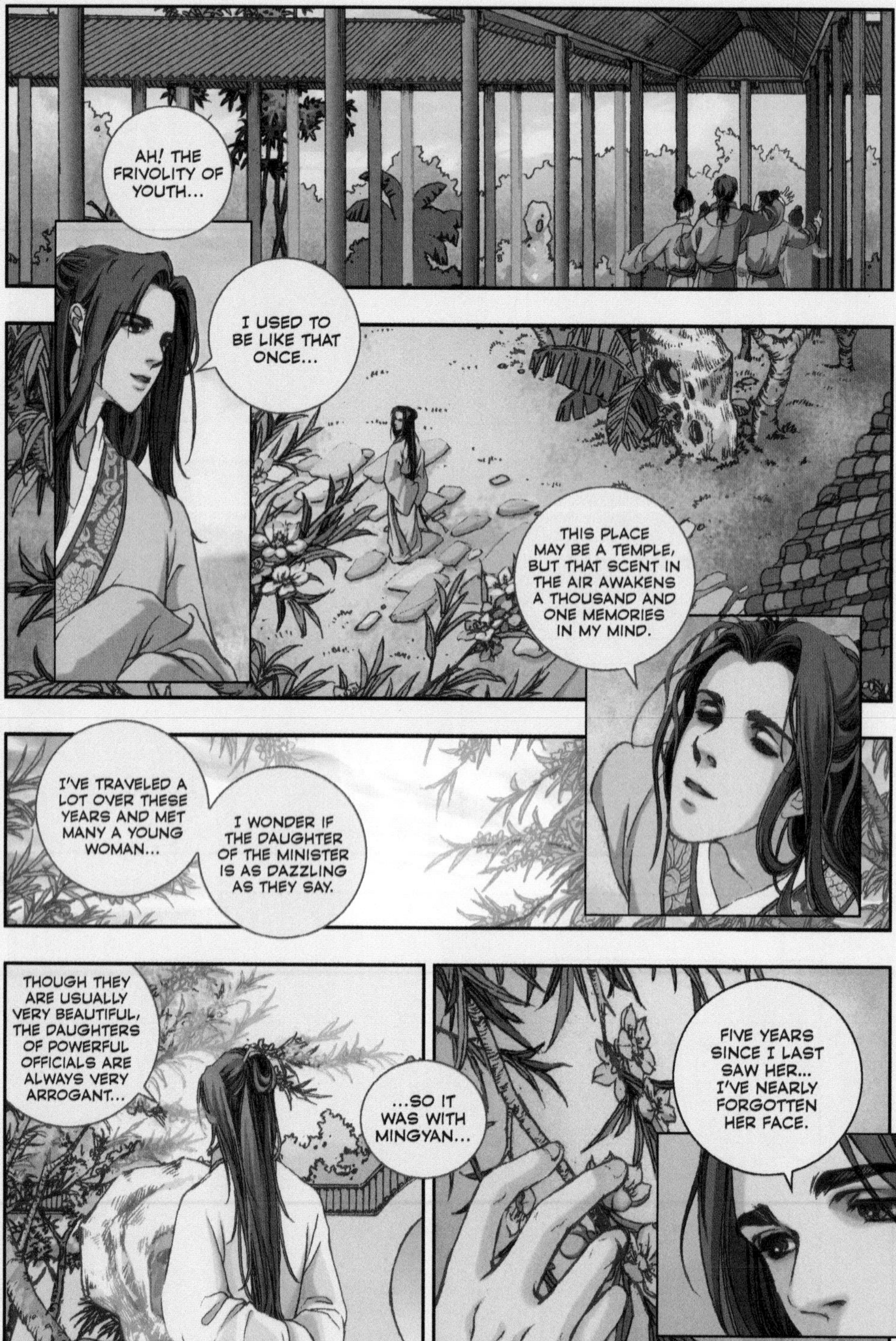
AH! THE FRIVOLITY OF YOUTH...
I USED TO BE LIKE THAT ONCE...
THIS PLACE MAY BE A TEMPLE, BUT THAT SCENT IN THE AIR AWAKENS A THOUSAND AND ONE MEMORIES IN MY MIND.
I'VE TRAVELED A LOT OVER THESE YEARS AND MET MANY A YOUNG WOMAN...
I WONDER IF THE DAUGHTER OF THE MINISTER IS AS DAZZLING AS THEY SAY.
THOUGH THEY ARE USUALLY VERY BEAUTIFUL, THE DAUGHTERS OF POWERFUL OFFICIALS ARE ALWAYS VERY ARROGANT...
...SO IT WAS WITH MINGYAN...
FIVE YEARS SINCE I LAST SAW HER... I'VE NEARLY FORGOTTEN HER FACE.

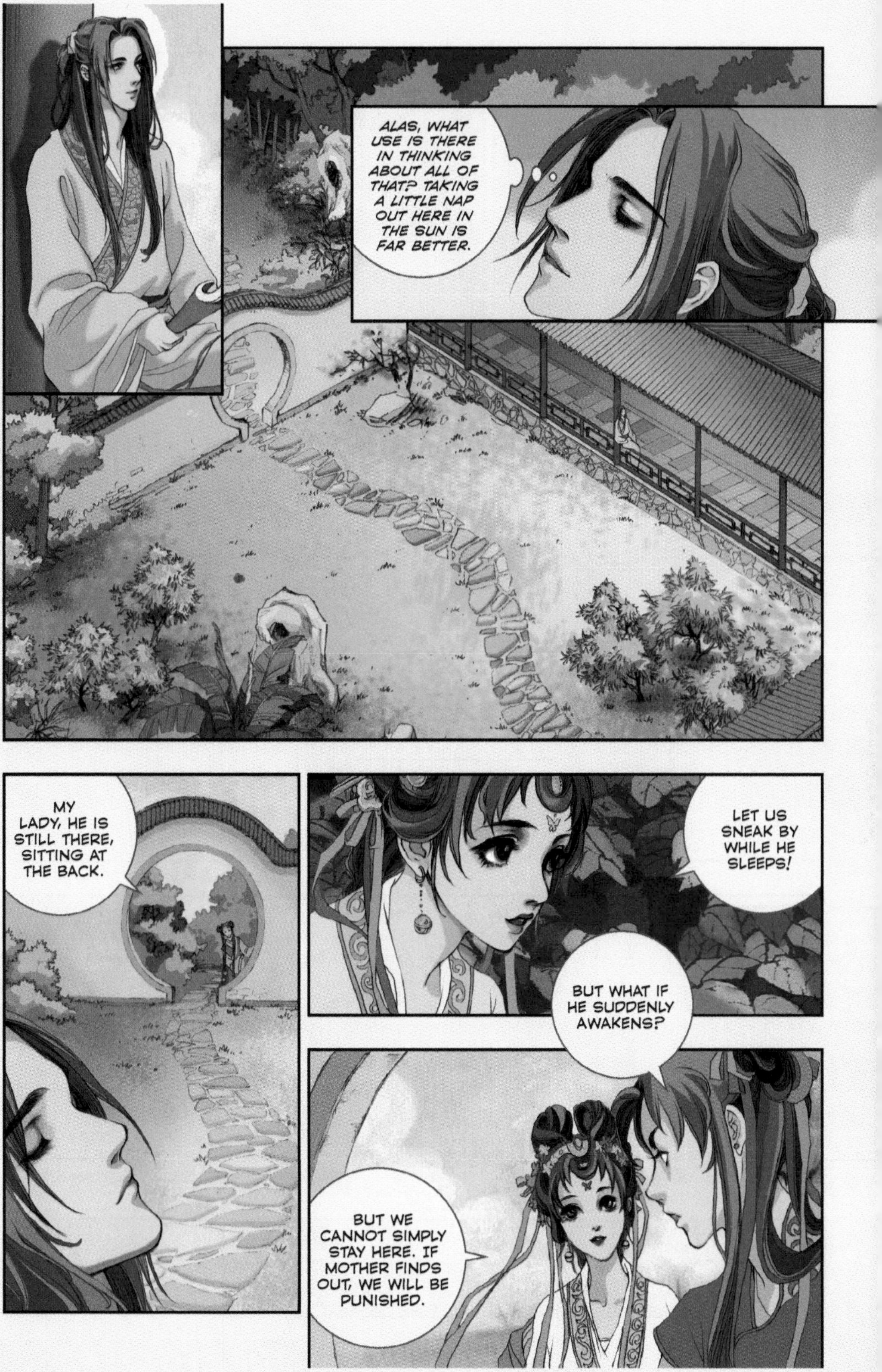
ALAS, WHAT USE IS THERE IN THINKING ABOUT ALL OF THAT? TAKING A LITTLE NAP OUT HERE IN THE SUN IS FAR BETTER.
MY LADY, HE IS STILL THERE, SITTING AT THE BACK.
LET US SNEAK BY WHILE HE SLEEPS!
BUT WHAT IF HE SUDDENLY AWAKENS?
BUT WE CANNOT SIMPLY STAY HERE. IF MOTHER FINDS OUT, WE WILL BE PUNISHED.

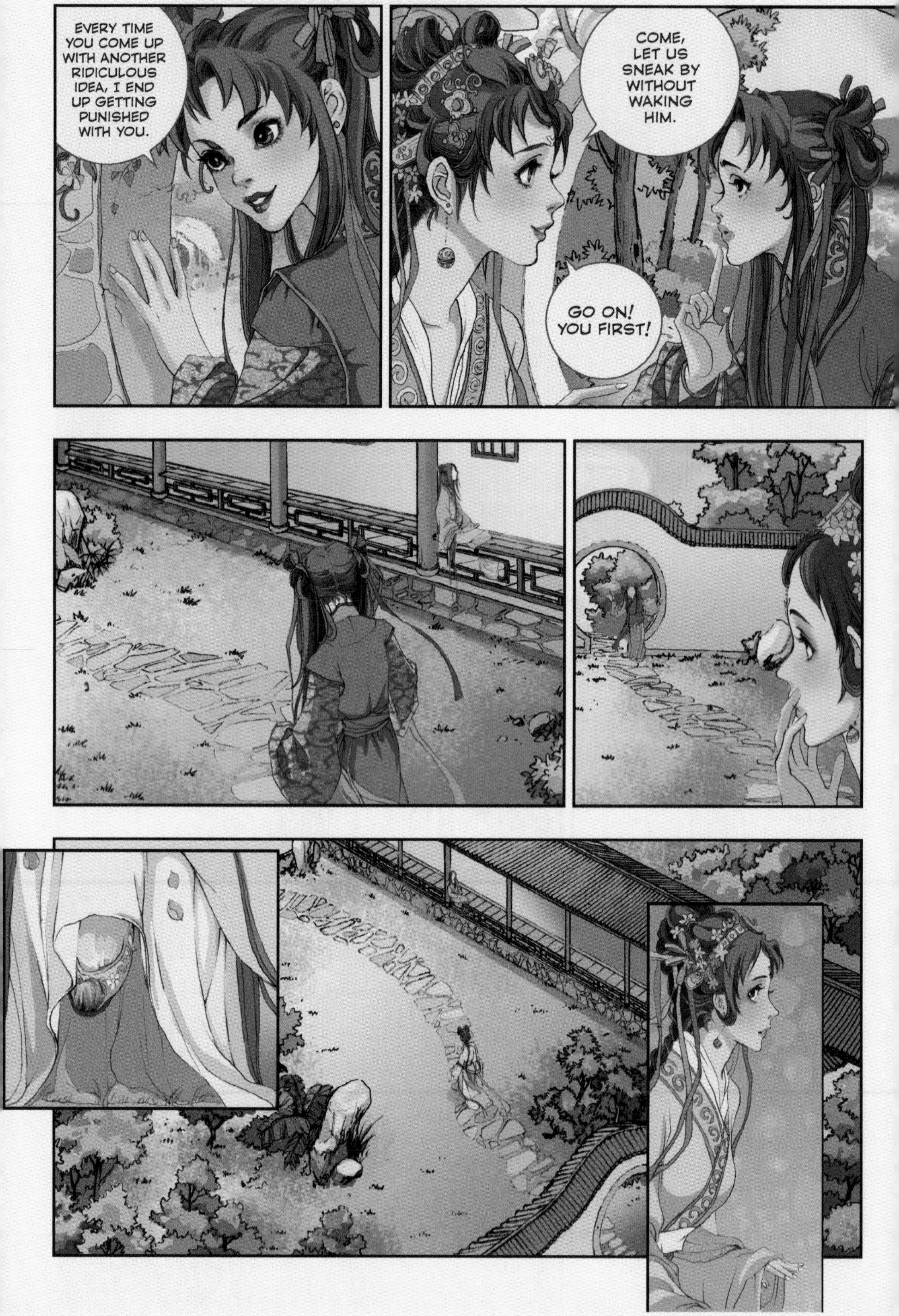
EVERY TIME YOU COME UP WITH ANOTHER RIDICULOUS IDEA, I END UP GETTING PUNISHED WITH YOU.
COME, LET US SNEAK BY WITHOUT WAKING HIM.
GO ON! YOU FIRST!

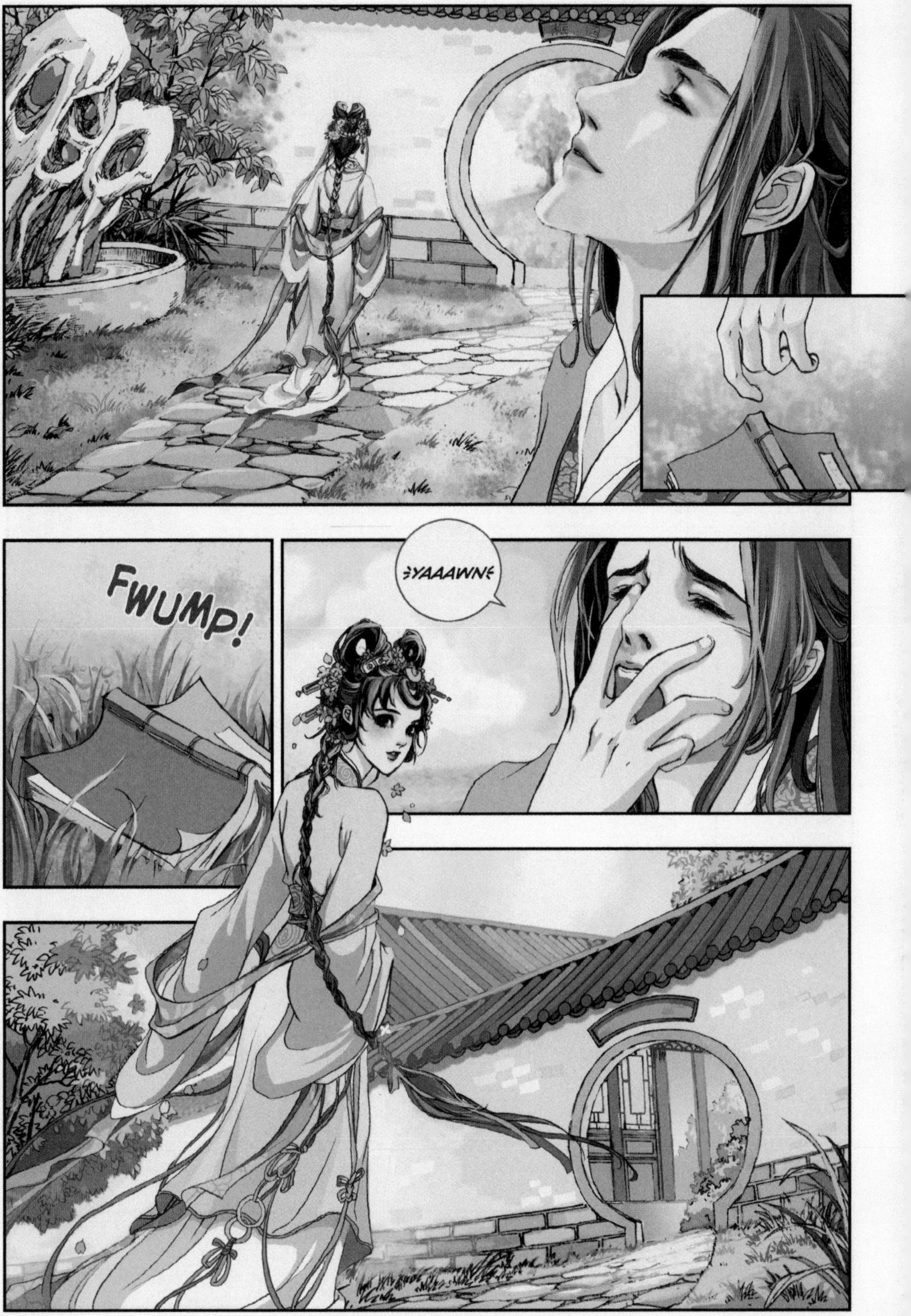
FWUMP!
YAAAWN

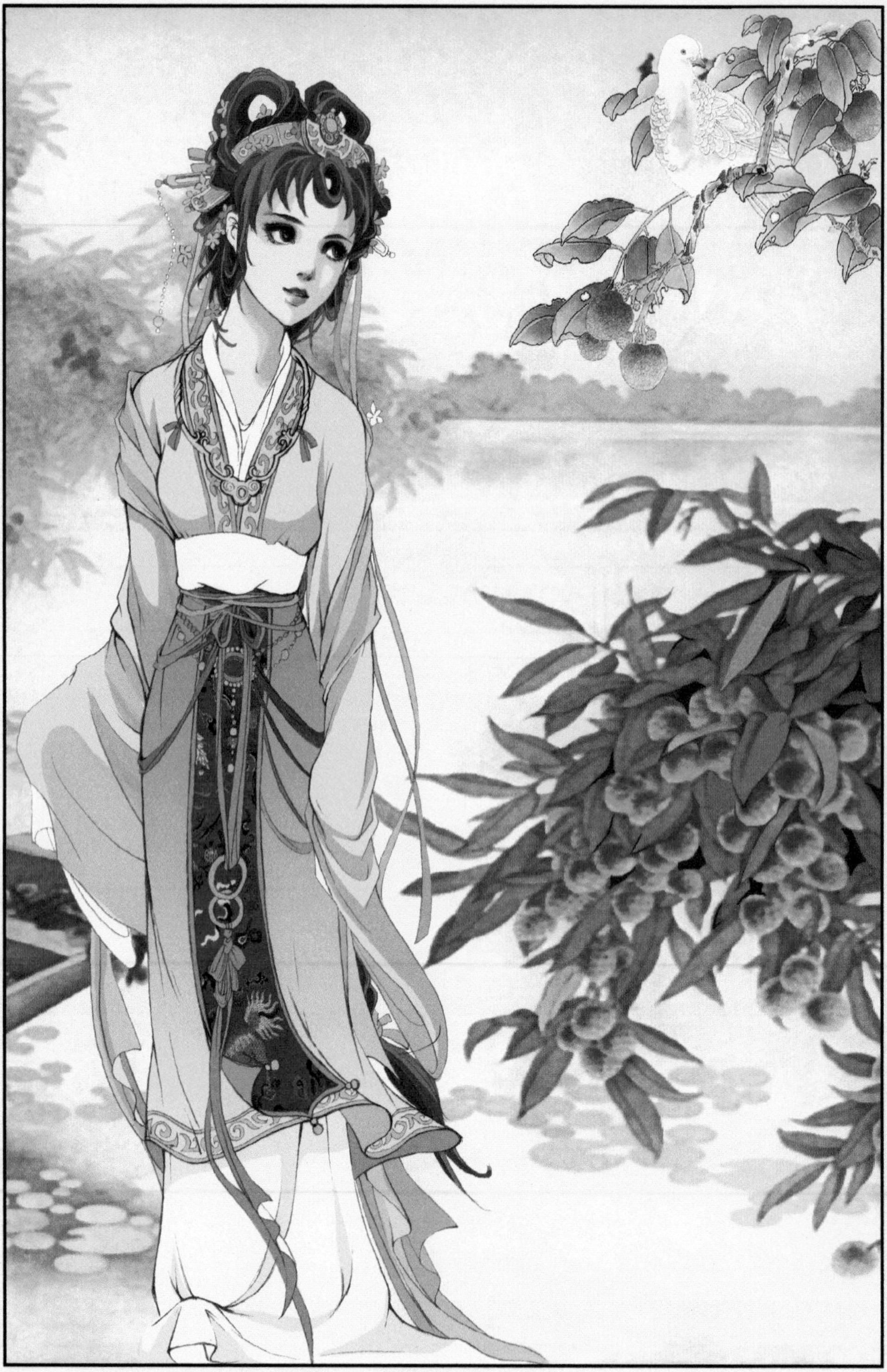

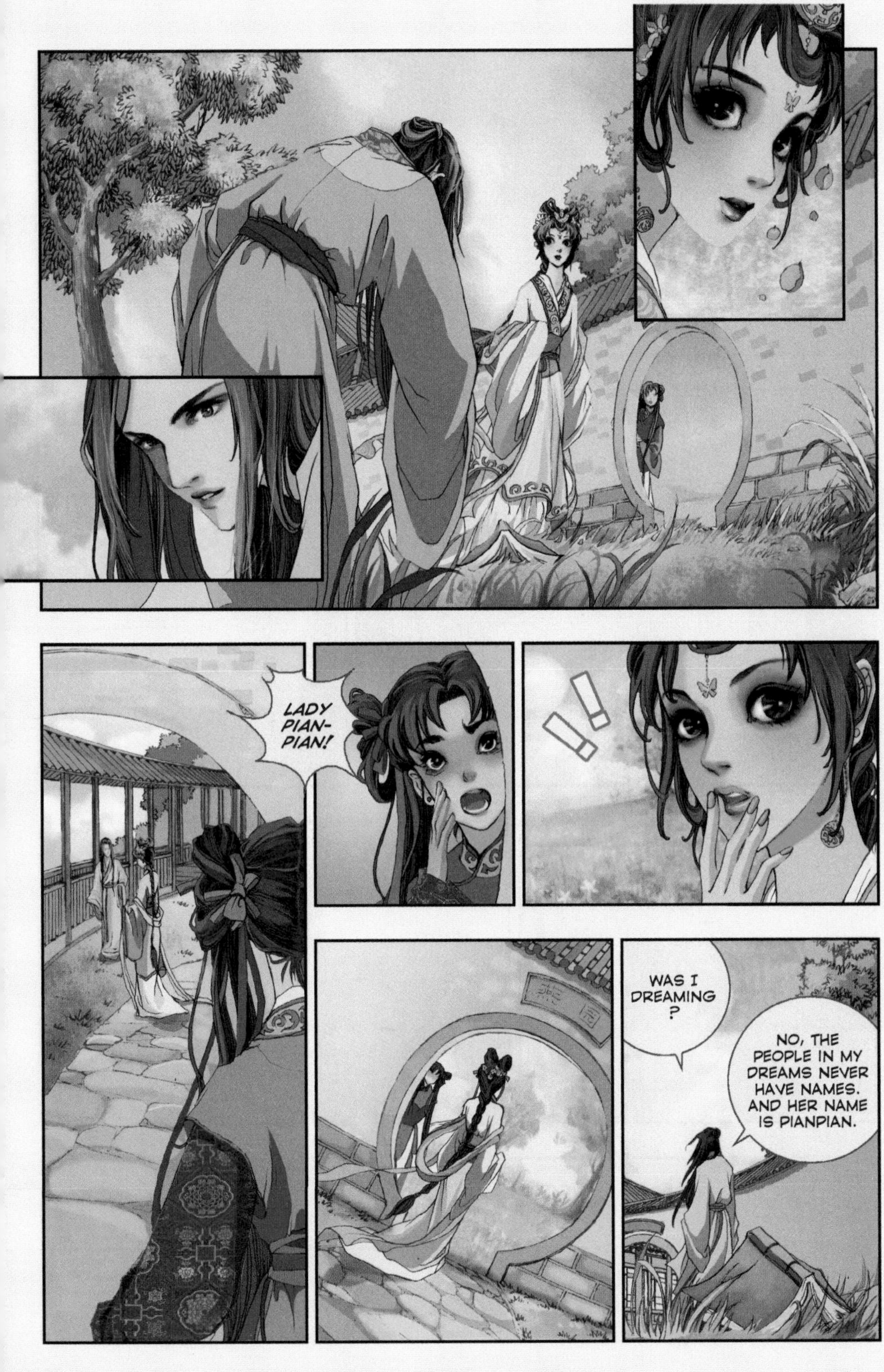
LADY PIAN-PIAN!
!!
WAS I DREAMING?
NO, THE PEOPLE IN MY DREAMS NEVER HAVE NAMES. AND HER NAME IS PIANPIAN.

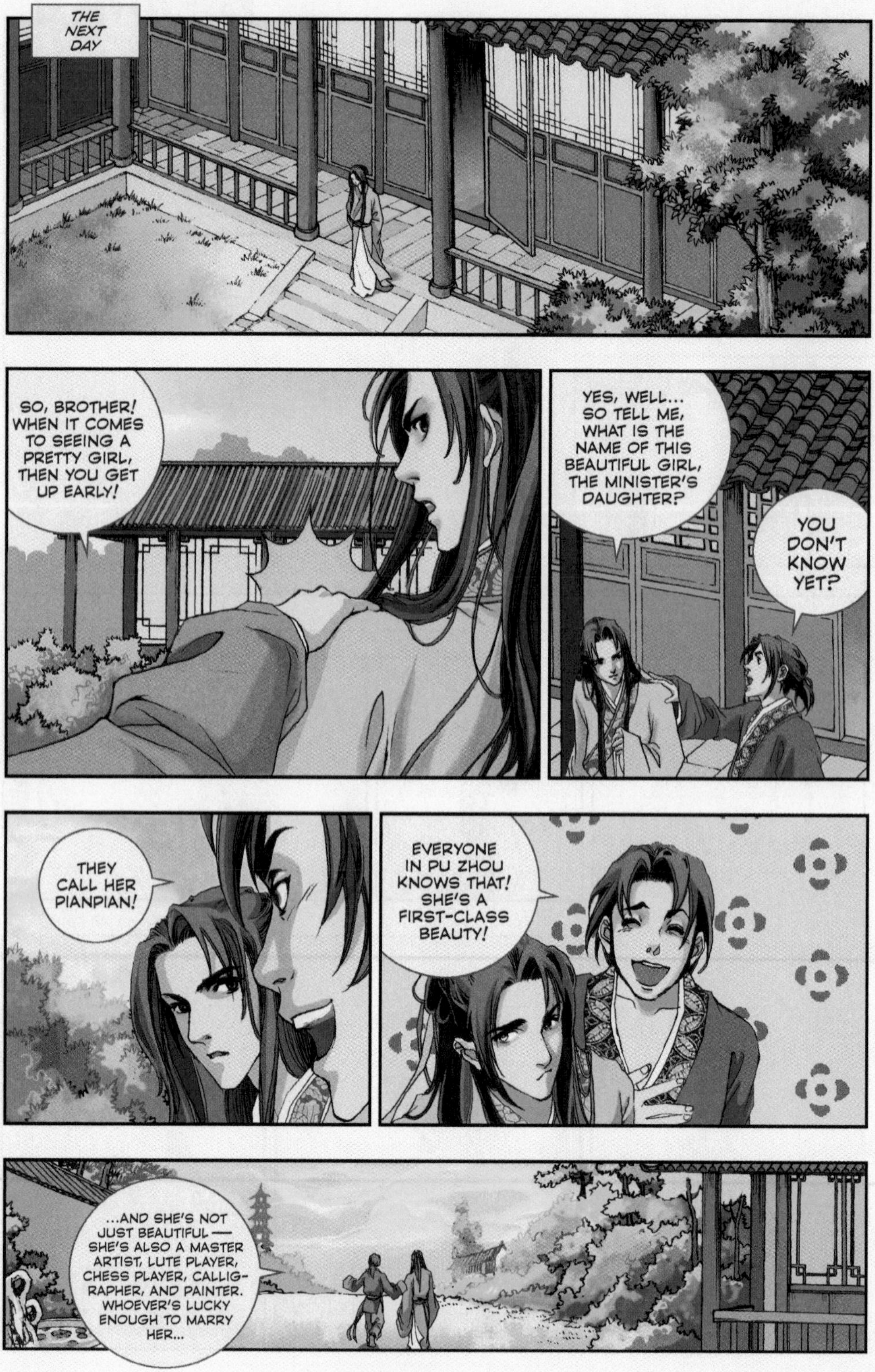
THE NEXT DAY
SO, BROTHER! WHEN IT COMES TO SEEING A PRETTY GIRL, THEN YOU GET UP EARLY!
YES, WELL... SO TELL ME, WHAT IS THE NAME OF THIS BEAUTIFUL GIRL, THE MINISTER'S DAUGHTER?
YOU DON'T KNOW YET?
THEY CALL HER PIANPIAN!
EVERYONE IN PU ZHOU KNOWS THAT! SHE'S A FIRST-CLASS BEAUTY!
...AND SHE'S NOT JUST BEAUTIFUL — SHE'S ALSO A MASTER ARTIST, LUTE PLAYER, CHESS PLAYER, CALLIGRAPHER, AND PAINTER. WHOEVER'S LUCKY ENOUGH TO MARRY HER...

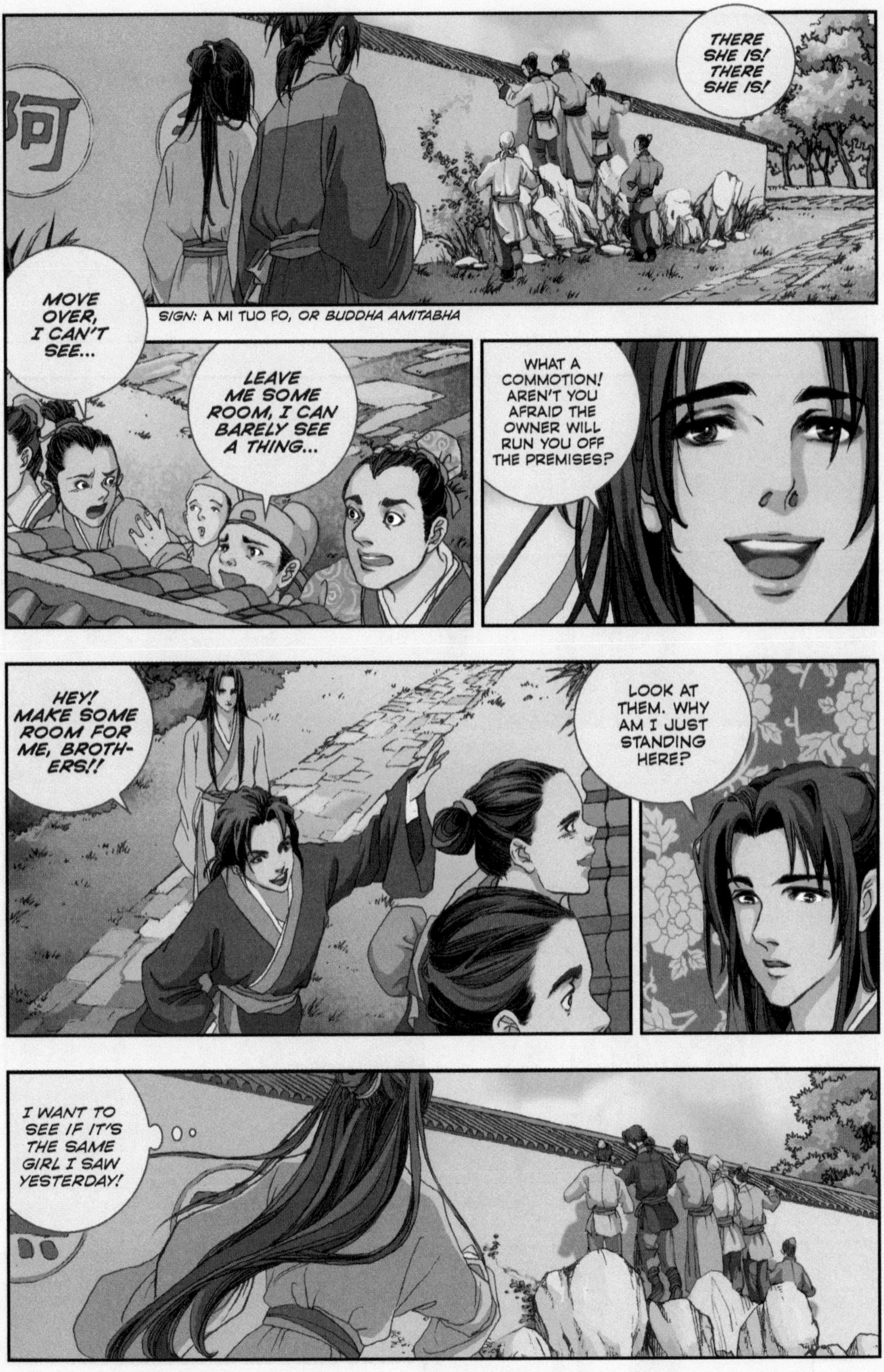
THERE SHE IS! THERE SHE IS!
MOVE OVER, I CAN'T SEE...
SIGN: A MI TUO FO, OR BUDDHA AMITABHA
LEAVE ME SOME ROOM, I CAN BARELY SEE A THING...
WHAT A COMMOTION! AREN'T YOU AFRAID THE OWNER WILL RUN YOU OFF THE PREMISES?
HEY! MAKE SOME ROOM FOR ME, BROTH-ERS!!
LOOK AT THEM. WHY AM I JUST STANDING HERE?
I WANT TO SEE IF IT'S THE SAME GIRL I SAW YESTERDAY!

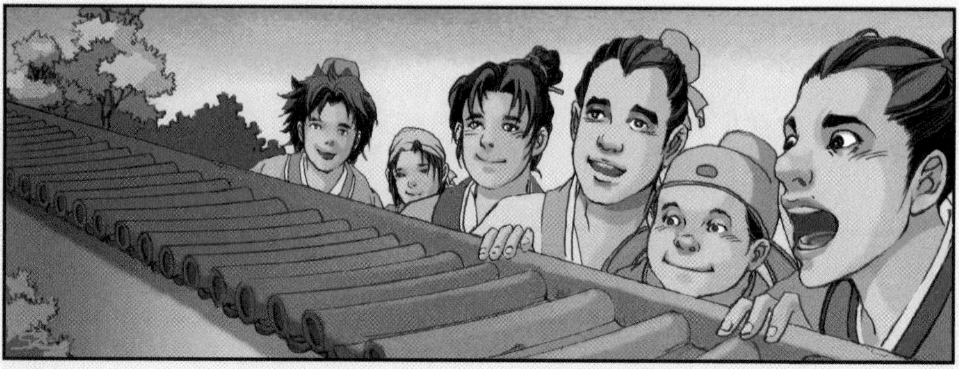

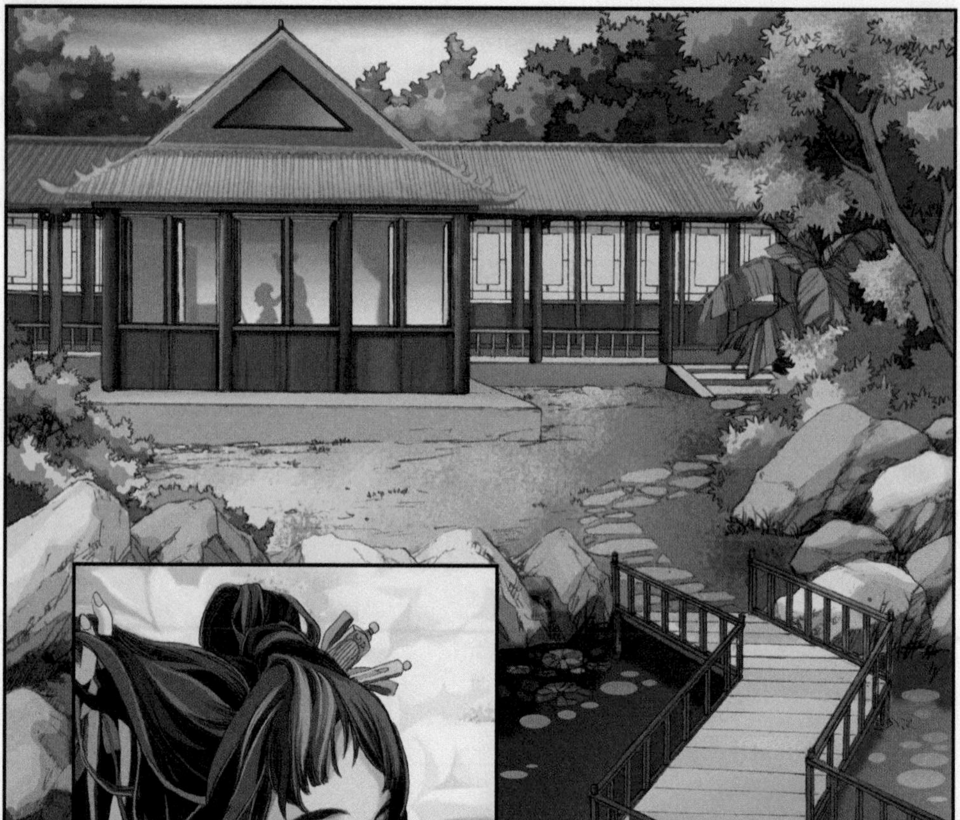

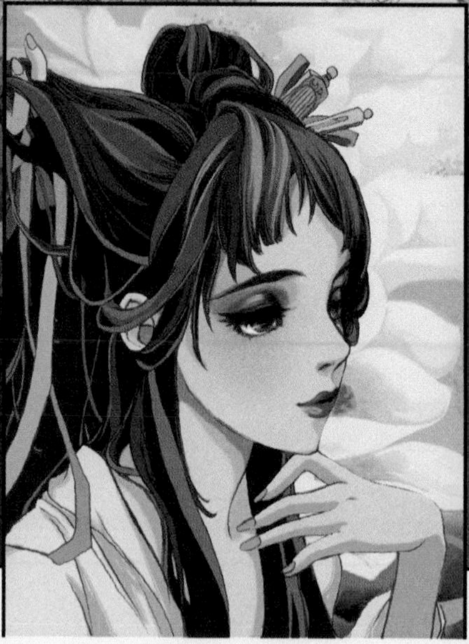

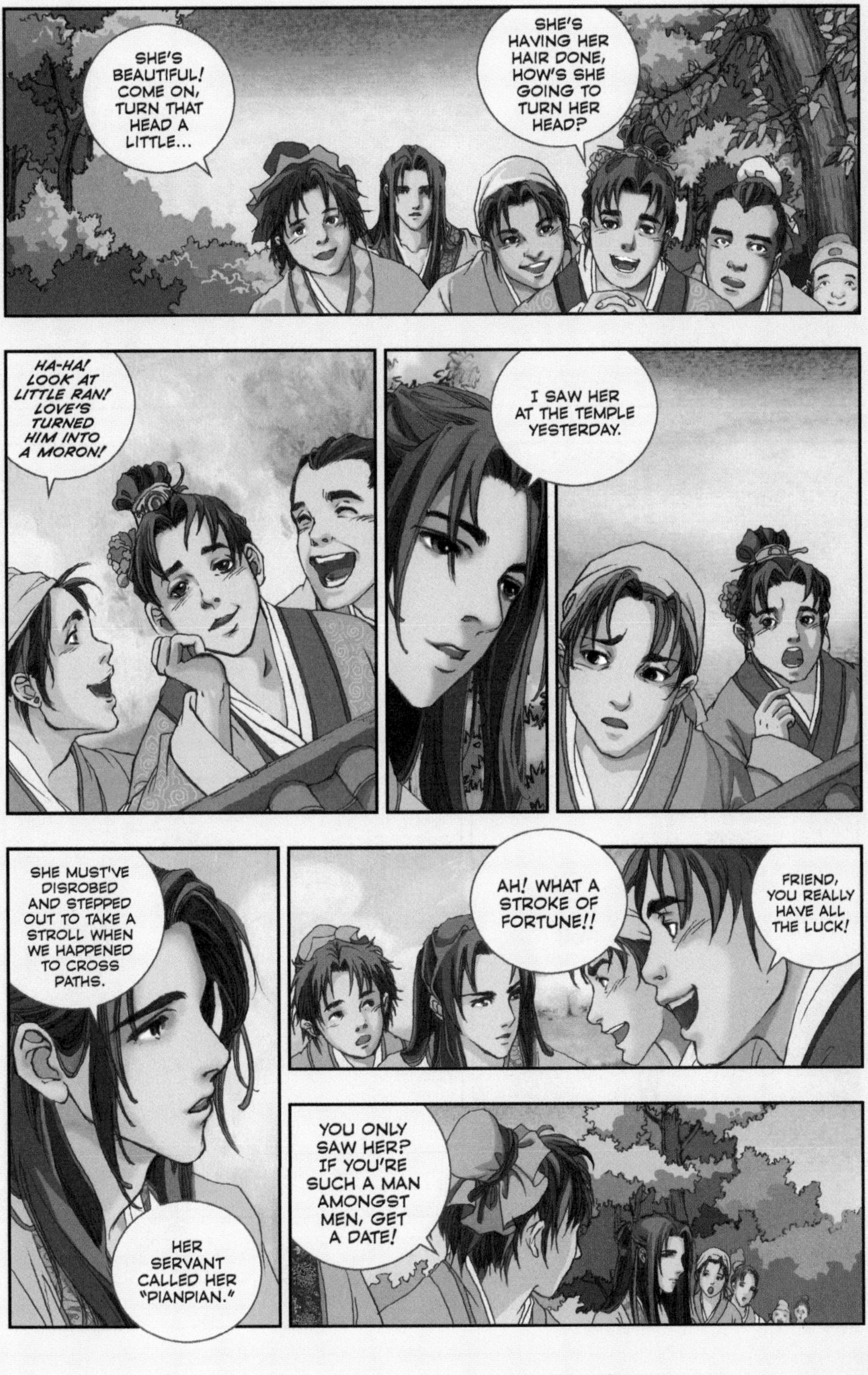
SHE'S BEAUTIFUL! COME ON, TURN THAT HEAD A LITTLE...
SHE'S HAVING HER HAIR DONE, HOW'S SHE GOING TO TURN HER HEAD?
HA-HA! LOOK AT LITTLE RAN! LOVE'S TURNED HIM INTO A MORON!
I SAW HER AT THE TEMPLE YESTERDAY.
SHE MUST'VE DISROBED AND STEPPED OUT TO TAKE A STROLL WHEN WE HAPPENED TO CROSS PATHS.
HER SERVANT CALLED HER "PIANPIAN."
AH! WHAT A STROKE OF FORTUNE!!
FRIEND, YOU REALLY HAVE ALL THE LUCK!
YOU ONLY SAW HER? IF YOU'RE SUCH A MAN AMONGST MEN, GET A DATE!

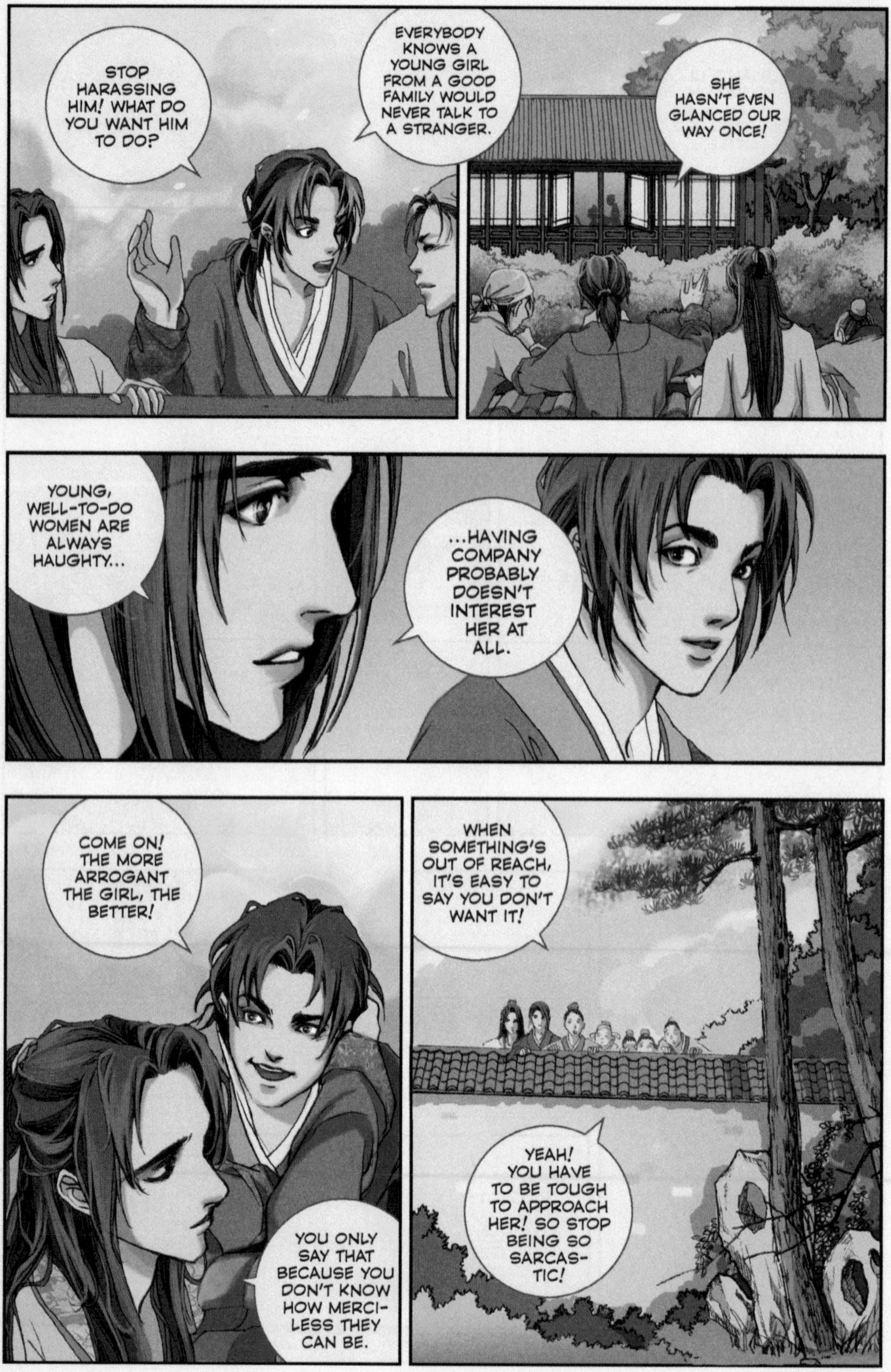
STOP HARASSING HIM! WHAT DO YOU WANT HIM TO DO?
EVERYBODY KNOWS A YOUNG GIRL FROM A GOOD FAMILY WOULD NEVER TALK TO A STRANGER.
SHE HASN'T EVEN GLANCED OUR WAY ONCE!
YOUNG, WELL-TO-DO WOMEN ARE ALWAYS HAUGHTY...
...HAVING COMPANY PROBABLY DOESN'T INTEREST HER AT ALL.
COME ON! THE MORE ARROGANT THE GIRL, THE BETTER!
YOU ONLY SAY THAT BECAUSE YOU DON'T KNOW HOW MERCI-LESS THEY CAN BE.
WHEN SOMETHING'S OUT OF REACH, IT'S EASY TO SAY YOU DON'T WANT IT!
YEAH! YOU HAVE TO BE TOUGH TO APPROACH HER! SO STOP BEING SO SARCAS-TIC!

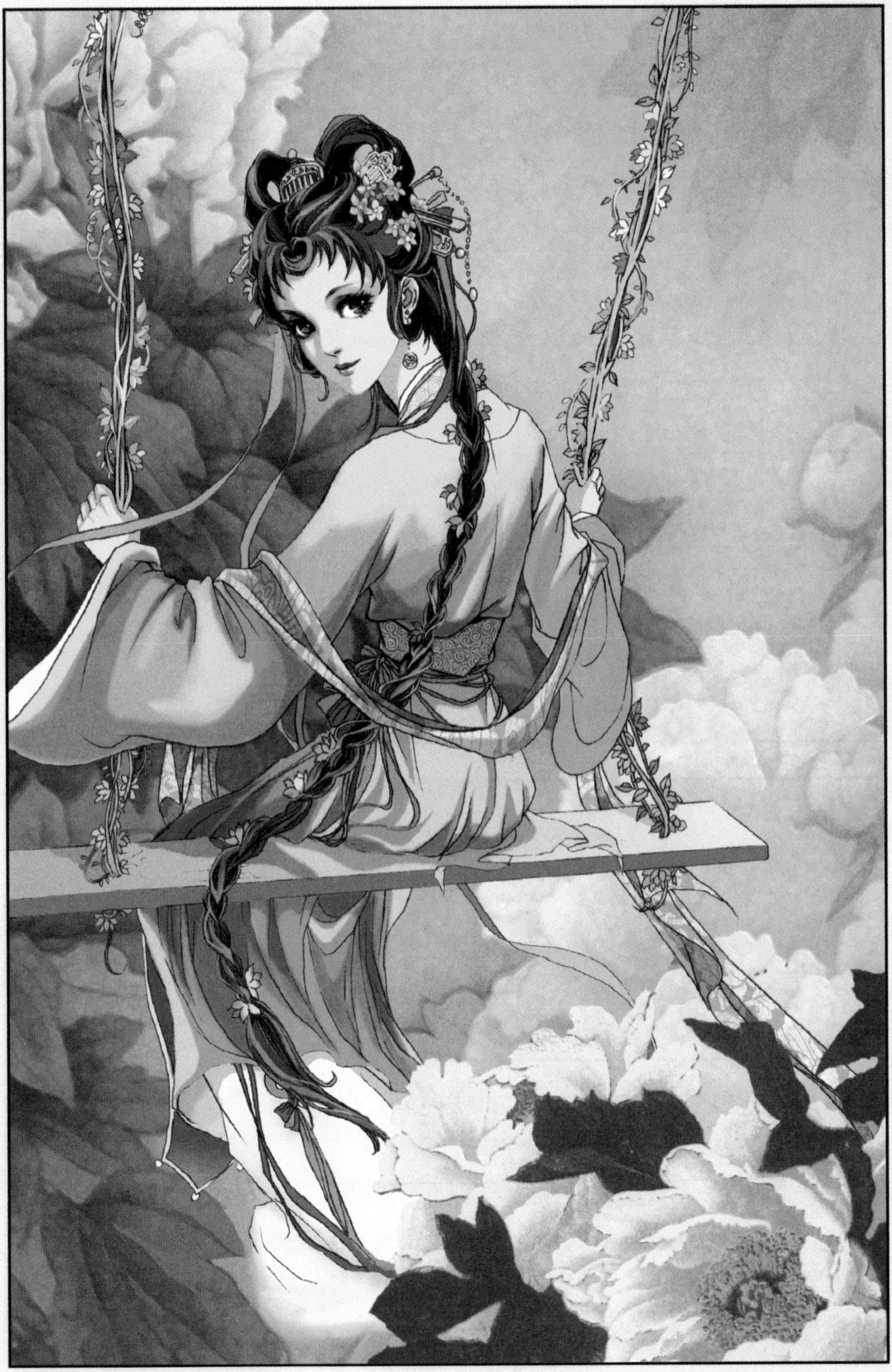

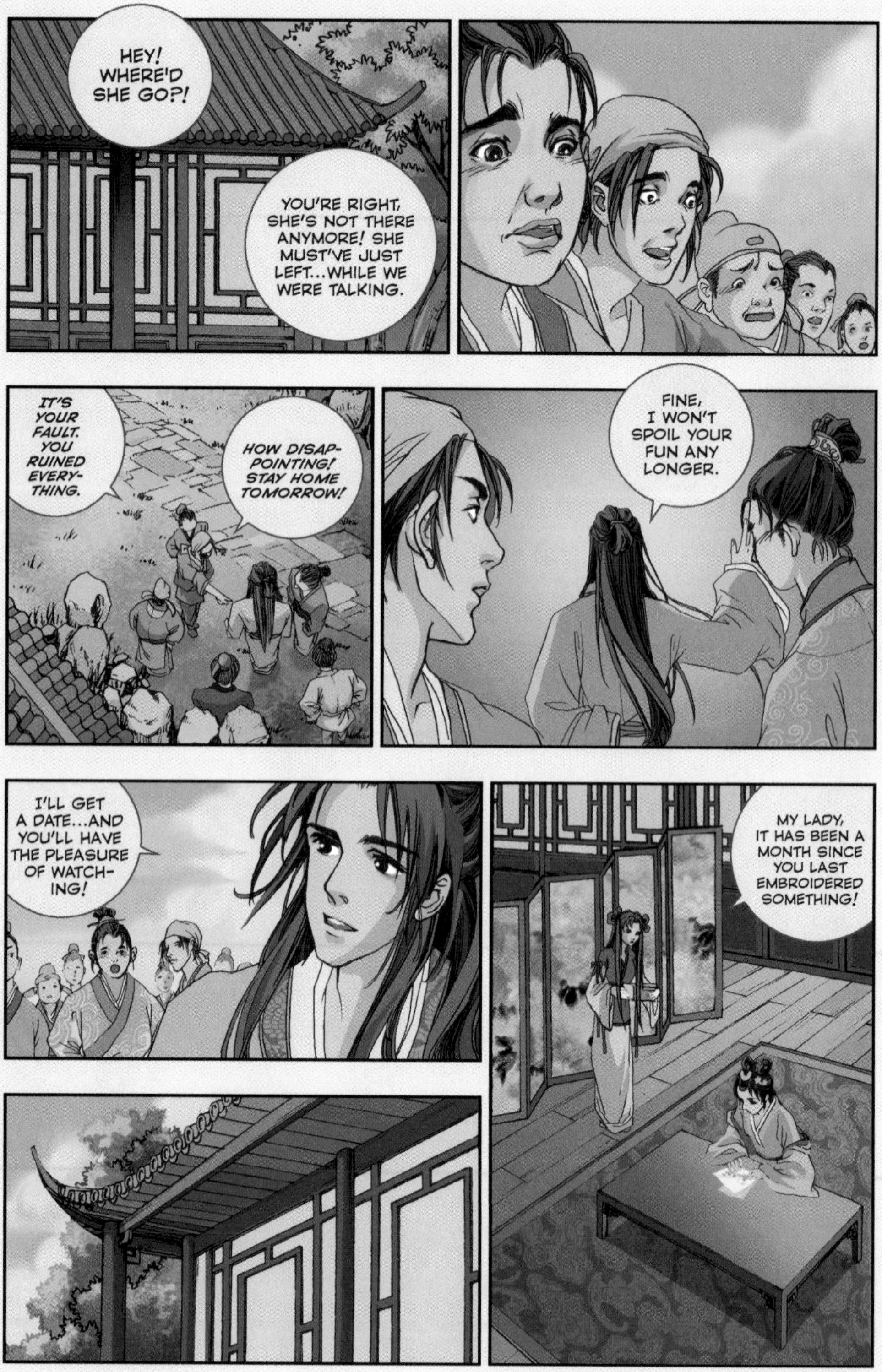
HEY! WHERE'D SHE GO?!
YOU'RE RIGHT, SHE'S NOT THERE ANYMORE! SHE MUST'VE JUST LEFT...WHILE WE WERE TALKING.
IT'S YOUR FAULT. YOU RUINED EVERY-THING.
HOW DISAP-POINTING! STAY HOME TOMORROW!
FINE, I WON'T SPOIL YOUR FUN ANY LONGER.
I'LL GET A DATE...AND YOU'LL HAVE THE PLEASURE OF WATCH-ING!
MY LADY, IT HAS BEEN A MONTH SINCE YOU LAST EMBROIDERED SOMETHING!

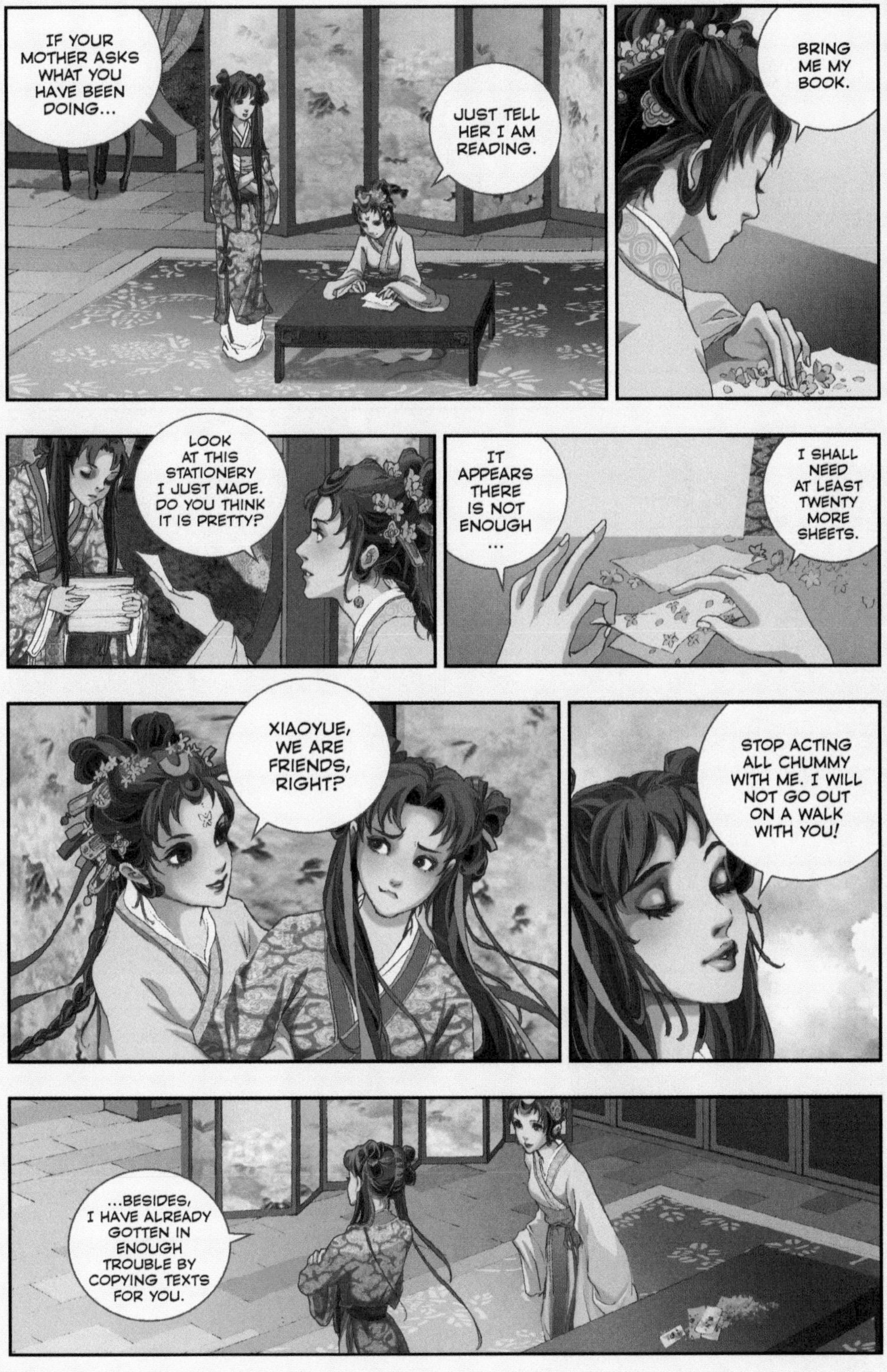
IF YOUR MOTHER ASKS WHAT YOU HAVE BEEN DOING...
JUST TELL HER I AM READING.
BRING ME MY BOOK.
LOOK AT THIS STATIONERY I JUST MADE. DO YOU THINK IT IS PRETTY?
IT APPEARS THERE IS NOT ENOUGH ...
I SHALL NEED AT LEAST TWENTY MORE SHEETS.
XIAOYUE, WE ARE FRIENDS, RIGHT?
STOP ACTING ALL CHUMMY WITH ME. I WILL NOT GO OUT ON A WALK WITH YOU!
...BESIDES, I HAVE ALREADY GOTTEN IN ENOUGH TROUBLE BY COPYING TEXTS FOR YOU.

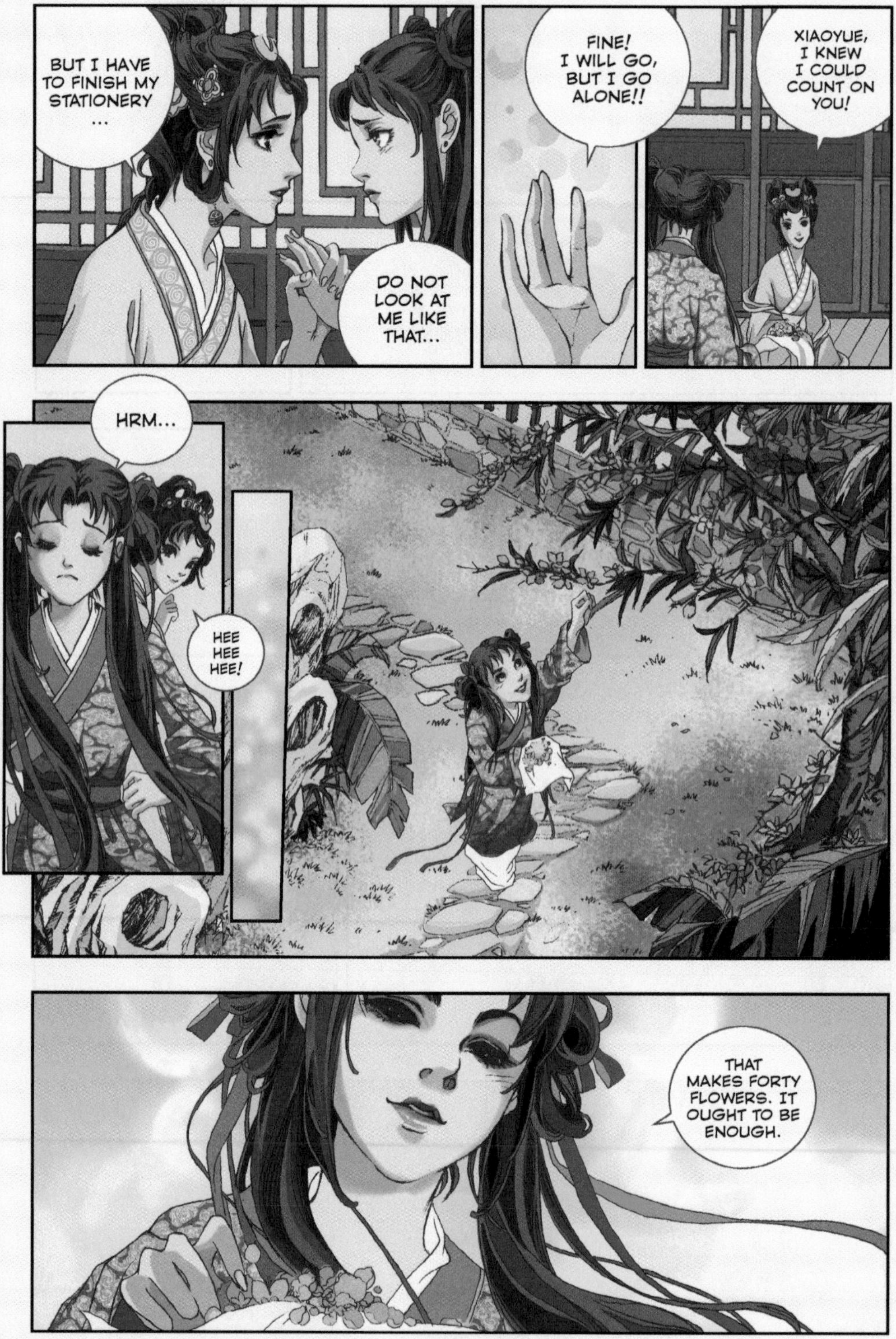
BUT I HAVE TO FINISH MY STATIONERY ...
DO NOT LOOK AT ME LIKE THAT...
FINE! I WILL GO, BUT I GO ALONE!!
XIAOYUE, I KNEW I COULD COUNT ON YOU!
HRM...
HEE HEE HEE!
THAT MAKES FORTY FLOWERS. IT OUGHT TO BE ENOUGH.

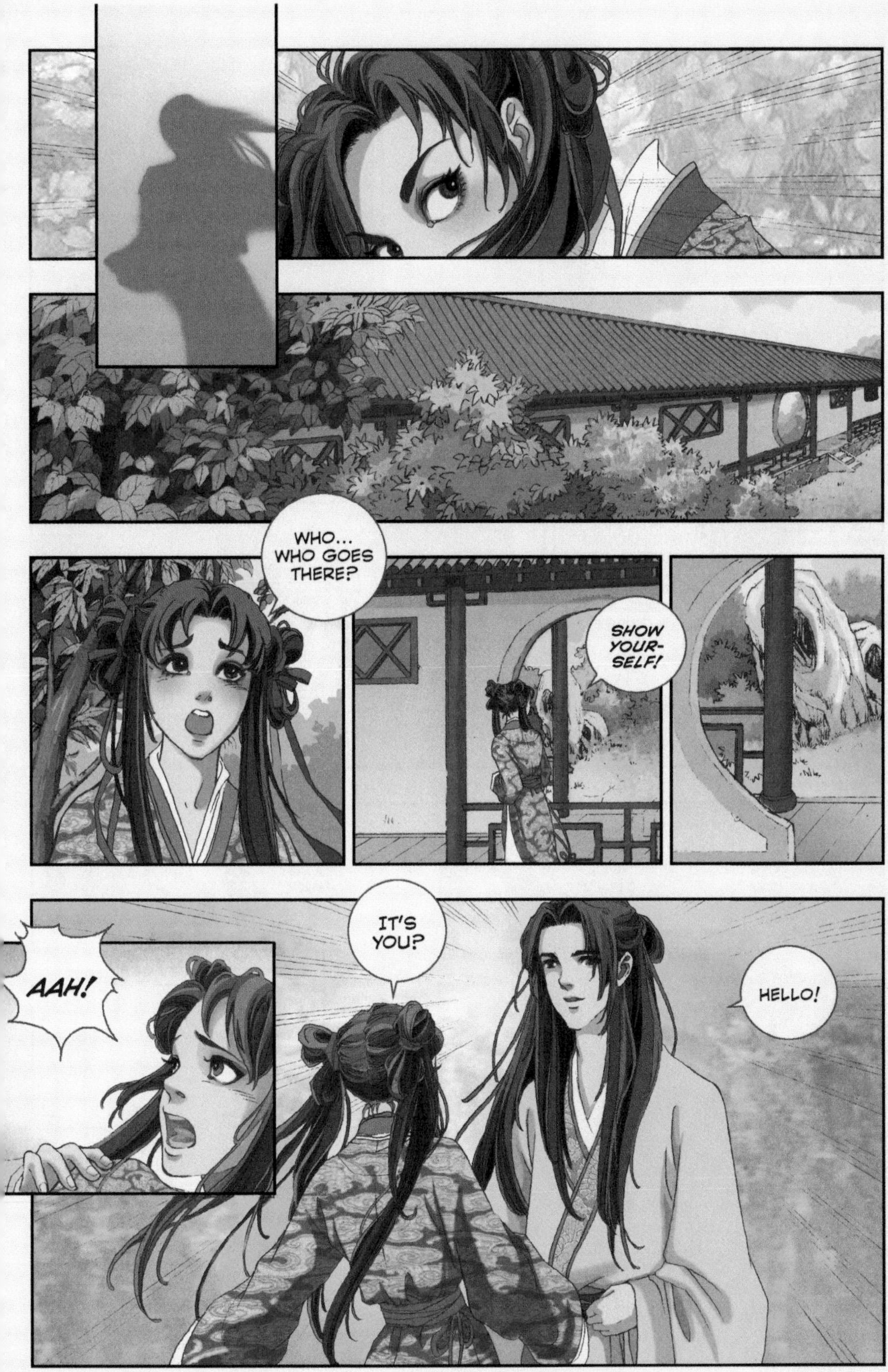
WHO... WHO GOES THERE?
SHOW YOUR-SELF!
AAH!
IT'S YOU?
HELLO!

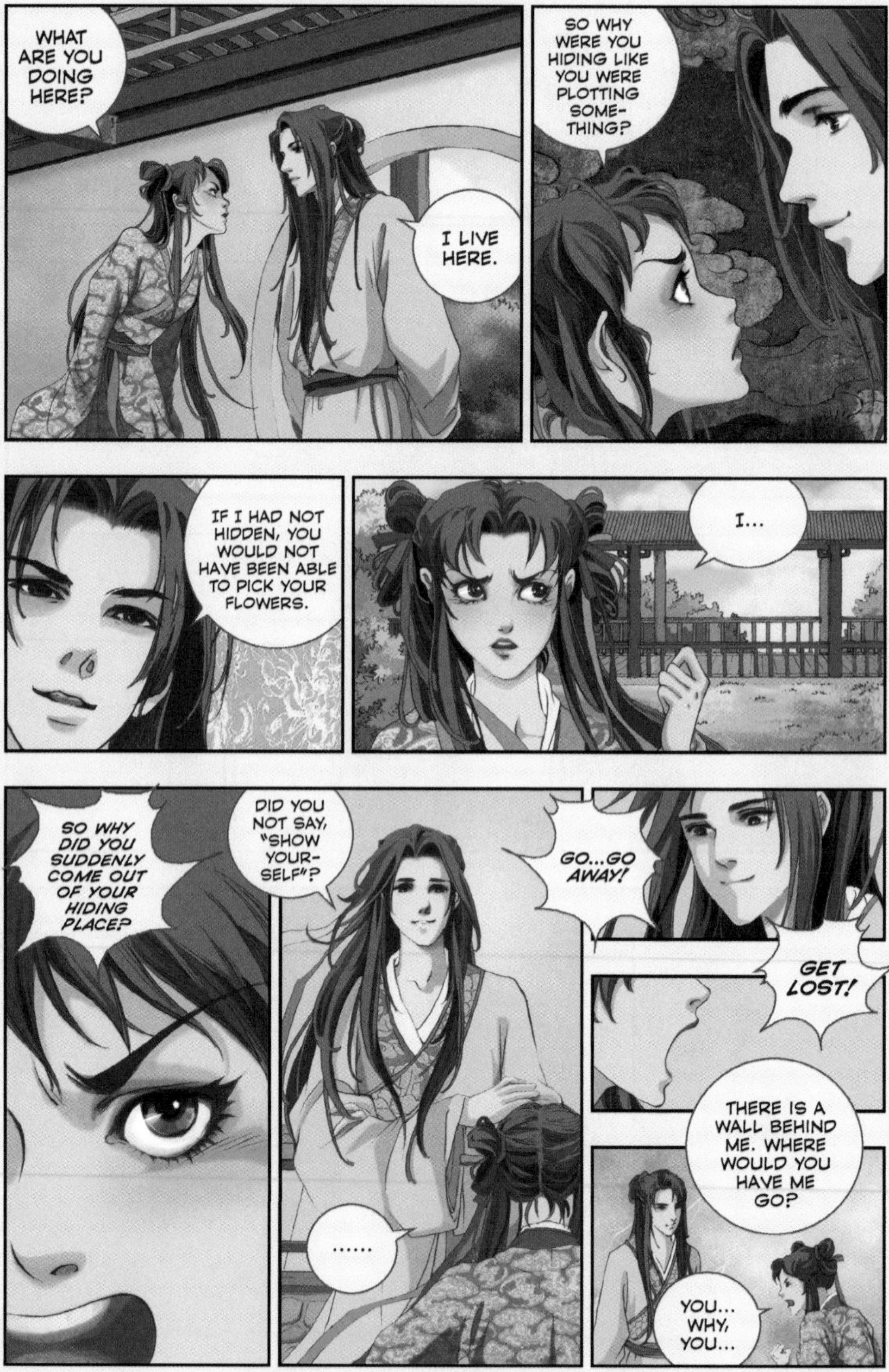
WHAT ARE YOU DOING HERE?
I LIVE HERE.
SO WHY WERE YOU HIDING LIKE YOU WERE PLOTTING SOME-THING?
IF I HAD NOT HIDDEN, YOU WOULD NOT HAVE BEEN ABLE TO PICK YOUR FLOWERS.
I...
SO WHY DID YOU SUDDENLY COME OUT OF YOUR HIDING PLACE?
DID YOU NOT SAY, "SHOW YOUR-SELF"?
......
GO...GO AWAY!
GET LOST!
THERE IS A WALL BEHIND ME. WHERE WOULD YOU HAVE ME GO?
YOU... WHY, YOU...

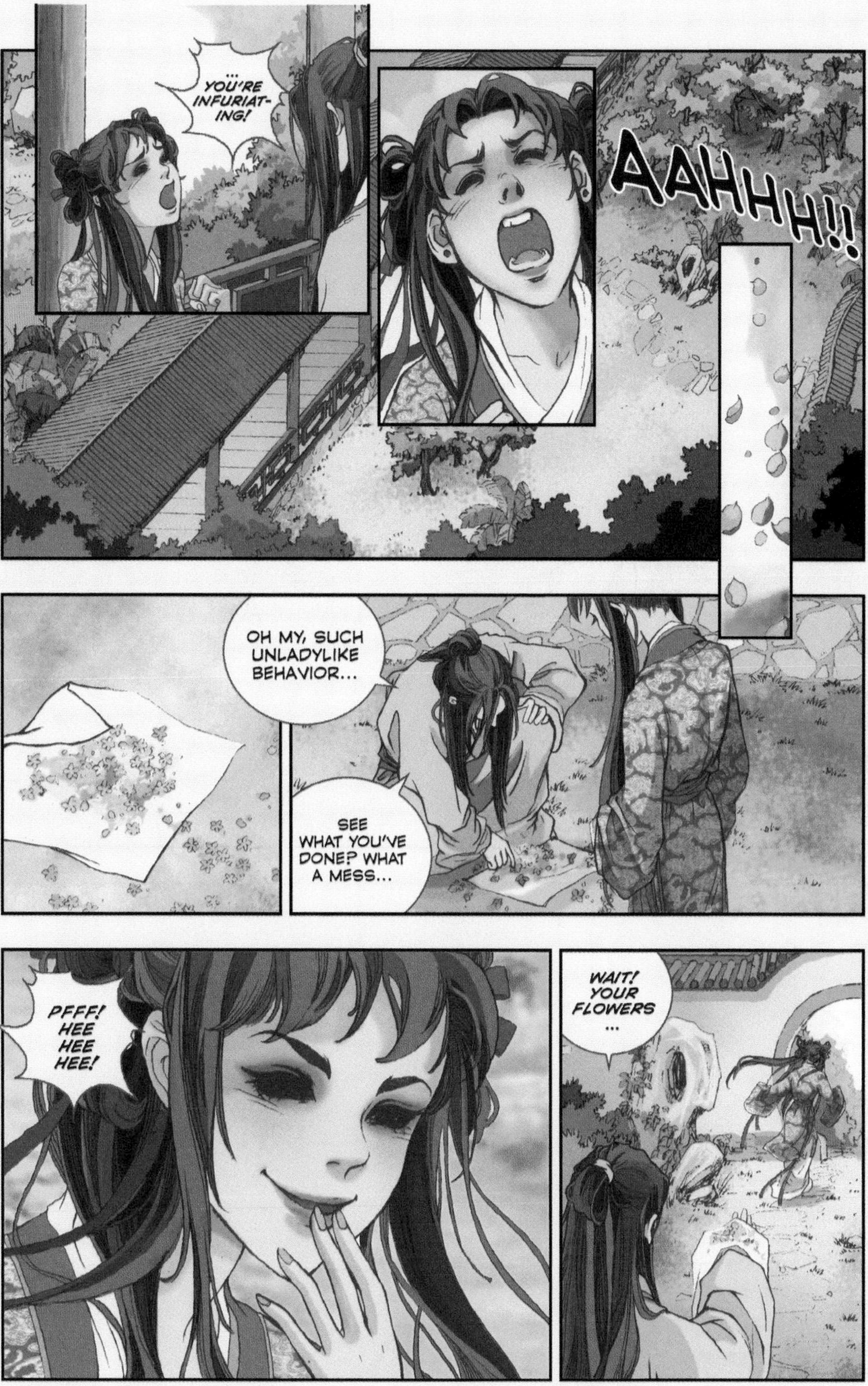

... YOU'RE INFURIATING!
AAHHHH!!
OH MY, SUCH UNLADYLIKE BEHAVIOR...
SEE WHAT YOU'VE DONE? WHAT A MESS...
PFFF! HEE HEE HEE!
WAIT! YOUR FLOWERS ...

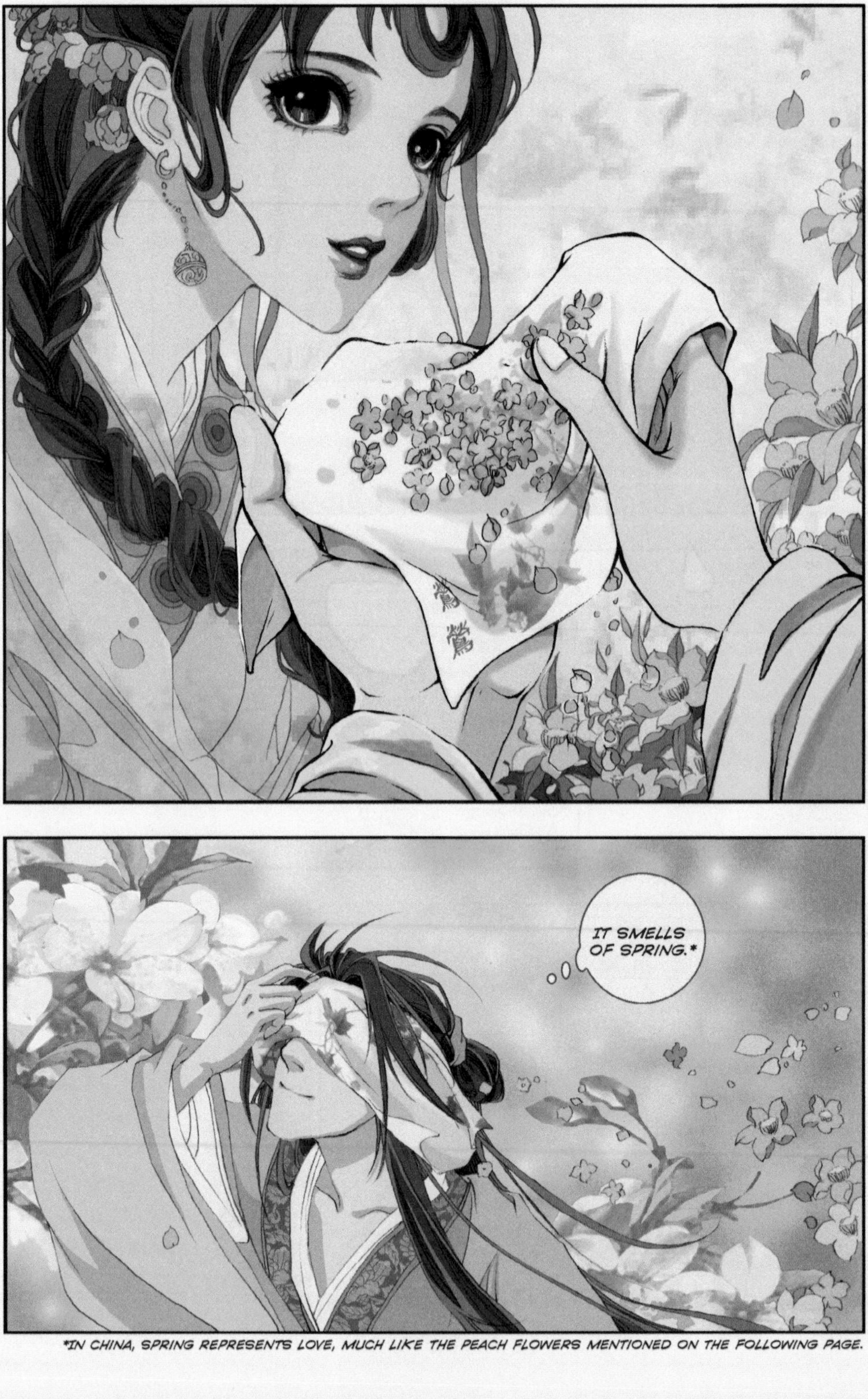
IT SMELLS OF SPRING.*

*IN CHINA, SPRING REPRESENTS LOVE, MUCH LIKE THE PEACH FLOWERS MENTIONED ON THE FOLLOWING PAGE.

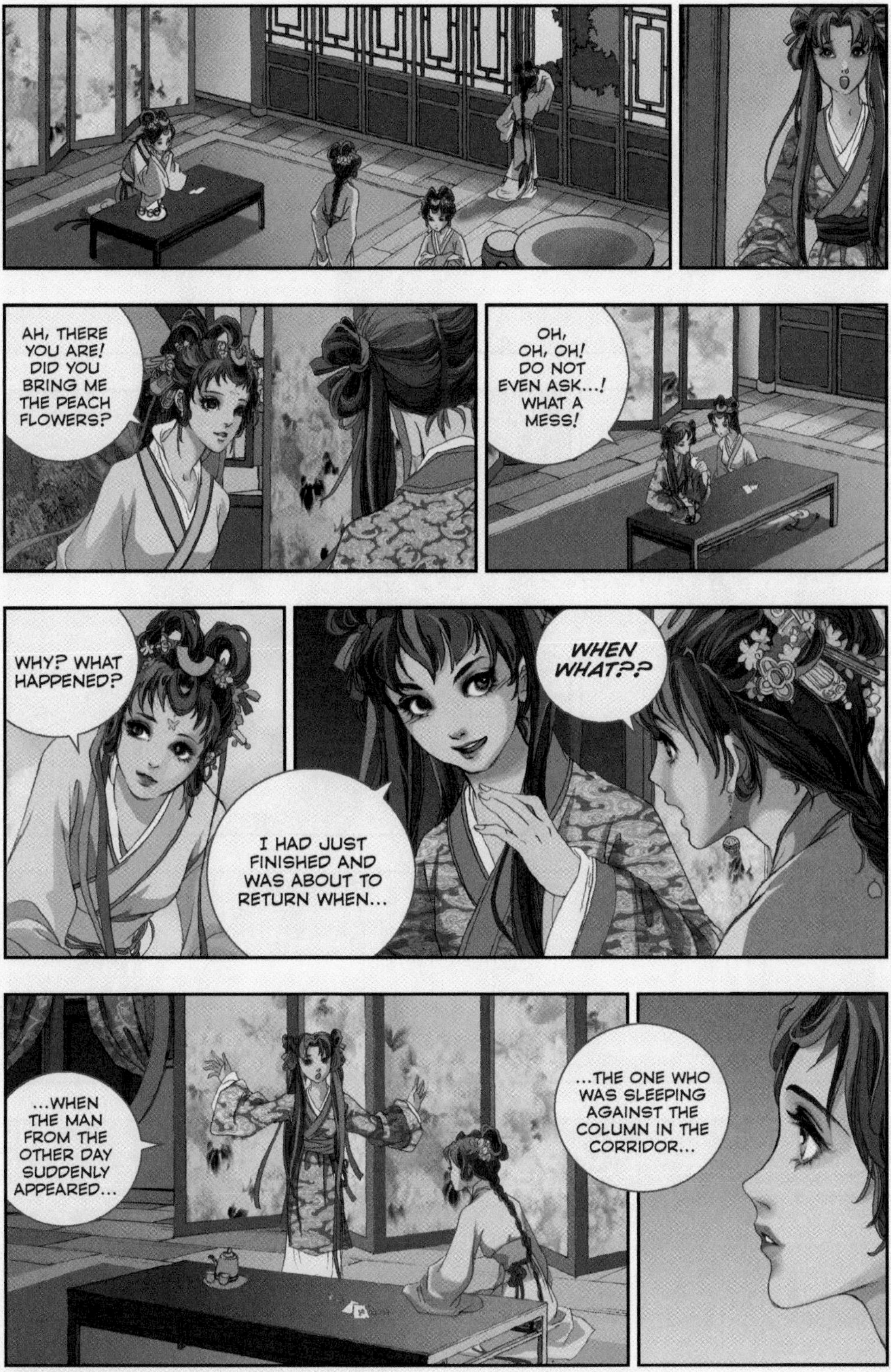
AH, THERE YOU ARE! DID YOU BRING ME THE PEACH FLOWERS?
OH, OH, OH! DO NOT EVEN ASK...! WHAT A MESS!
WHY? WHAT HAPPENED?
I HAD JUST FINISHED AND WAS ABOUT TO RETURN WHEN...
WHEN WHAT??
...WHEN THE MAN FROM THE OTHER DAY SUDDENLY APPEARED...
...THE ONE WHO WAS SLEEPING AGAINST THE COLUMN IN THE CORRIDOR...

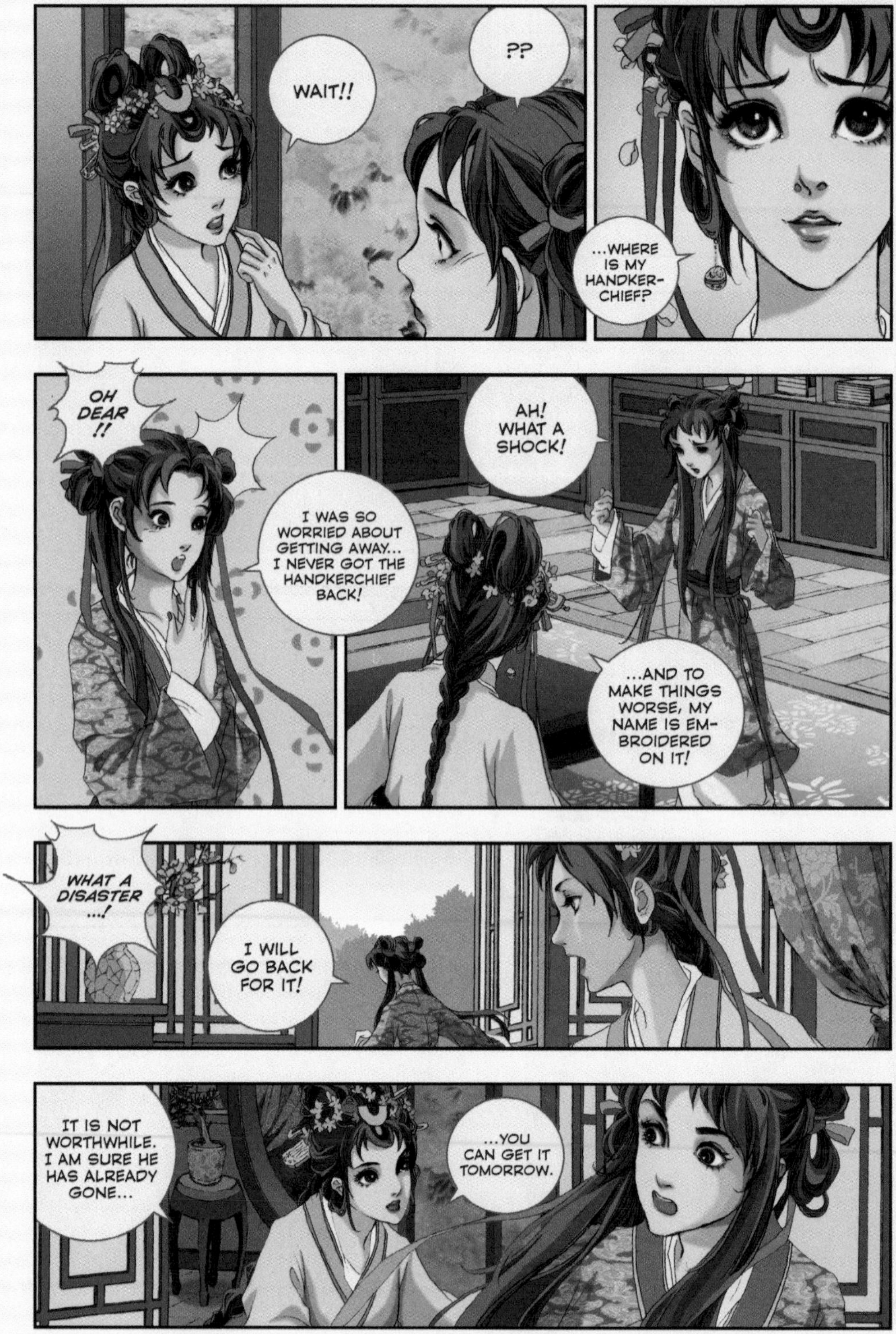
WAIT!!
??
...WHERE IS MY HANDKER-CHIEF?
OH DEAR !!
I WAS SO WORRIED ABOUT GETTING AWAY... I NEVER GOT THE HANDKERCHIEF BACK!
AH! WHAT A SHOCK!
...AND TO MAKE THINGS WORSE, MY NAME IS EM-BROIDERED ON IT!
WHAT A DISASTER ...!
I WILL GO BACK FOR IT!
IT IS NOT WORTHWHILE. I AM SURE HE HAS ALREADY GONE...
...YOU CAN GET IT TOMORROW.

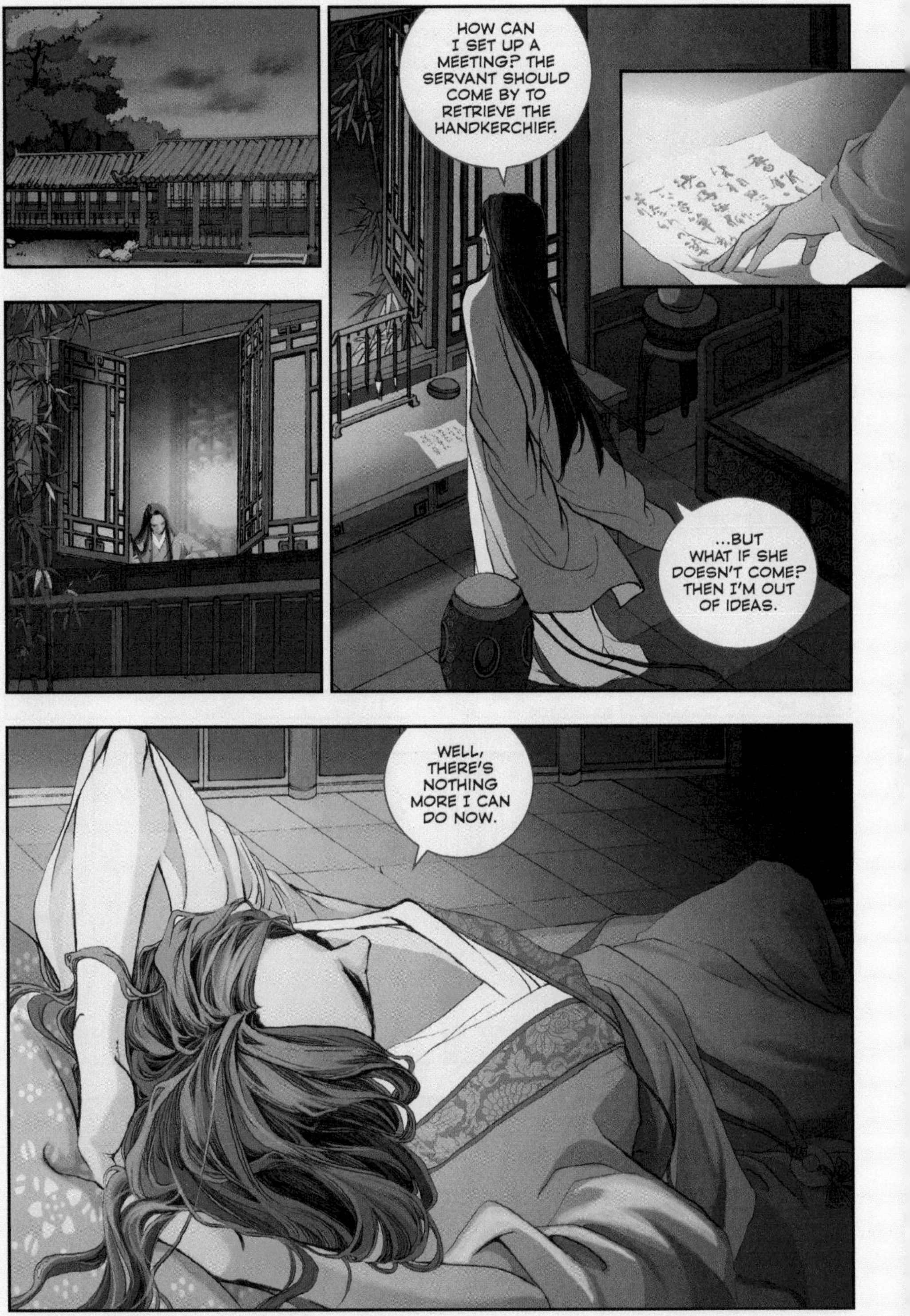
HOW CAN I SET UP A MEETING? THE SERVANT SHOULD COME BY TO RETRIEVE THE HANDKERCHIEF.
...BUT WHAT IF SHE DOESN'T COME? THEN I'M OUT OF IDEAS.
WELL, THERE'S NOTHING MORE I CAN DO NOW.

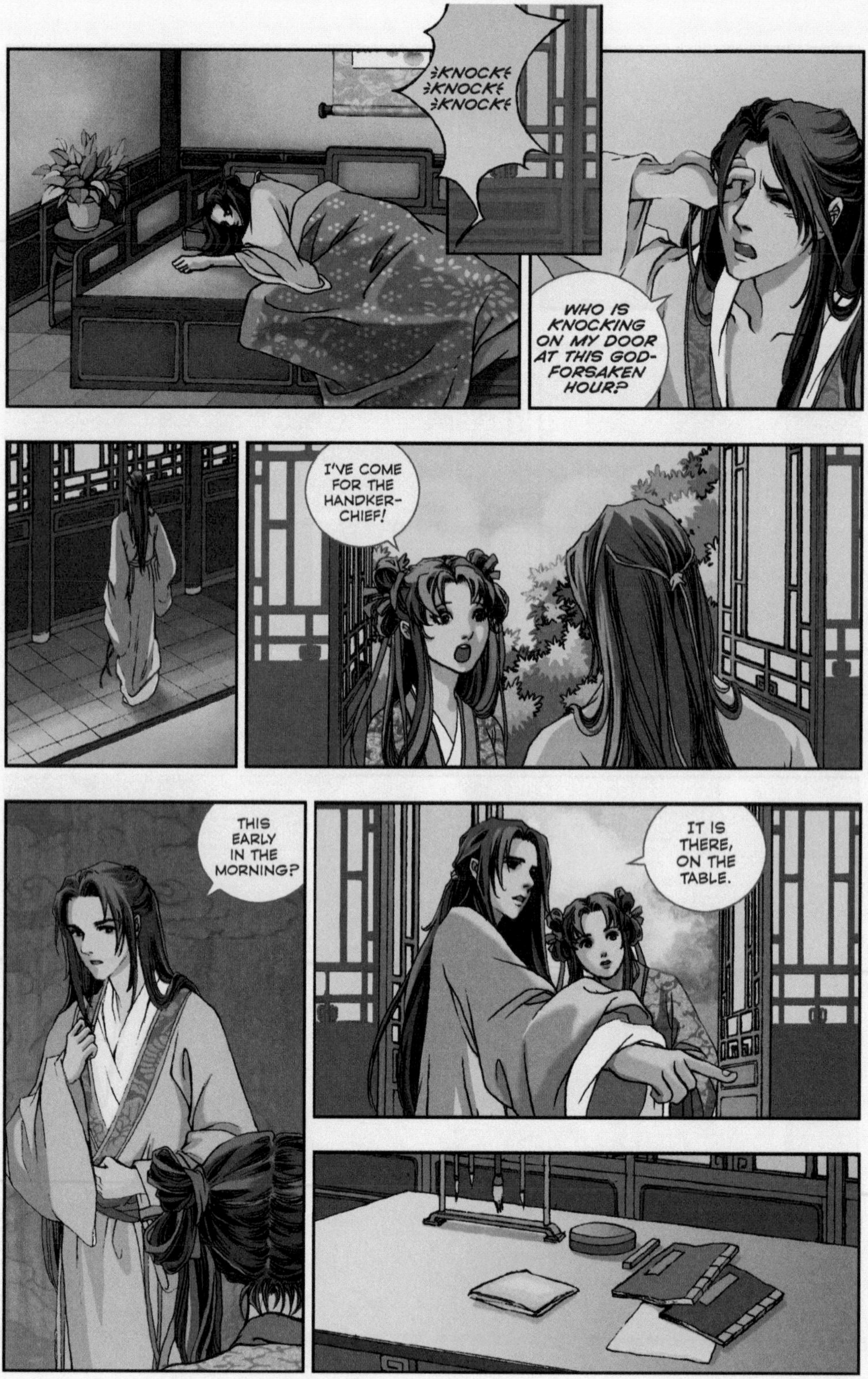

KNOCK KNOCK KNOCK
WHO IS KNOCKING ON MY DOOR AT THIS GOD-FORSAKEN HOUR?
I'VE COME FOR THE HANDKER-CHIEF!
THIS EARLY IN THE MORNING?
IT IS THERE, ON THE TABLE.

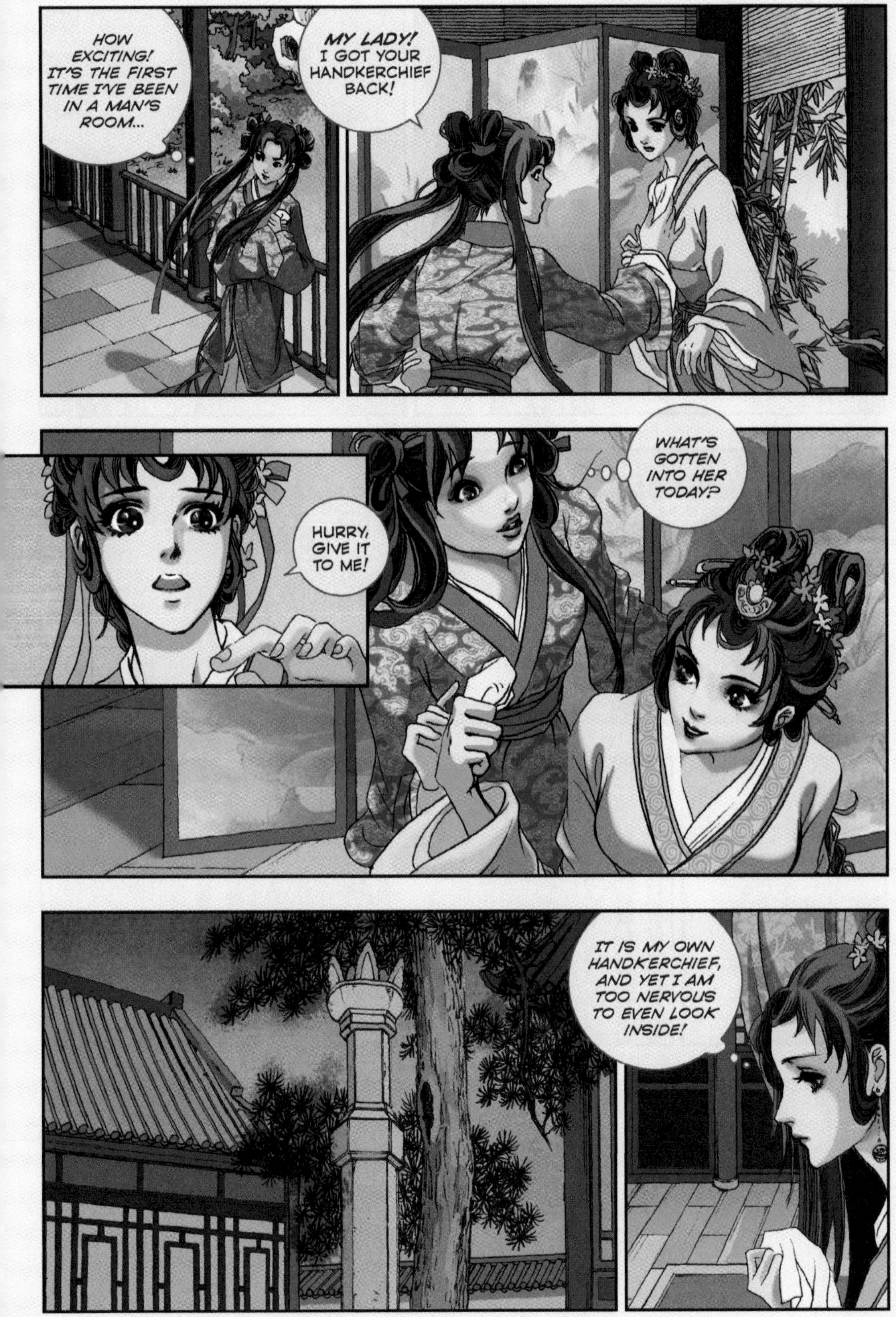
HOW EXCITING! IT'S THE FIRST TIME I'VE BEEN IN A MAN'S ROOM...
MY LADY! I GOT YOUR HANDKERCHIEF BACK!
HURRY, GIVE IT TO ME!
WHAT'S GOTTEN INTO HER TODAY?
IT IS MY OWN HANDKERCHIEF, AND YET I AM TOO NERVOUS TO EVEN LOOK INSIDE!

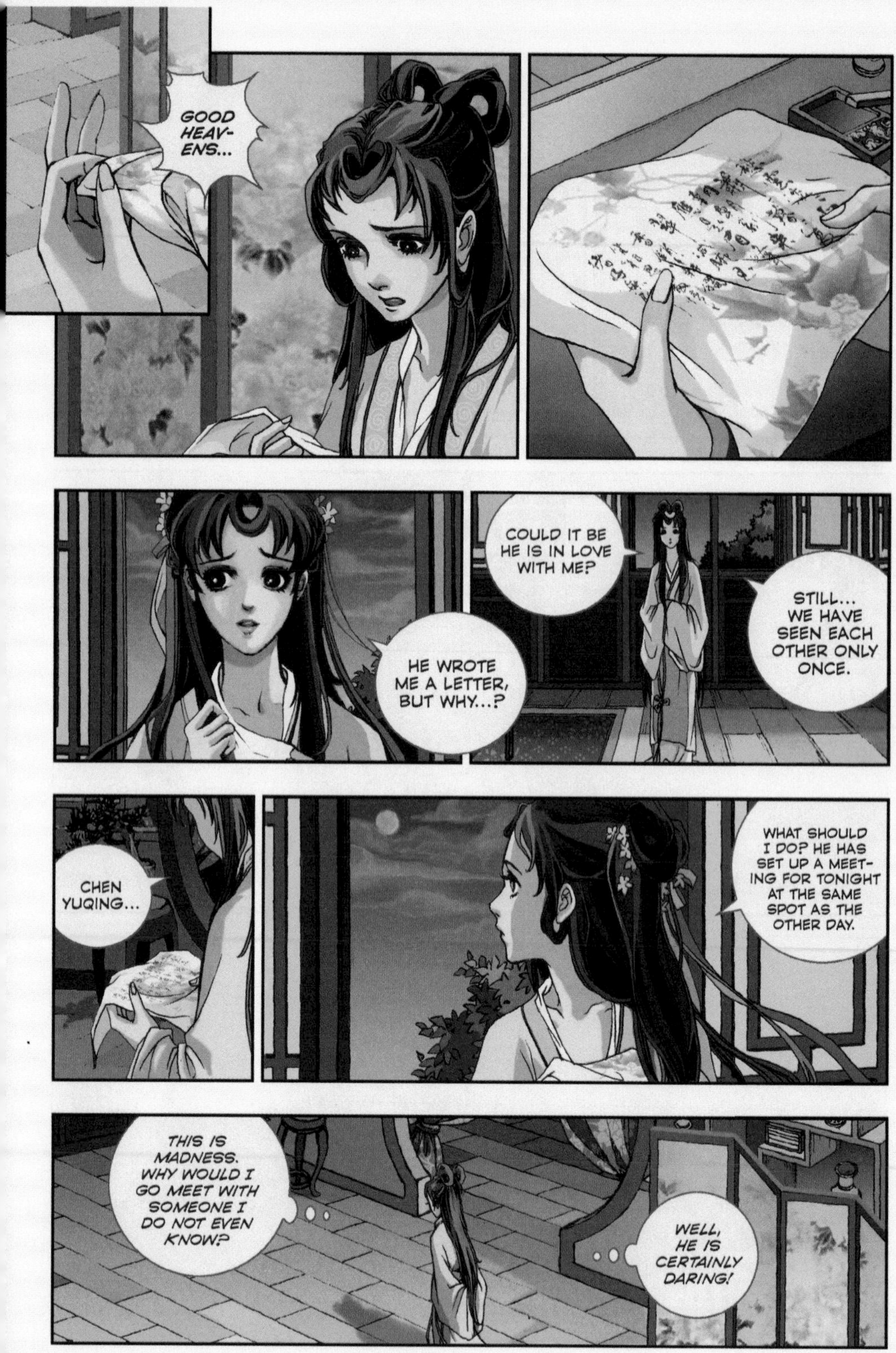
GOOD HEAV-ENS...
HE WROTE ME A LETTER, BUT WHY...?
COULD IT BE HE IS IN LOVE WITH ME?
STILL... WE HAVE SEEN EACH OTHER ONLY ONCE.
CHEN YUQING...
WHAT SHOULD I DO? HE HAS SET UP A MEET-ING FOR TONIGHT AT THE SAME SPOT AS THE OTHER DAY.
THIS IS MADNESS. WHY WOULD I GO MEET WITH SOMEONE I DO NOT EVEN KNOW?
WELL, HE IS CERTAINLY DARING!

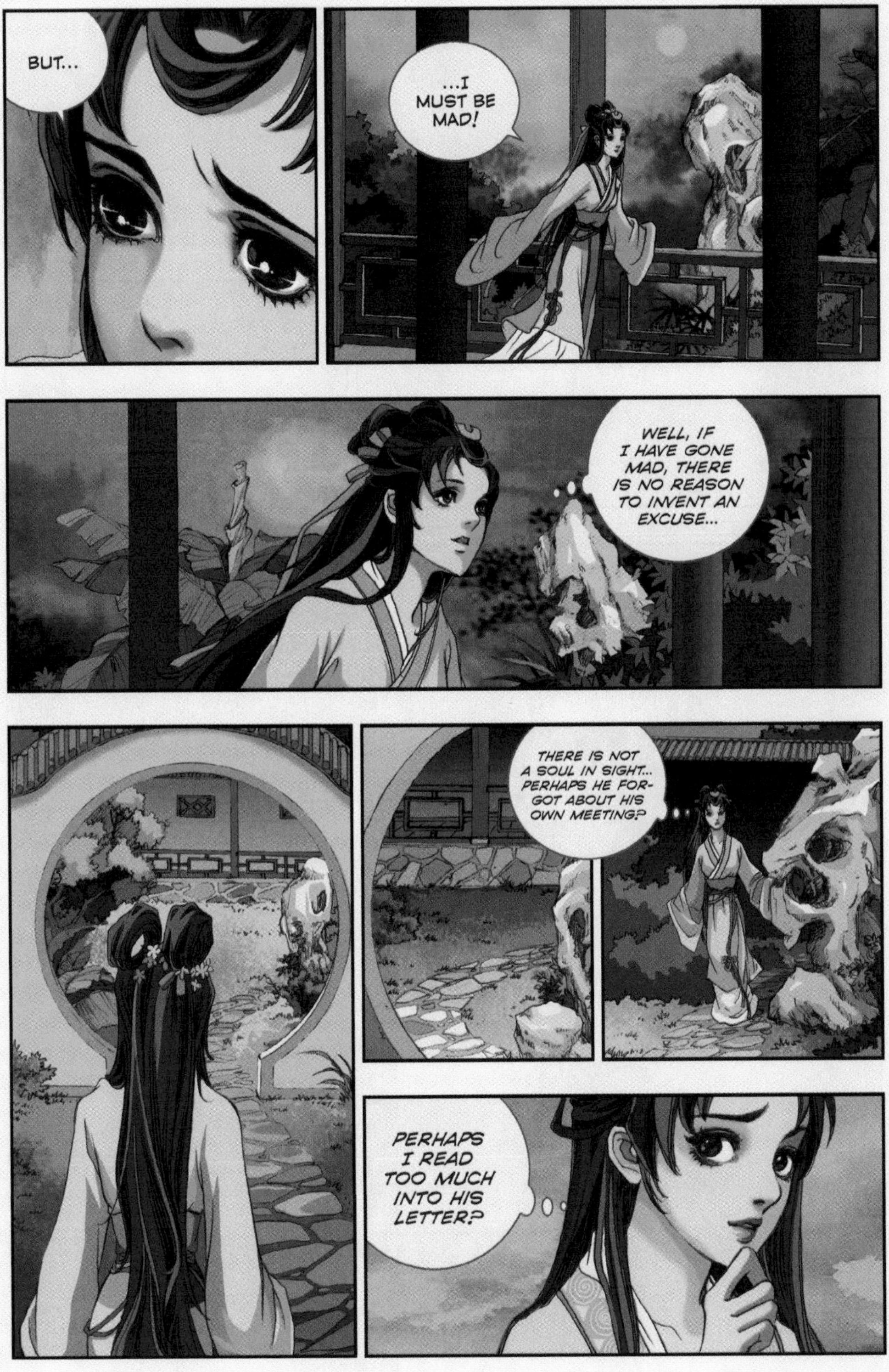
BUT...
...I MUST BE MAD!
WELL, IF I HAVE GONE MAD, THERE IS NO REASON TO INVENT AN EXCUSE...
THERE IS NOT A SOUL IN SIGHT... PERHAPS HE FORGOT ABOUT HIS OWN MEETING?
PERHAPS I READ TOO MUCH INTO HIS LETTER?

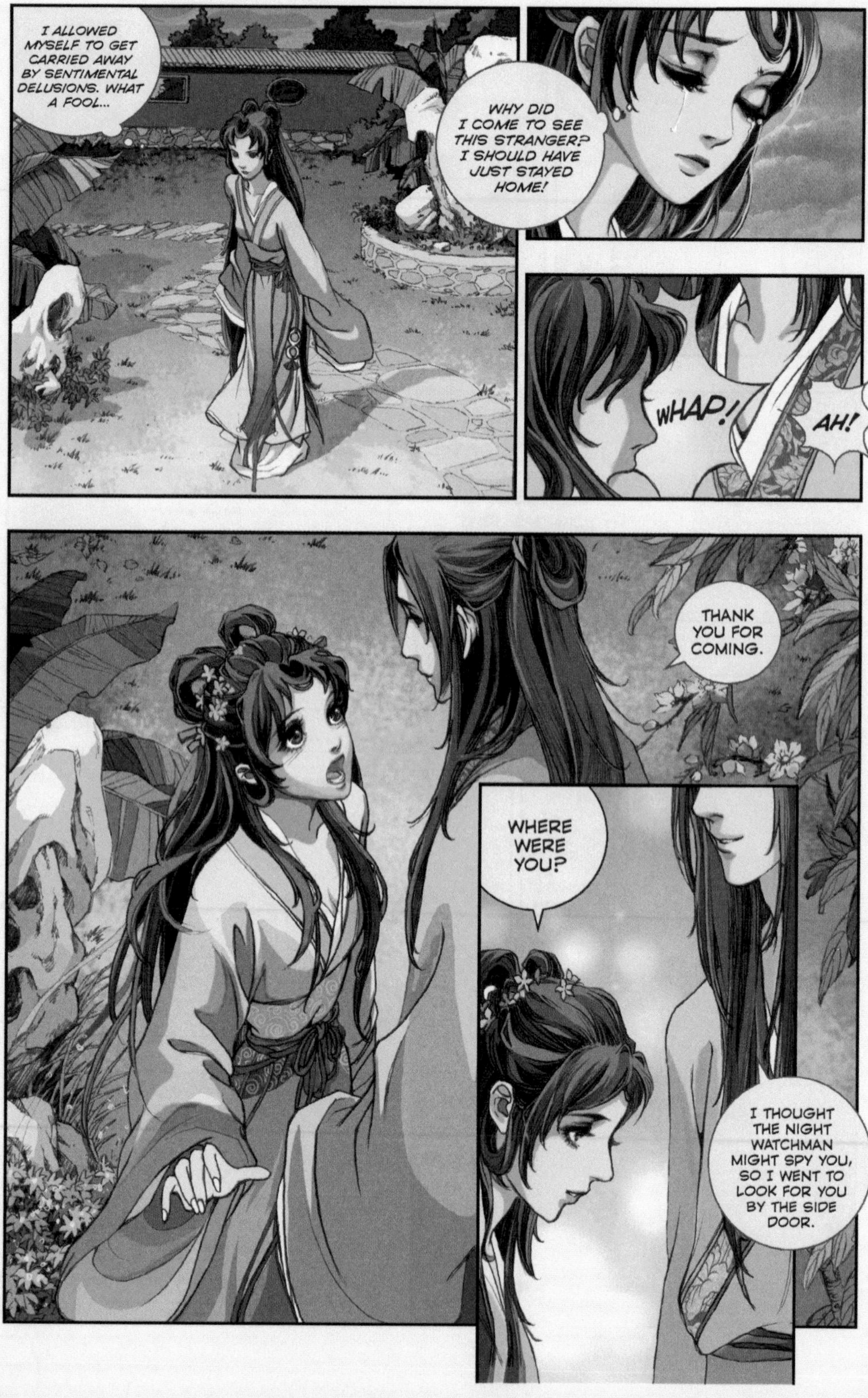
I ALLOWED MYSELF TO GET CARRIED AWAY BY SENTIMENTAL DELUSIONS. WHAT A FOOL...
WHY DID I COME TO SEE THIS STRANGER? I SHOULD HAVE JUST STAYED HOME!
WHAP!
AH!
THANK YOU FOR COMING.
WHERE WERE YOU?
I THOUGHT THE NIGHT WATCHMAN MIGHT SPY YOU, SO I WENT TO LOOK FOR YOU BY THE SIDE DOOR.

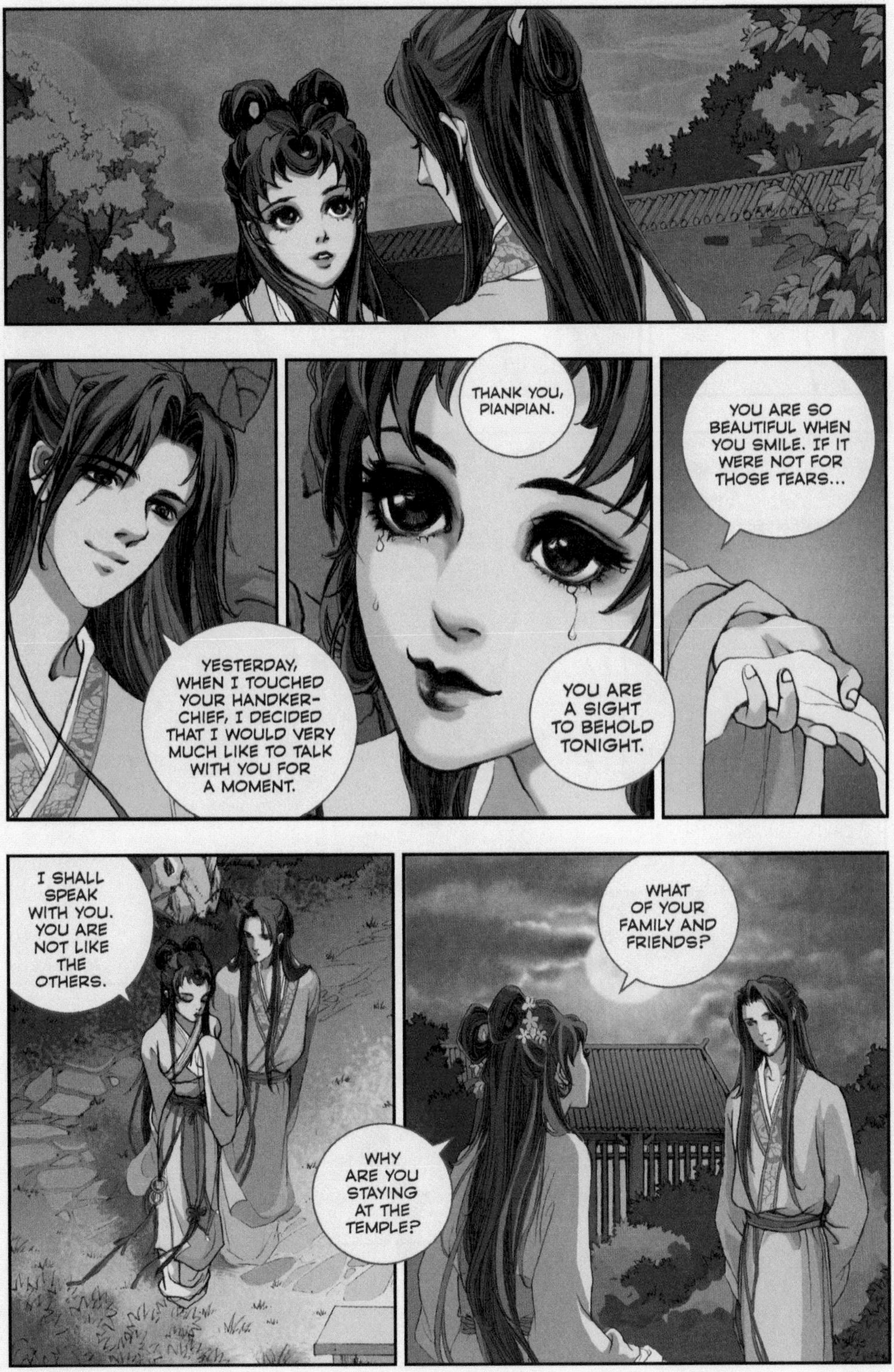
YESTERDAY, WHEN I TOUCHED YOUR HANDKER-CHIEF, I DECIDED THAT I WOULD VERY MUCH LIKE TO TALK WITH YOU FOR A MOMENT.
THANK YOU, PIANPIAN.
YOU ARE A SIGHT TO BEHOLD TONIGHT.
YOU ARE SO BEAUTIFUL WHEN YOU SMILE. IF IT WERE NOT FOR THOSE TEARS...
I SHALL SPEAK WITH YOU. YOU ARE NOT LIKE THE OTHERS.
WHAT OF YOUR FAMILY AND FRIENDS?
WHY ARE YOU STAYING AT THE TEMPLE?

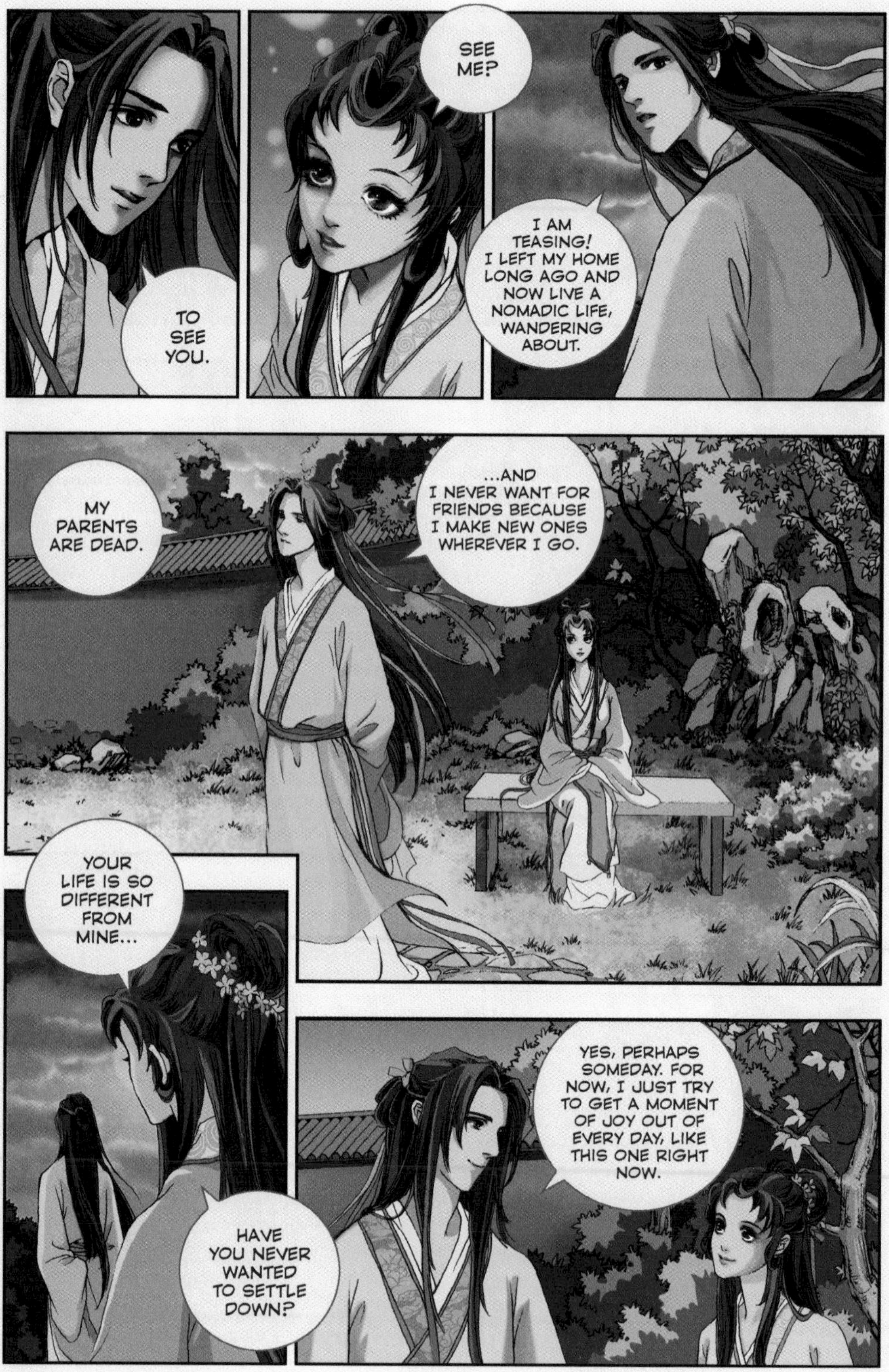
TO SEE YOU.
SEE ME?
I AM TEASING! I LEFT MY HOME LONG AGO AND NOW LIVE A NOMADIC LIFE, WANDERING ABOUT.
MY PARENTS ARE DEAD.
...AND I NEVER WANT FOR FRIENDS BECAUSE I MAKE NEW ONES WHEREVER I GO.
YOUR LIFE IS SO DIFFERENT FROM MINE...
HAVE YOU NEVER WANTED TO SETTLE DOWN?
YES, PERHAPS SOMEDAY. FOR NOW, I JUST TRY TO GET A MOMENT OF JOY OUT OF EVERY DAY, LIKE THIS ONE RIGHT NOW.

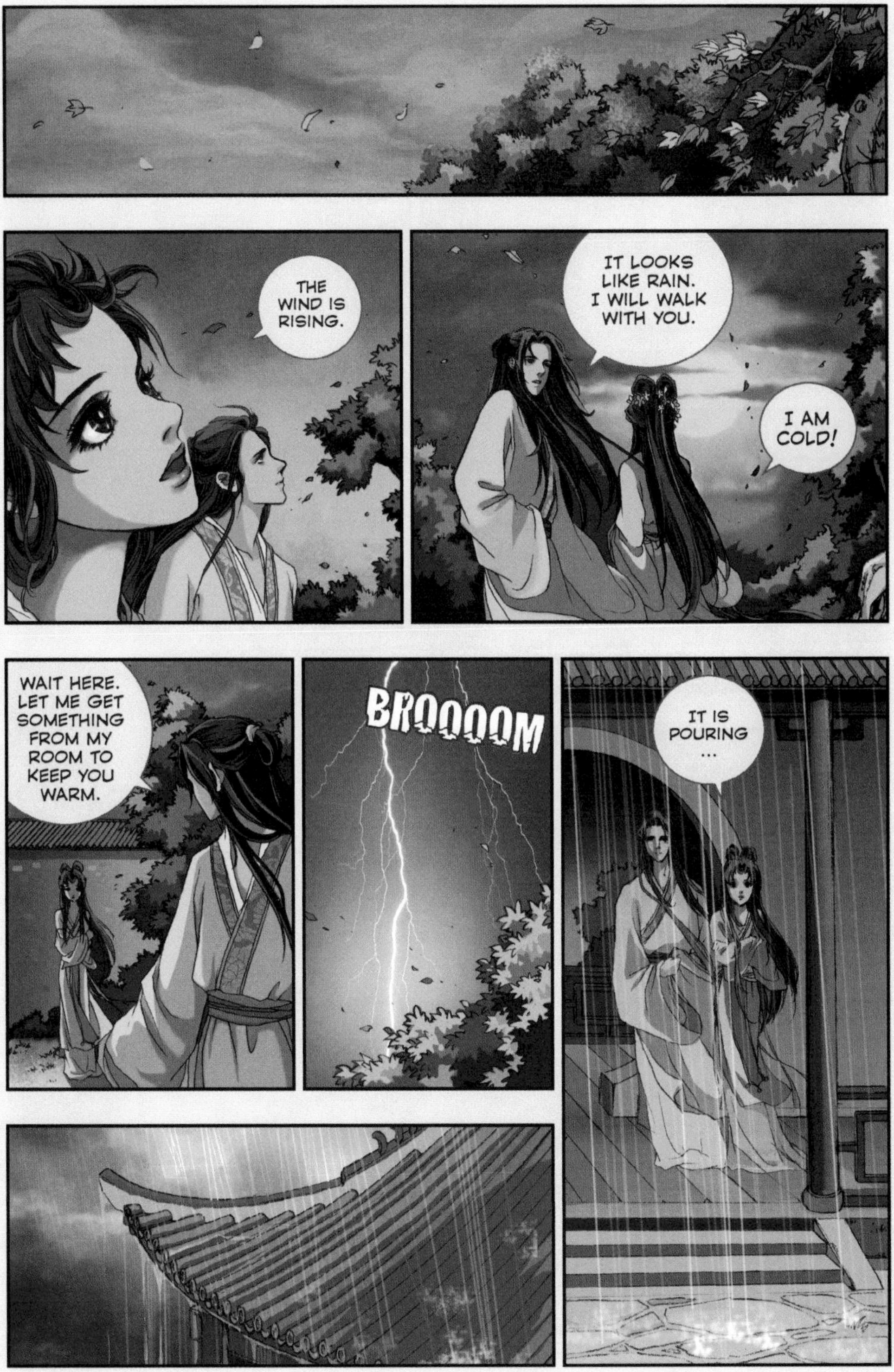
THE WIND IS RISING.
IT LOOKS LIKE RAIN. I WILL WALK WITH YOU.
I AM COLD!
WAIT HERE. LET ME GET SOMETHING FROM MY ROOM TO KEEP YOU WARM.
BROOOOM
IT IS POURING ...

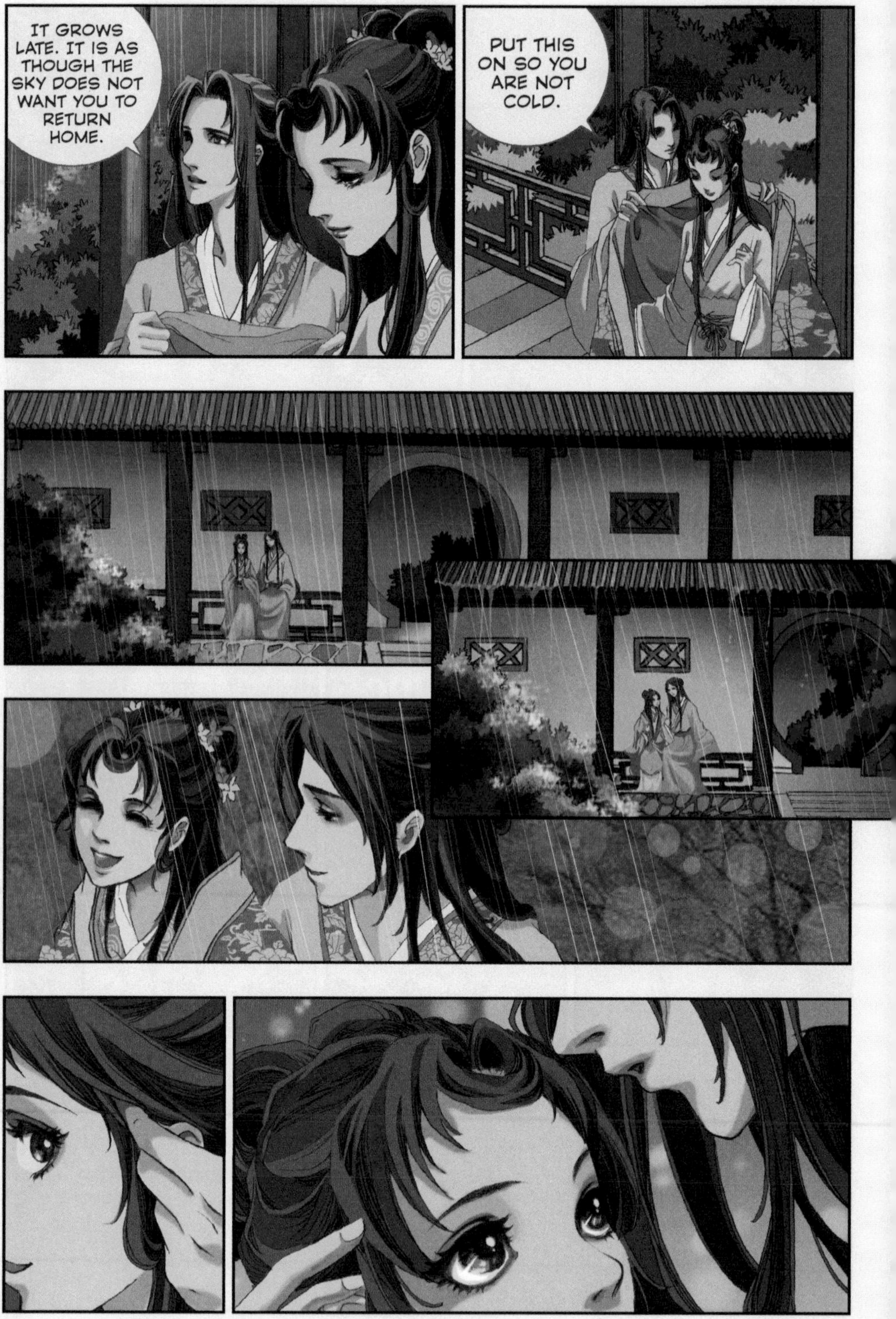
IT GROWS LATE. IT IS AS THOUGH THE SKY DOES NOT WANT YOU TO RETURN HOME.
PUT THIS ON SO YOU ARE NOT COLD.

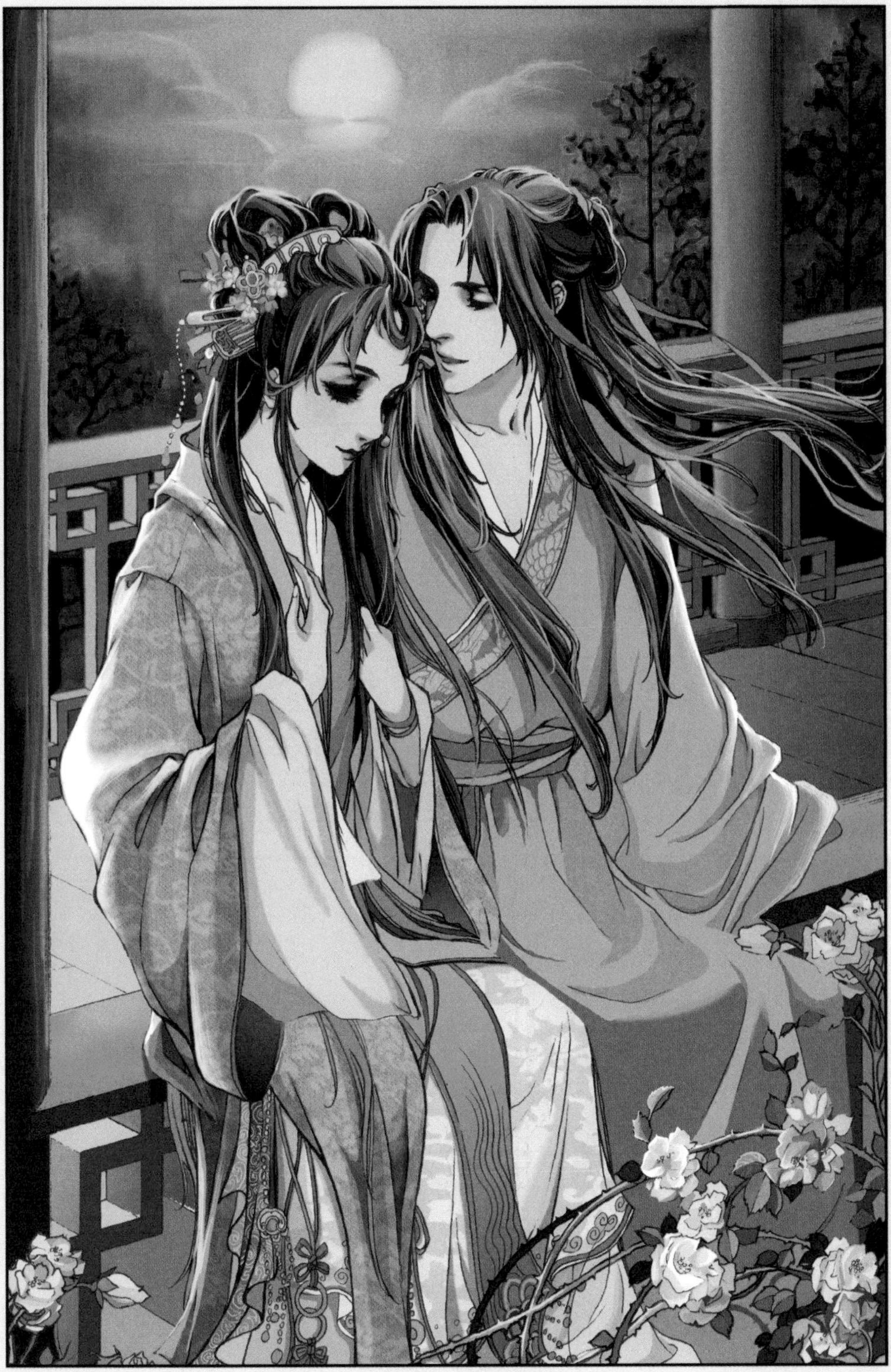

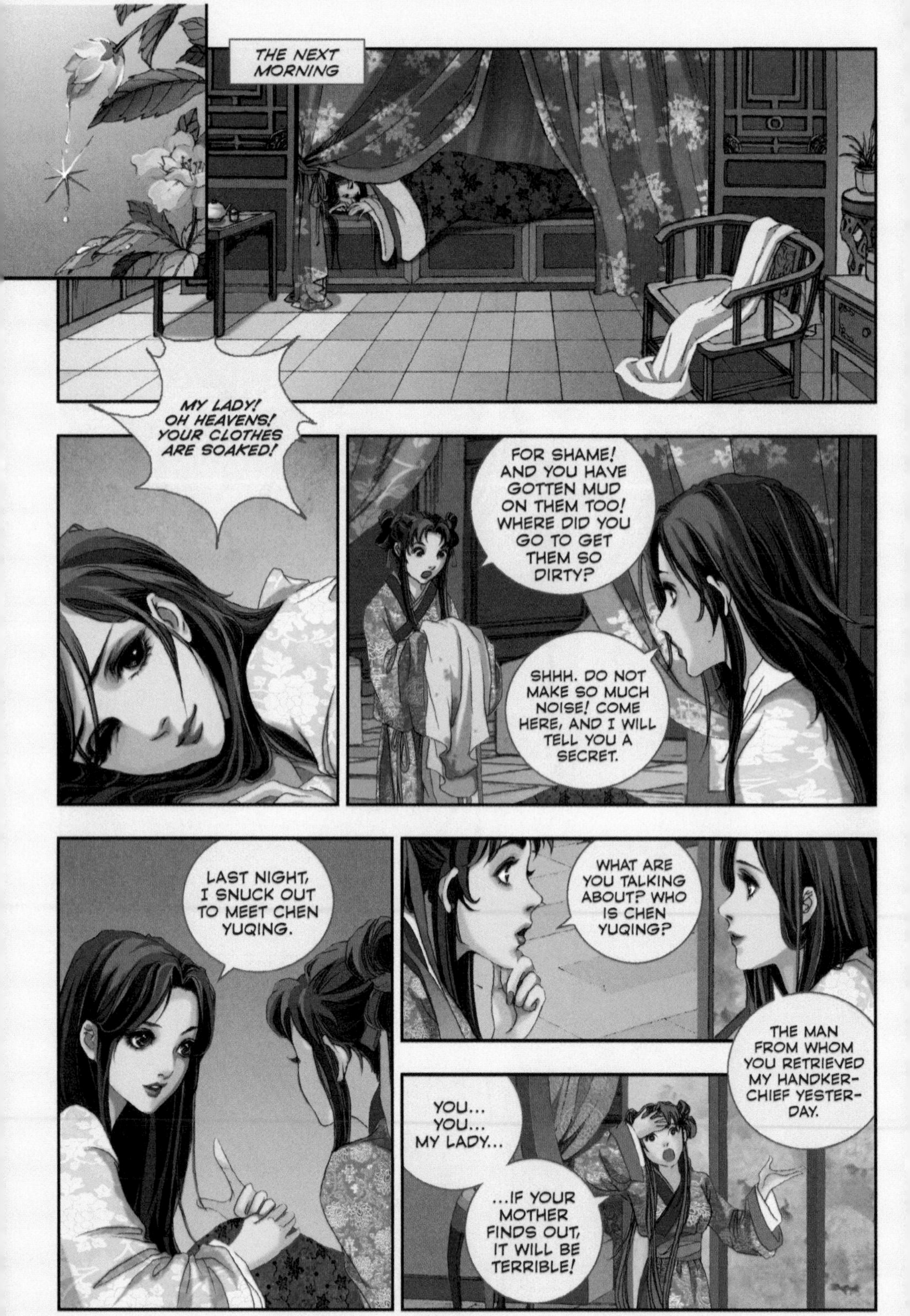
THE NEXT MORNING
MY LADY! OH HEAVENS! YOUR CLOTHES ARE SOAKED!
FOR SHAME! AND YOU HAVE GOTTEN MUD ON THEM TOO! WHERE DID YOU GO TO GET THEM SO DIRTY?
SHHH. DO NOT MAKE SO MUCH NOISE! COME HERE, AND I WILL TELL YOU A SECRET.
LAST NIGHT, I SNUCK OUT TO MEET CHEN YUQING.
WHAT ARE YOU TALKING ABOUT? WHO IS CHEN YUQING?
THE MAN FROM WHOM YOU RETRIEVED MY HANDKER-CHIEF YESTER-DAY.
YOU... YOU... MY LADY...
...IF YOUR MOTHER FINDS OUT, IT WILL BE TERRIBLE!

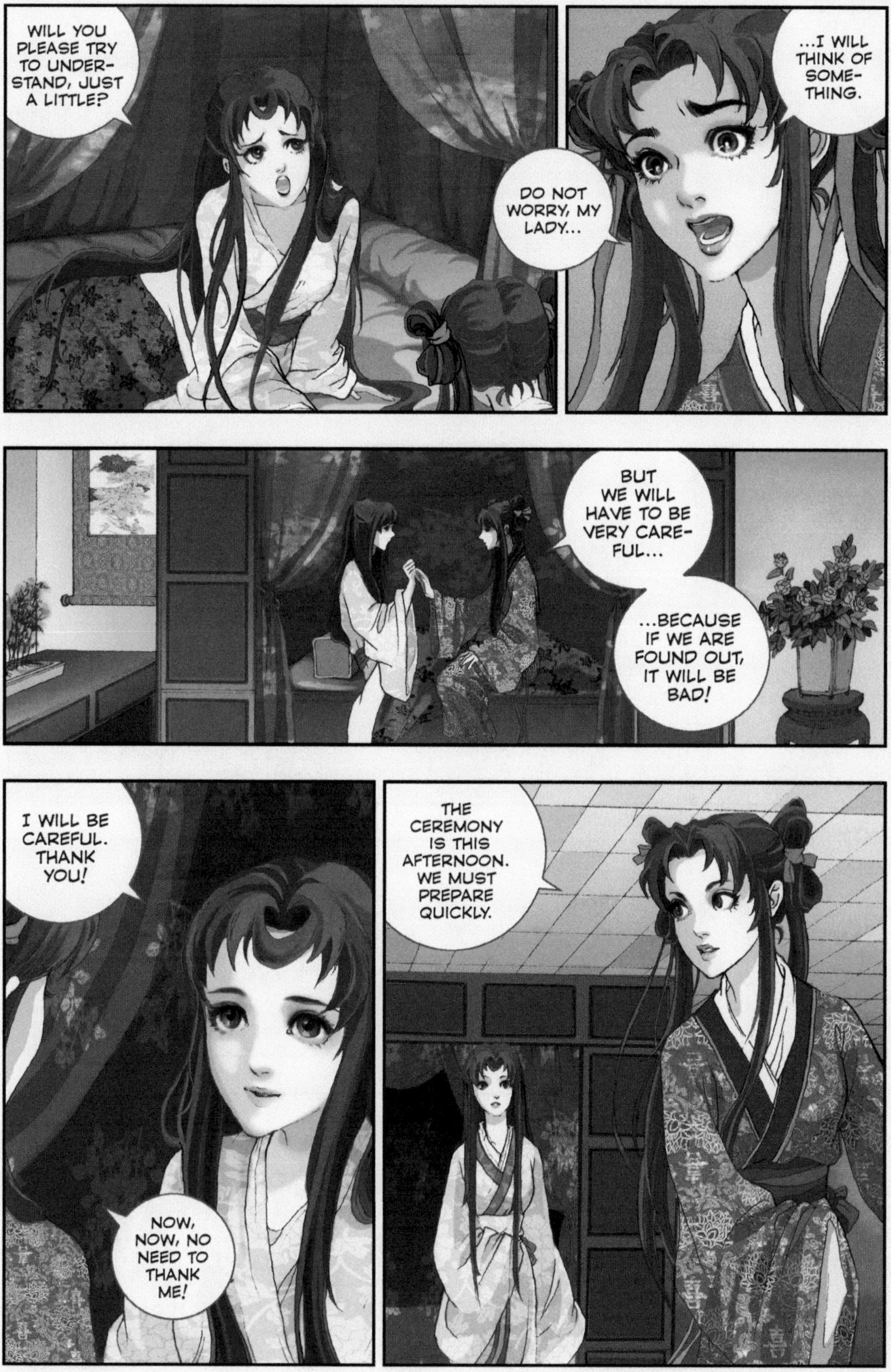
WILL YOU PLEASE TRY TO UNDER-STAND, JUST A LITTLE?
DO NOT WORRY, MY LADY...
...I WILL THINK OF SOME-THING.
BUT WE WILL HAVE TO BE VERY CARE-FUL...
...BECAUSE IF WE ARE FOUND OUT, IT WILL BE BAD!
I WILL BE CAREFUL. THANK YOU!
NOW, NOW, NO NEED TO THANK ME!
THE CEREMONY IS THIS AFTERNOON. WE MUST PREPARE QUICKLY.

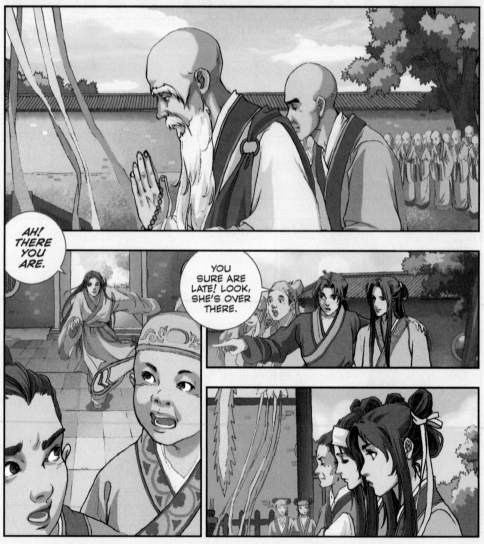

AH! THERE YOU ARE.

YOU SURE ARE LATE! LOOK, SHE'S OVER THERE.

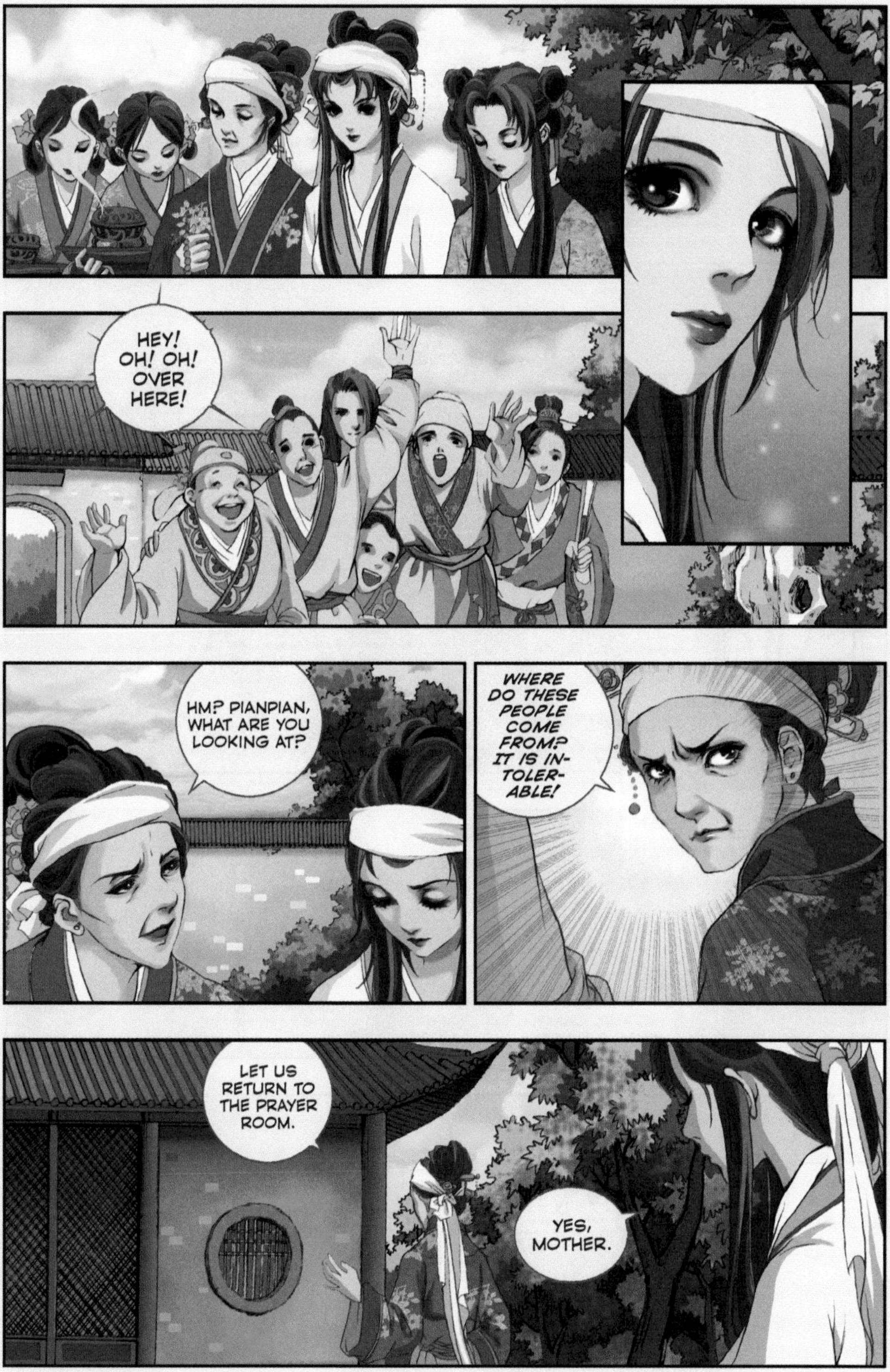
HEY! OH! OH! OVER HERE!
HM? PIANPIAN, WHAT ARE YOU LOOKING AT?
WHERE DO THESE PEOPLE COME FROM? IT IS INTOLERABLE!
LET US RETURN TO THE PRAYER ROOM.
YES, MOTHER.

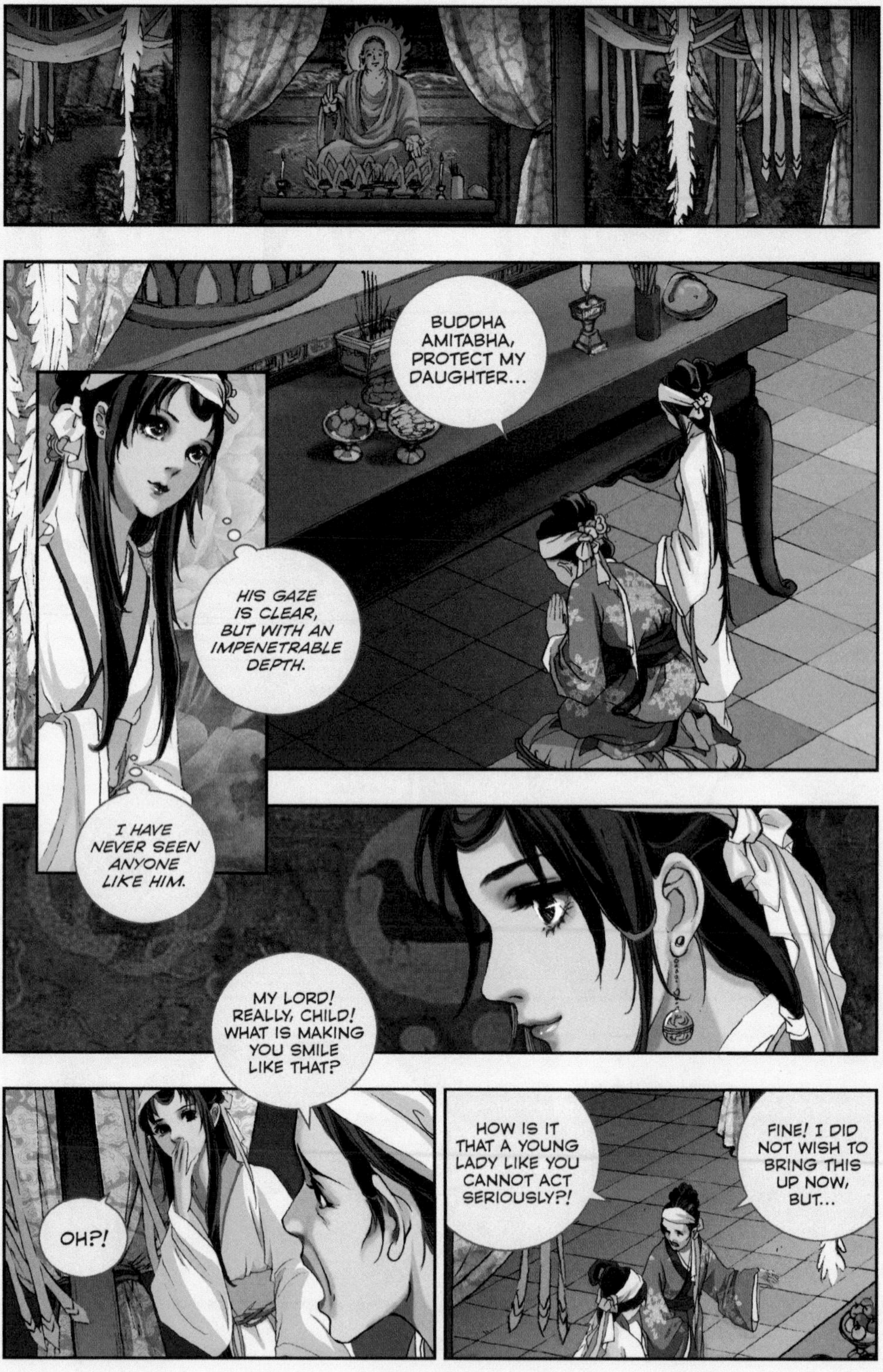
BUDDHA AMITABHA, PROTECT MY DAUGHTER...
HIS GAZE IS CLEAR, BUT WITH AN IMPENETRABLE DEPTH.
I HAVE NEVER SEEN ANYONE LIKE HIM.
MY LORD! REALLY, CHILD! WHAT IS MAKING YOU SMILE LIKE THAT?
OH?!
HOW IS IT THAT A YOUNG LADY LIKE YOU CANNOT ACT SERIOUSLY?!
FINE! I DID NOT WISH TO BRING THIS UP NOW, BUT...

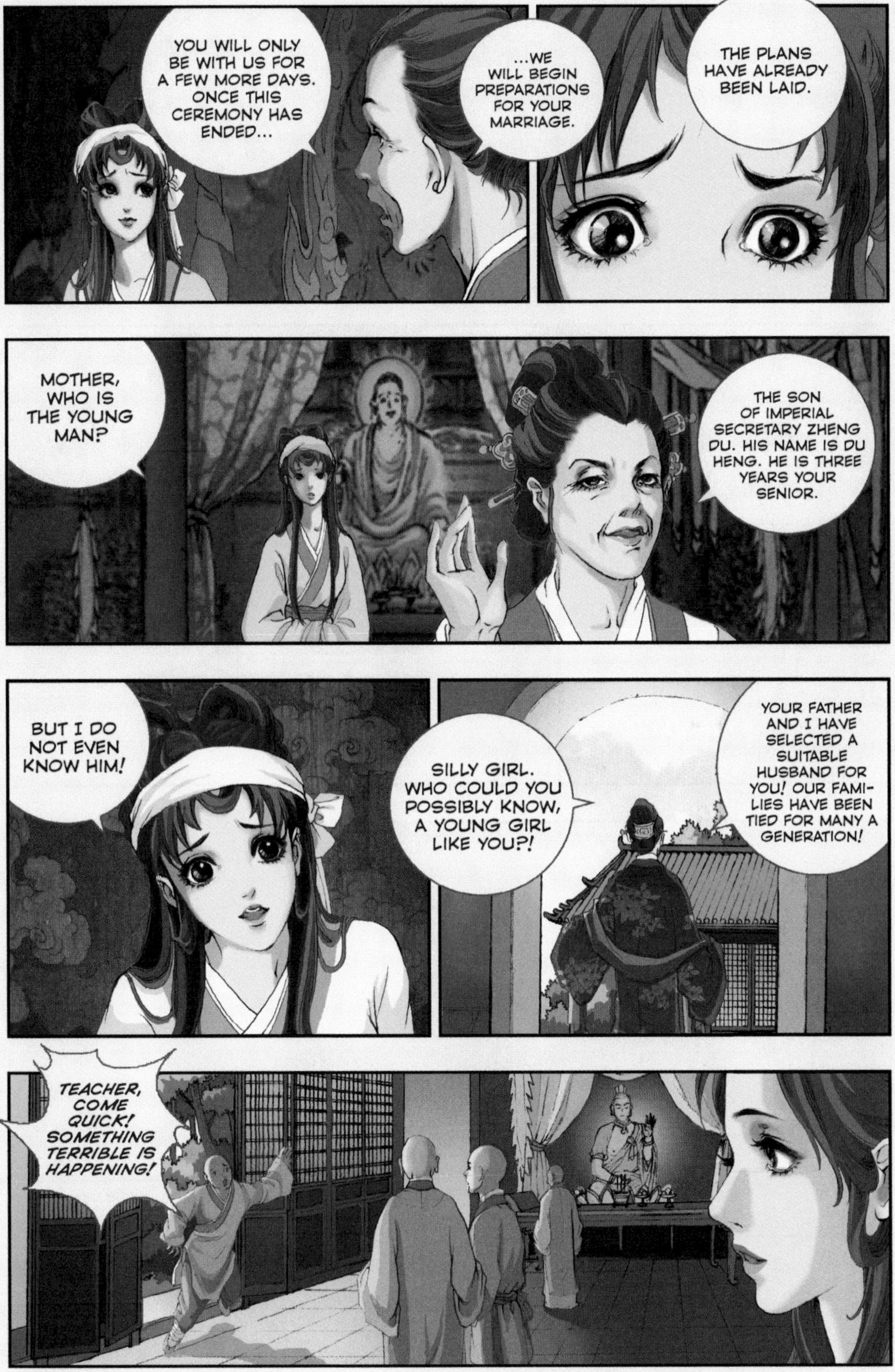
YOU WILL ONLY BE WITH US FOR A FEW MORE DAYS. ONCE THIS CEREMONY HAS ENDED...
...WE WILL BEGIN PREPARATIONS FOR YOUR MARRIAGE.
THE PLANS HAVE ALREADY BEEN LAID.
MOTHER, WHO IS THE YOUNG MAN?
THE SON OF IMPERIAL SECRETARY ZHENG DU. HIS NAME IS DU HENG. HE IS THREE YEARS YOUR SENIOR.
BUT I DO NOT EVEN KNOW HIM!
SILLY GIRL. WHO COULD YOU POSSIBLY KNOW, A YOUNG GIRL LIKE YOU?!
YOUR FATHER AND I HAVE SELECTED A SUITABLE HUSBAND FOR YOU! OUR FAMILIES HAVE BEEN TIED FOR MANY A GENERATION!
TEACHER, COME QUICK! SOMETHING TERRIBLE IS HAPPENING!

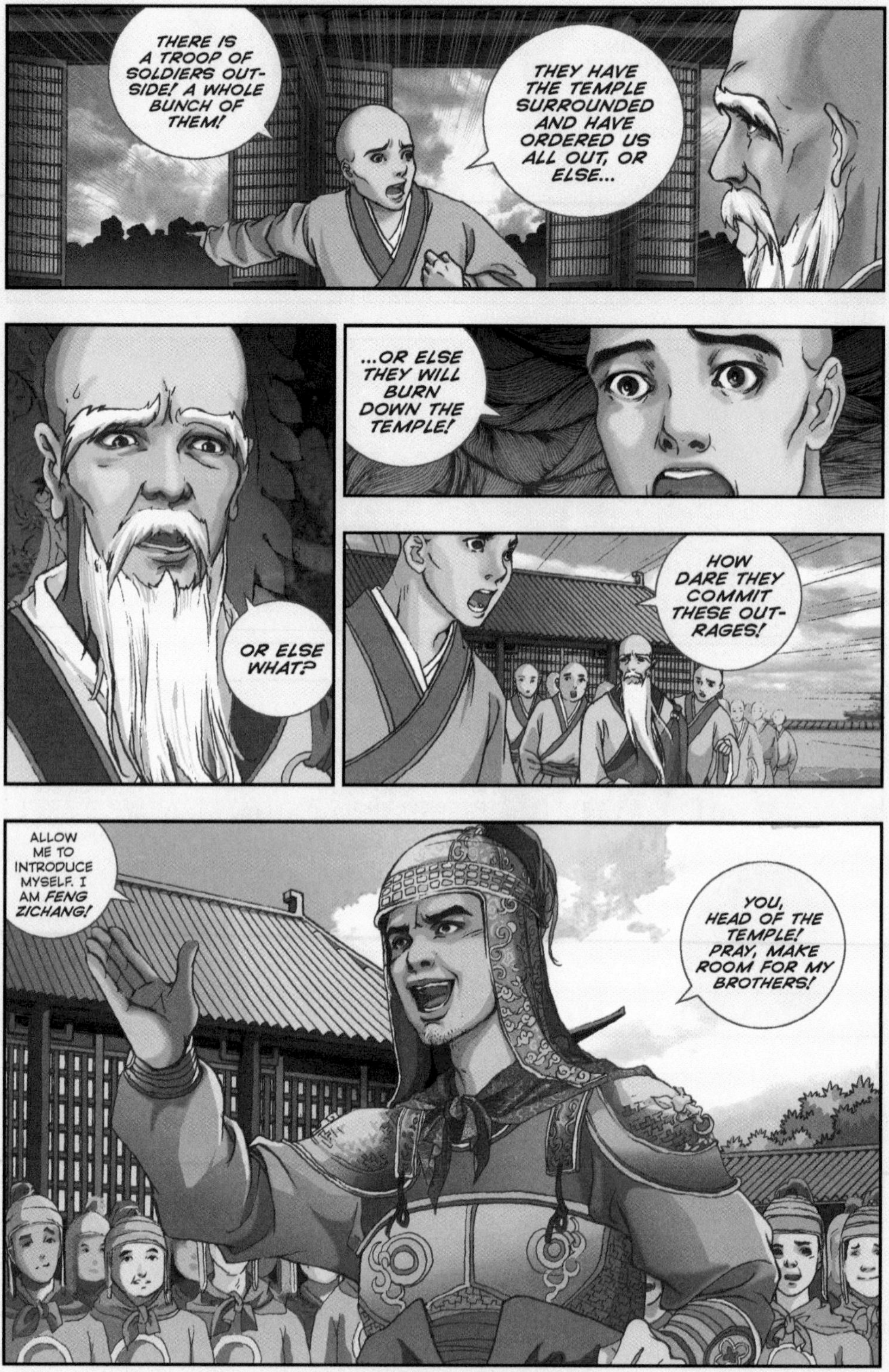
THERE IS A TROOP OF SOLDIERS OUT-SIDE! A WHOLE BUNCH OF THEM!
THEY HAVE THE TEMPLE SURROUNDED AND HAVE ORDERED US ALL OUT, OR ELSE...
OR ELSE WHAT?
...OR ELSE THEY WILL BURN DOWN THE TEMPLE!
HOW DARE THEY COMMIT THESE OUT-RAGES!
ALLOW ME TO INTRODUCE MYSELF. I AM *FENG ZICHANG*!
YOU, HEAD OF THE TEMPLE! PRAY, MAKE ROOM FOR MY BROTHERS!

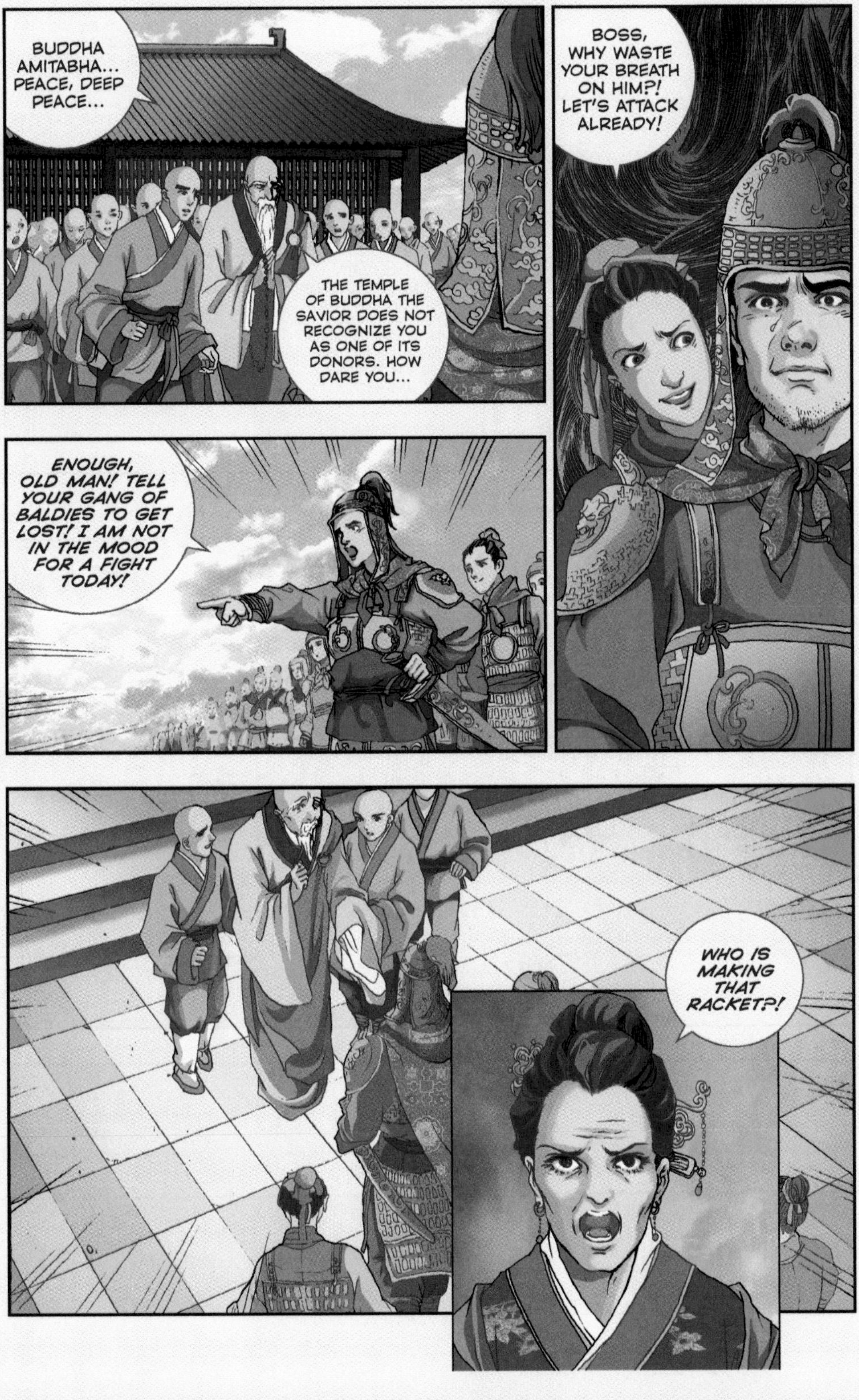
BUDDHA AMITABHA... PEACE, DEEP PEACE...
THE TEMPLE OF BUDDHA THE SAVIOR DOES NOT RECOGNIZE YOU AS ONE OF ITS DONORS. HOW DARE YOU...
BOSS, WHY WASTE YOUR BREATH ON HIM?! LET'S ATTACK ALREADY!
ENOUGH, OLD MAN! TELL YOUR GANG OF BALDIES TO GET LOST! I AM NOT IN THE MOOD FOR A FIGHT TODAY!
WHO IS MAKING THAT RACKET?!

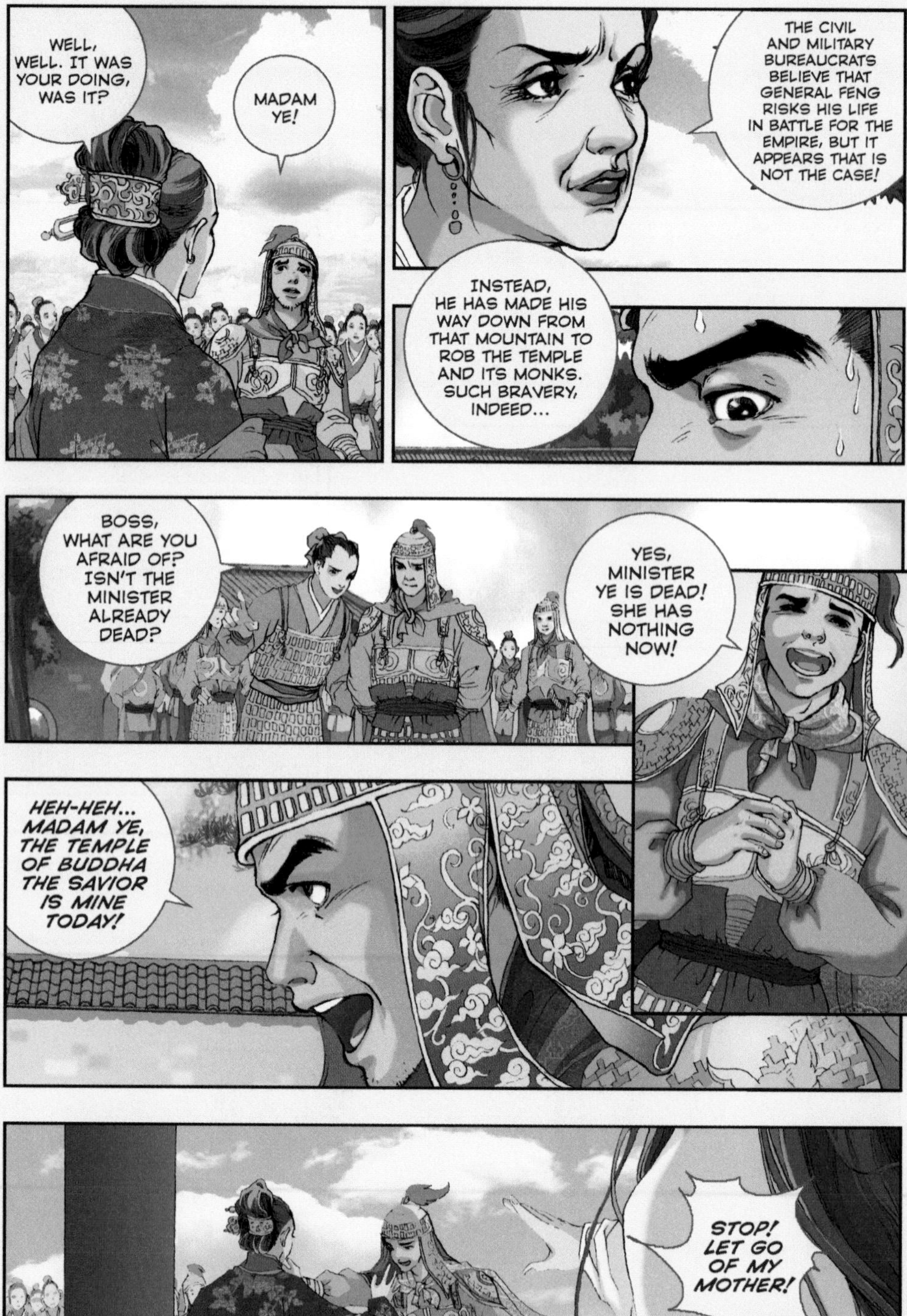
WELL, WELL. IT WAS YOUR DOING, WAS IT?
MADAM YE!
THE CIVIL AND MILITARY BUREAUCRATS BELIEVE THAT GENERAL FENG RISKS HIS LIFE IN BATTLE FOR THE EMPIRE, BUT IT APPEARS THAT IS NOT THE CASE!
INSTEAD, HE HAS MADE HIS WAY DOWN FROM THAT MOUNTAIN TO ROB THE TEMPLE AND ITS MONKS. SUCH BRAVERY, INDEED...
BOSS, WHAT ARE YOU AFRAID OF? ISN'T THE MINISTER ALREADY DEAD?
YES, MINISTER YE IS DEAD! SHE HAS NOTHING NOW!
HEH-HEH... MADAM YE, THE TEMPLE OF BUDDHA THE SAVIOR IS MINE TODAY!
STOP! LET GO OF MY MOTHER!

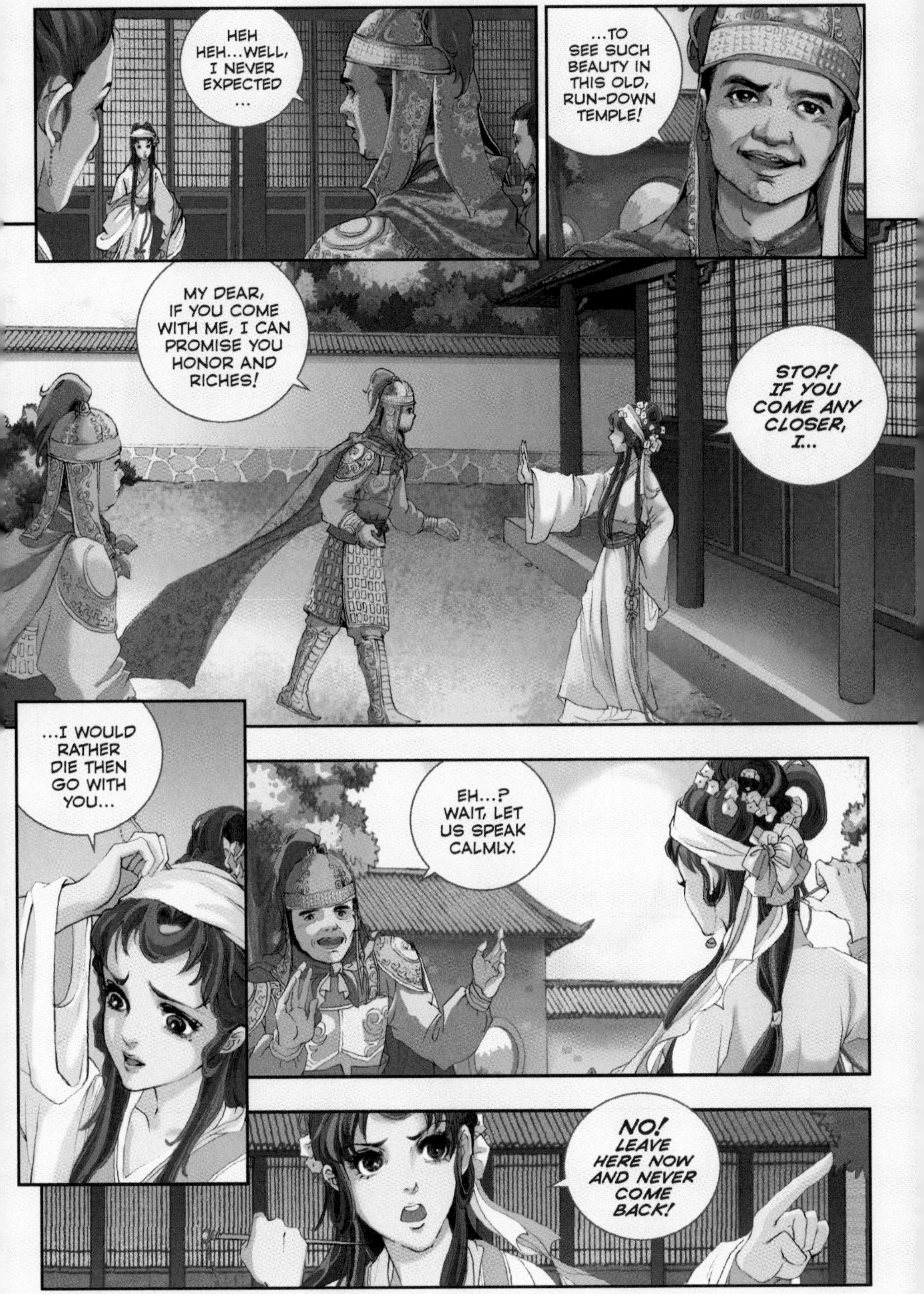
HEH HEH...WELL, I NEVER EXPECTED ...
...TO SEE SUCH BEAUTY IN THIS OLD, RUN-DOWN TEMPLE!
MY DEAR, IF YOU COME WITH ME, I CAN PROMISE YOU HONOR AND RICHES!
STOP! IF YOU COME ANY CLOSER, I...
...I WOULD RATHER DIE THEN GO WITH YOU...
EH...? WAIT, LET US SPEAK CALMLY.
NO! LEAVE HERE NOW AND NEVER COME BACK!

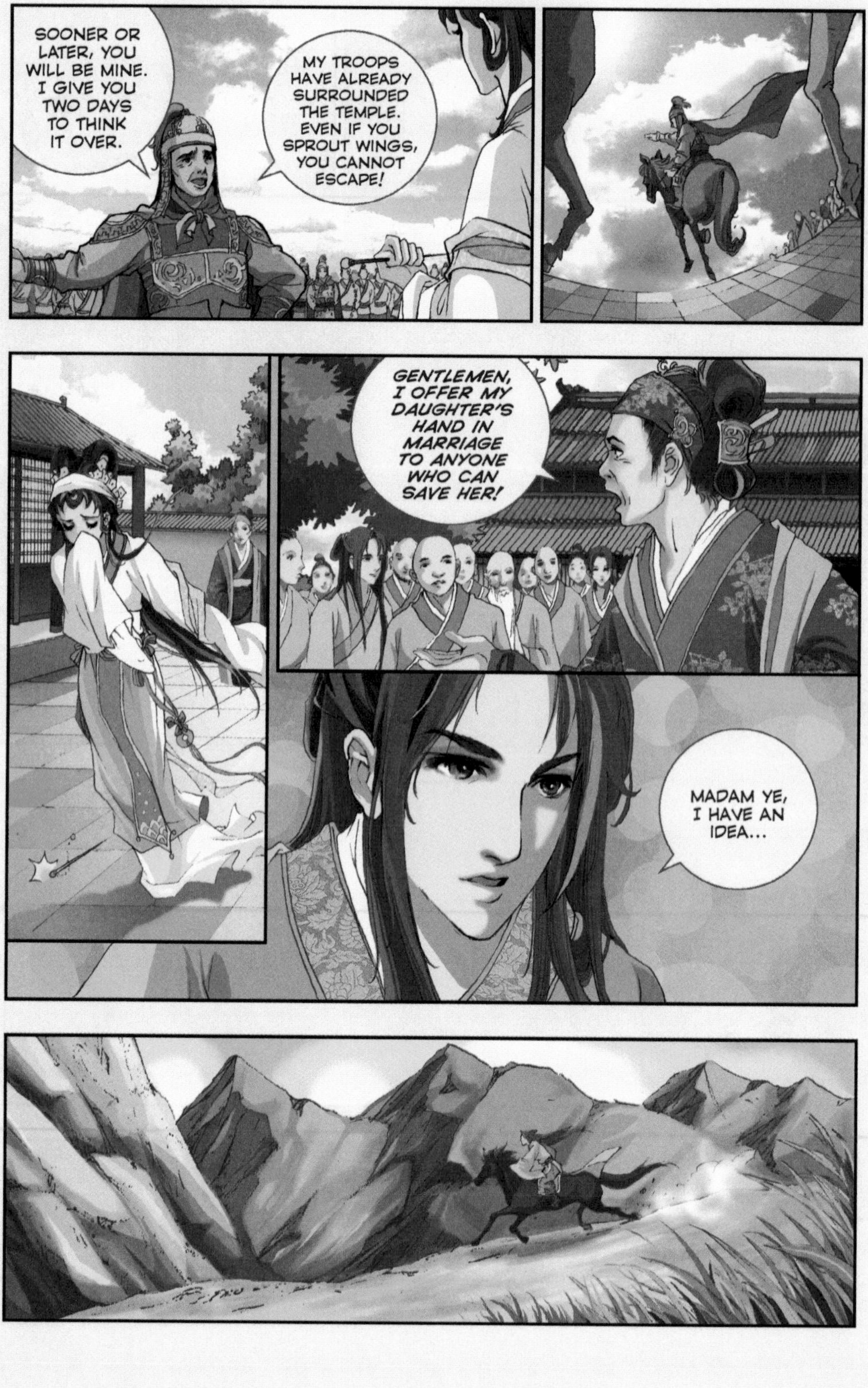
SOONER OR LATER, YOU WILL BE MINE. I GIVE YOU TWO DAYS TO THINK IT OVER.
MY TROOPS HAVE ALREADY SURROUNDED THE TEMPLE. EVEN IF YOU SPROUT WINGS, YOU CANNOT ESCAPE!
GENTLEMEN, I OFFER MY DAUGHTER'S HAND IN MARRIAGE TO ANYONE WHO CAN SAVE HER!
MADAM YE, I HAVE AN IDEA...

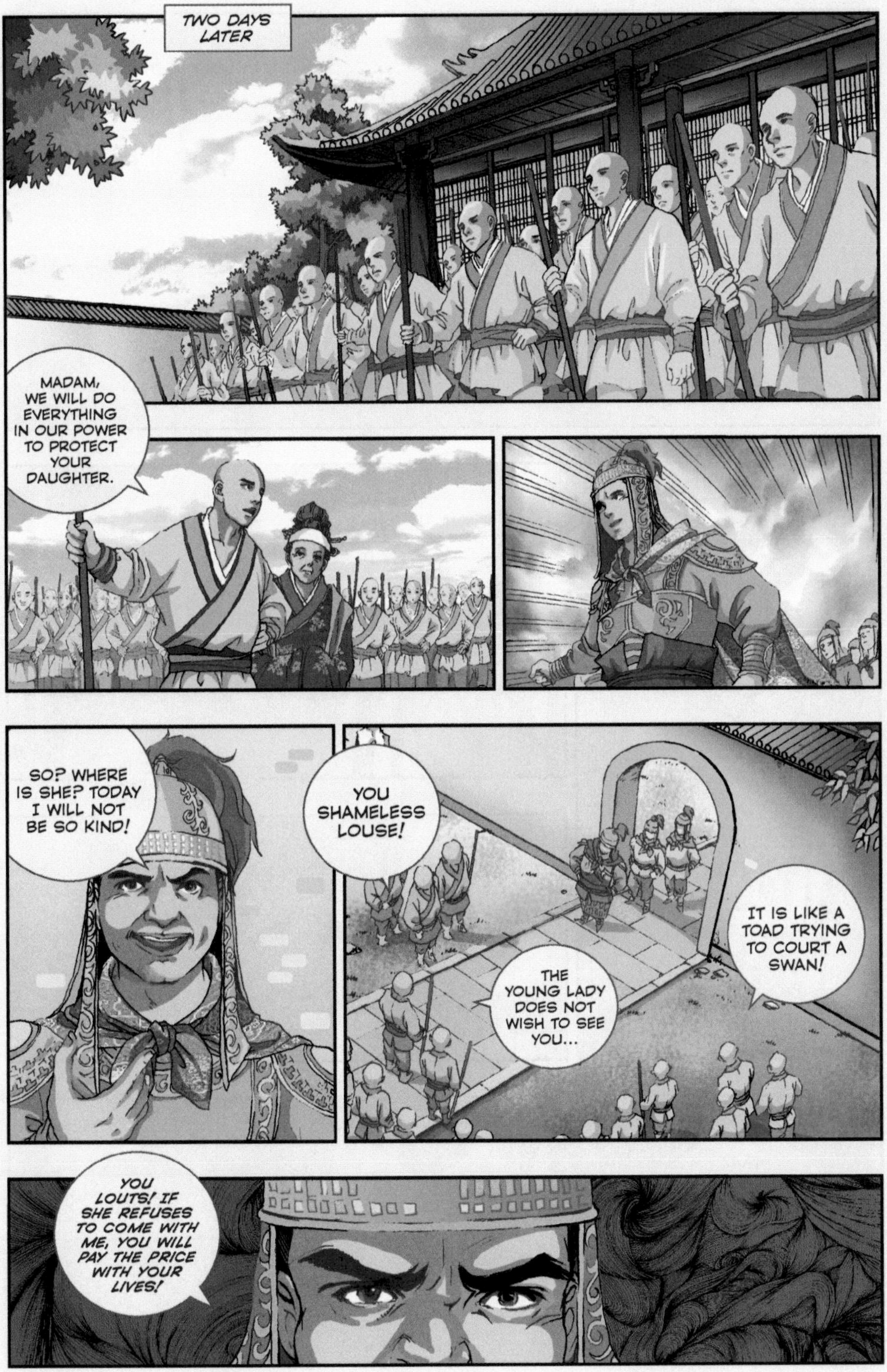
TWO DAYS LATER
MADAM, WE WILL DO EVERYTHING IN OUR POWER TO PROTECT YOUR DAUGHTER.
SO? WHERE IS SHE? TODAY I WILL NOT BE SO KIND!
YOU SHAMELESS LOUSE!
THE YOUNG LADY DOES NOT WISH TO SEE YOU...
IT IS LIKE A TOAD TRYING TO COURT A SWAN!
YOU LOUTS! IF SHE REFUSES TO COME WITH ME, YOU WILL PAY THE PRICE WITH YOUR LIVES!

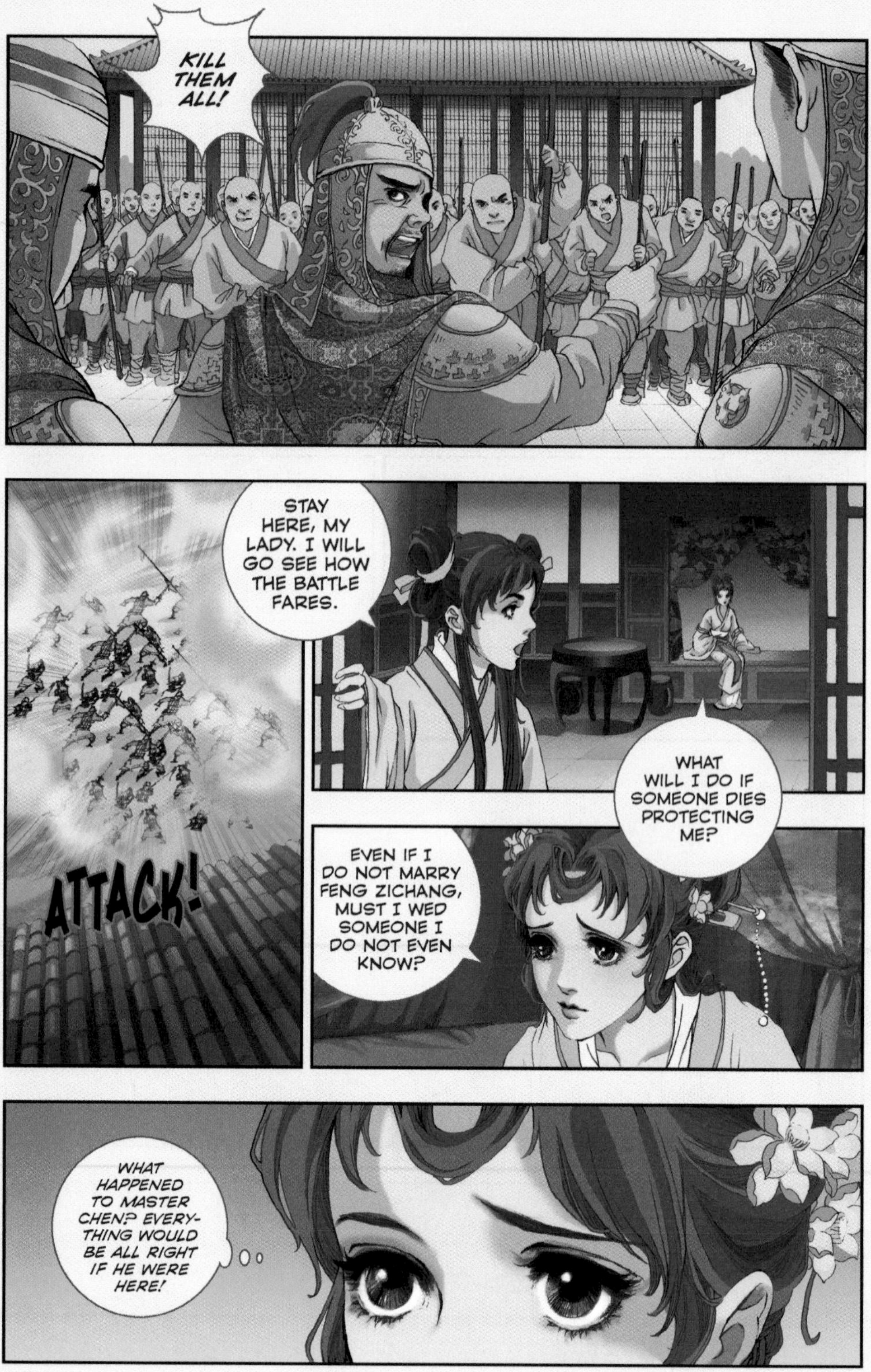
KILL THEM ALL!
ATTACK!
STAY HERE, MY LADY. I WILL GO SEE HOW THE BATTLE FARES.
WHAT WILL I DO IF SOMEONE DIES PROTECTING ME?
EVEN IF I DO NOT MARRY FENG ZICHANG, MUST I WED SOMEONE I DO NOT EVEN KNOW?
WHAT HAPPENED TO MASTER CHEN? EVERY-THING WOULD BE ALL RIGHT IF HE WERE HERE!

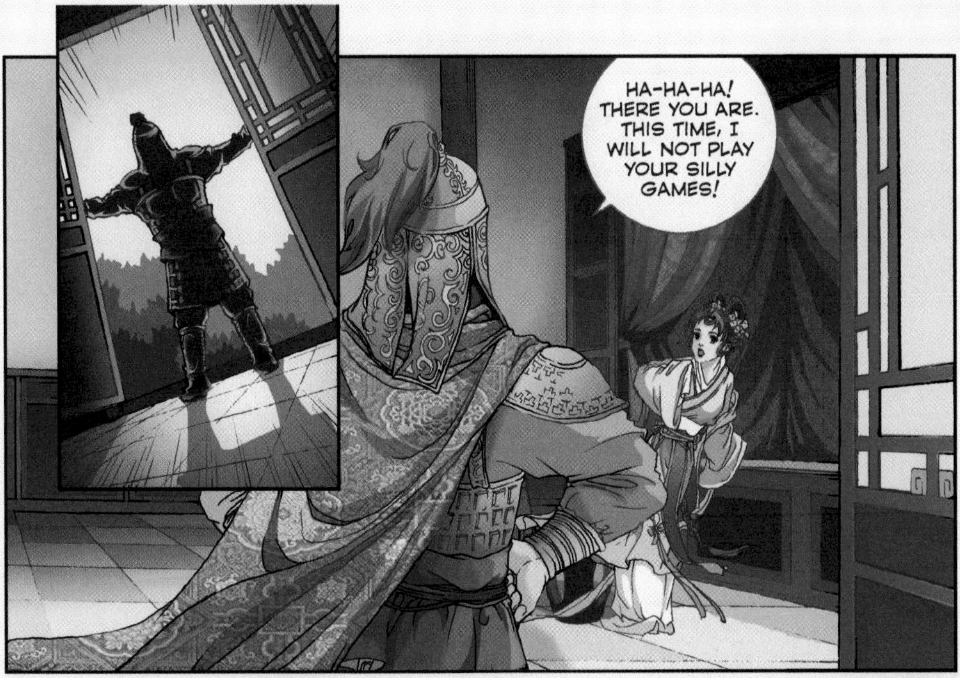
HA-HA-HA! THERE YOU ARE. THIS TIME, I WILL NOT PLAY YOUR SILLY GAMES!

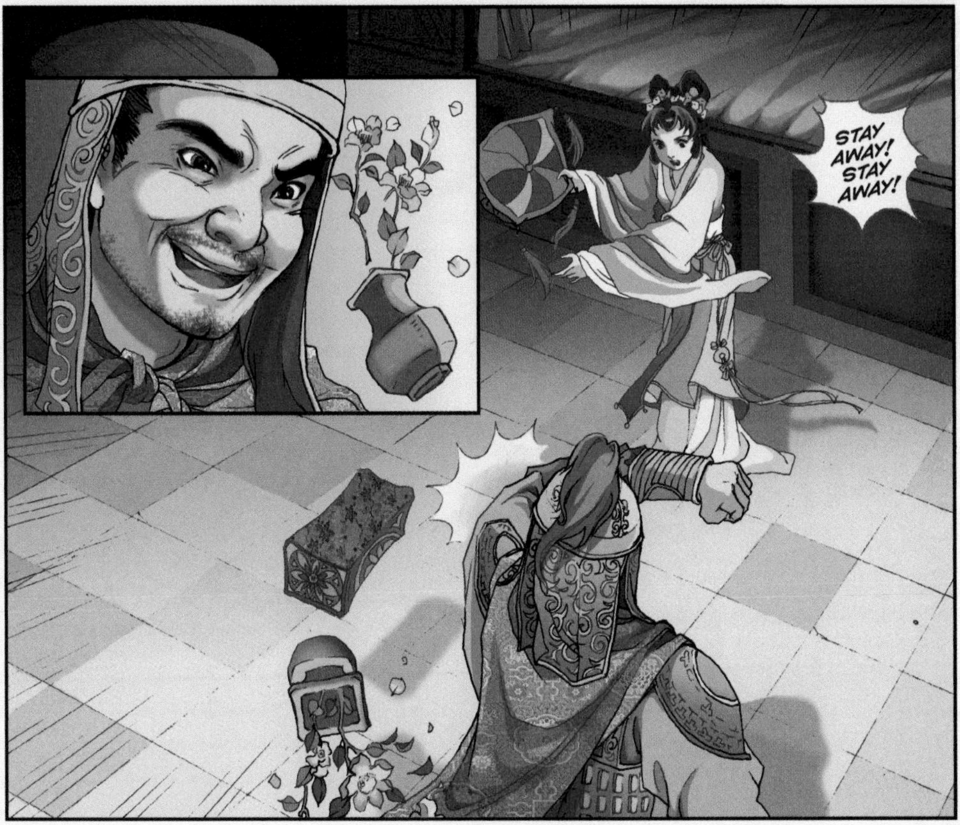
STAY AWAY! STAY AWAY!

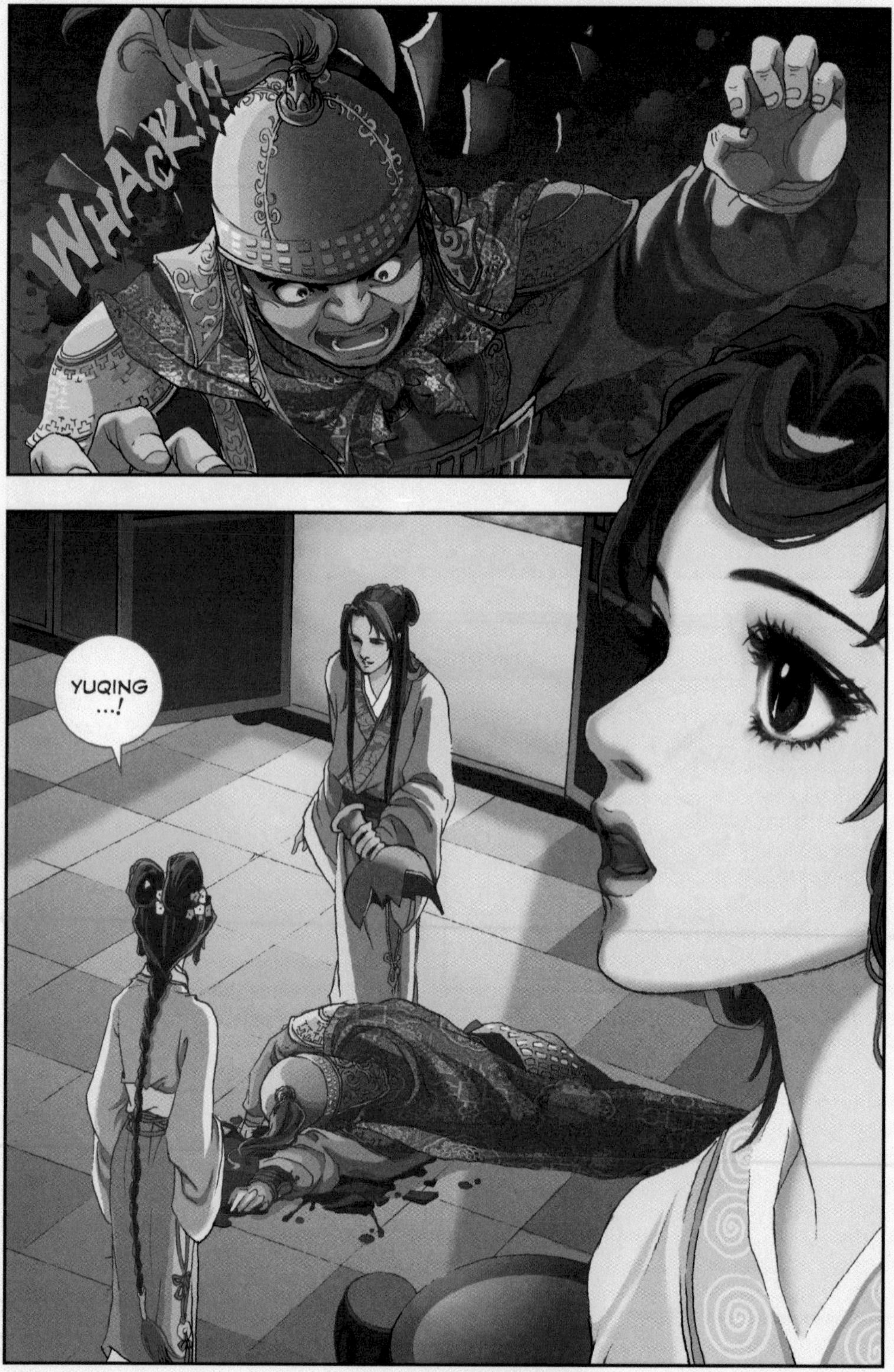
WHACK!!!
YUQING ...!

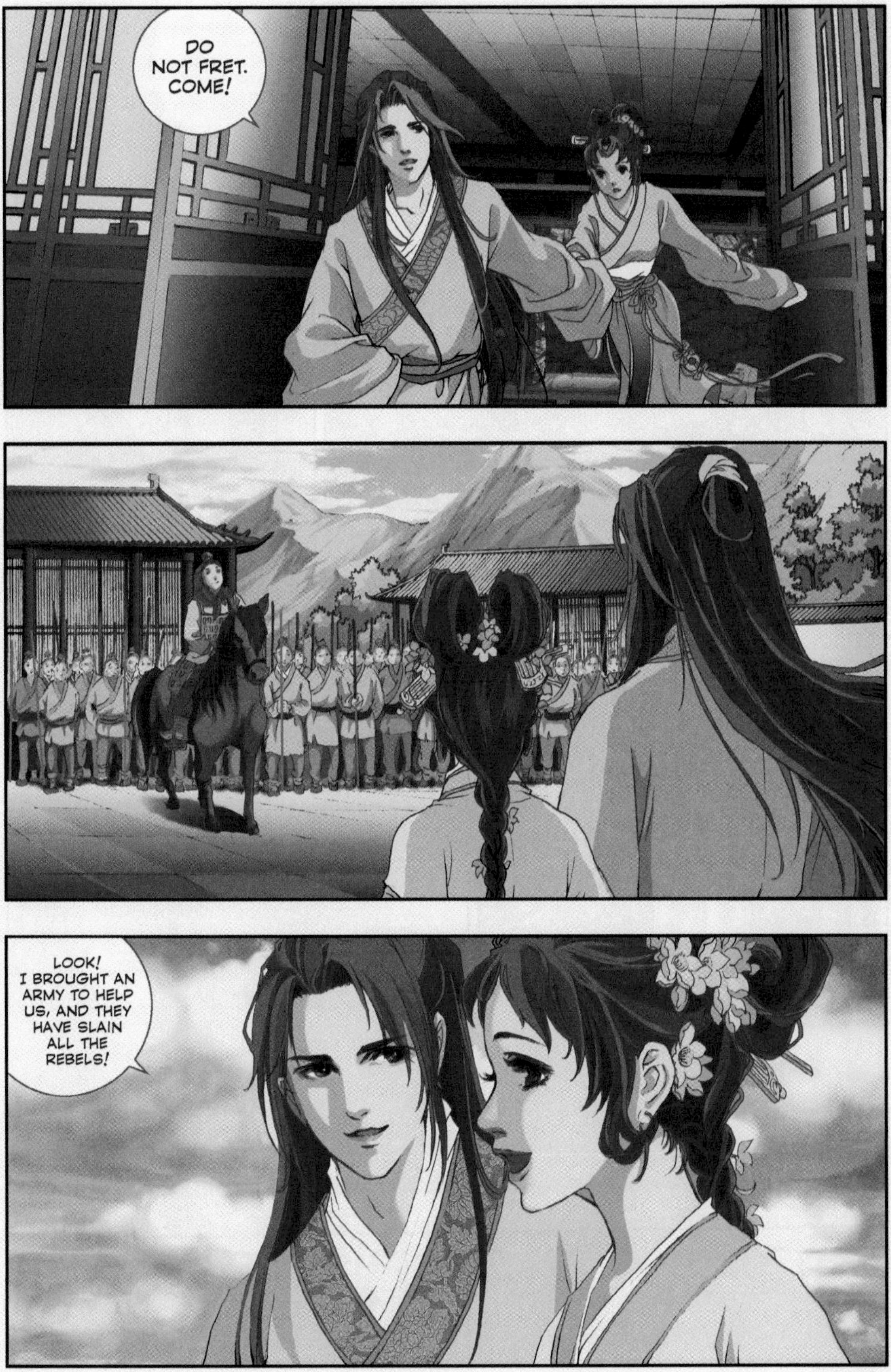
DO NOT FRET. COME!
LOOK! I BROUGHT AN ARMY TO HELP US, AND THEY HAVE SLAIN ALL THE REBELS!

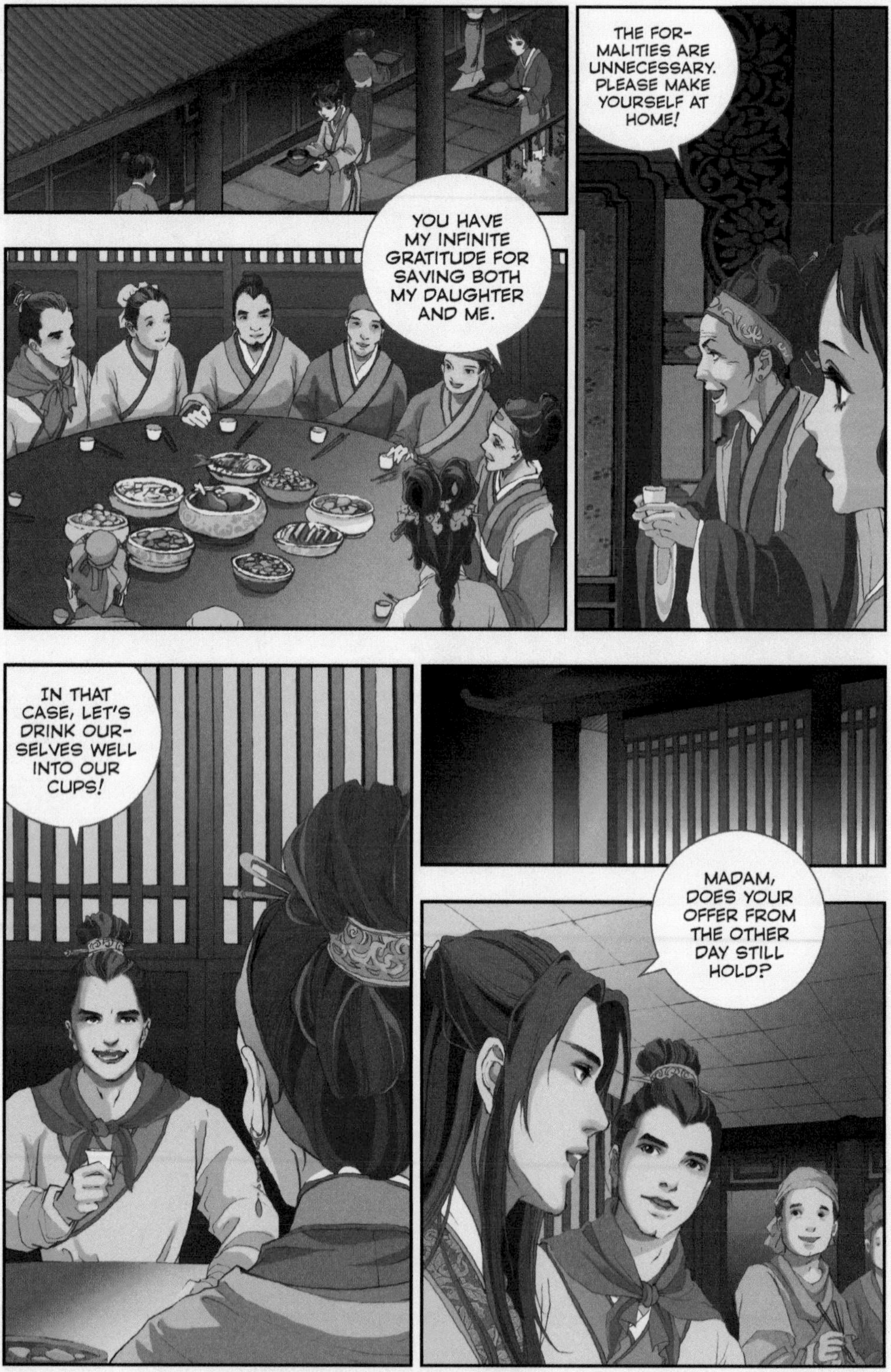
YOU HAVE MY INFINITE GRATITUDE FOR SAVING BOTH MY DAUGHTER AND ME.
THE FOR-MALITIES ARE UNNECESSARY. PLEASE MAKE YOURSELF AT HOME!
IN THAT CASE, LET'S DRINK OUR-SELVES WELL INTO OUR CUPS!
MADAM, DOES YOUR OFFER FROM THE OTHER DAY STILL HOLD?

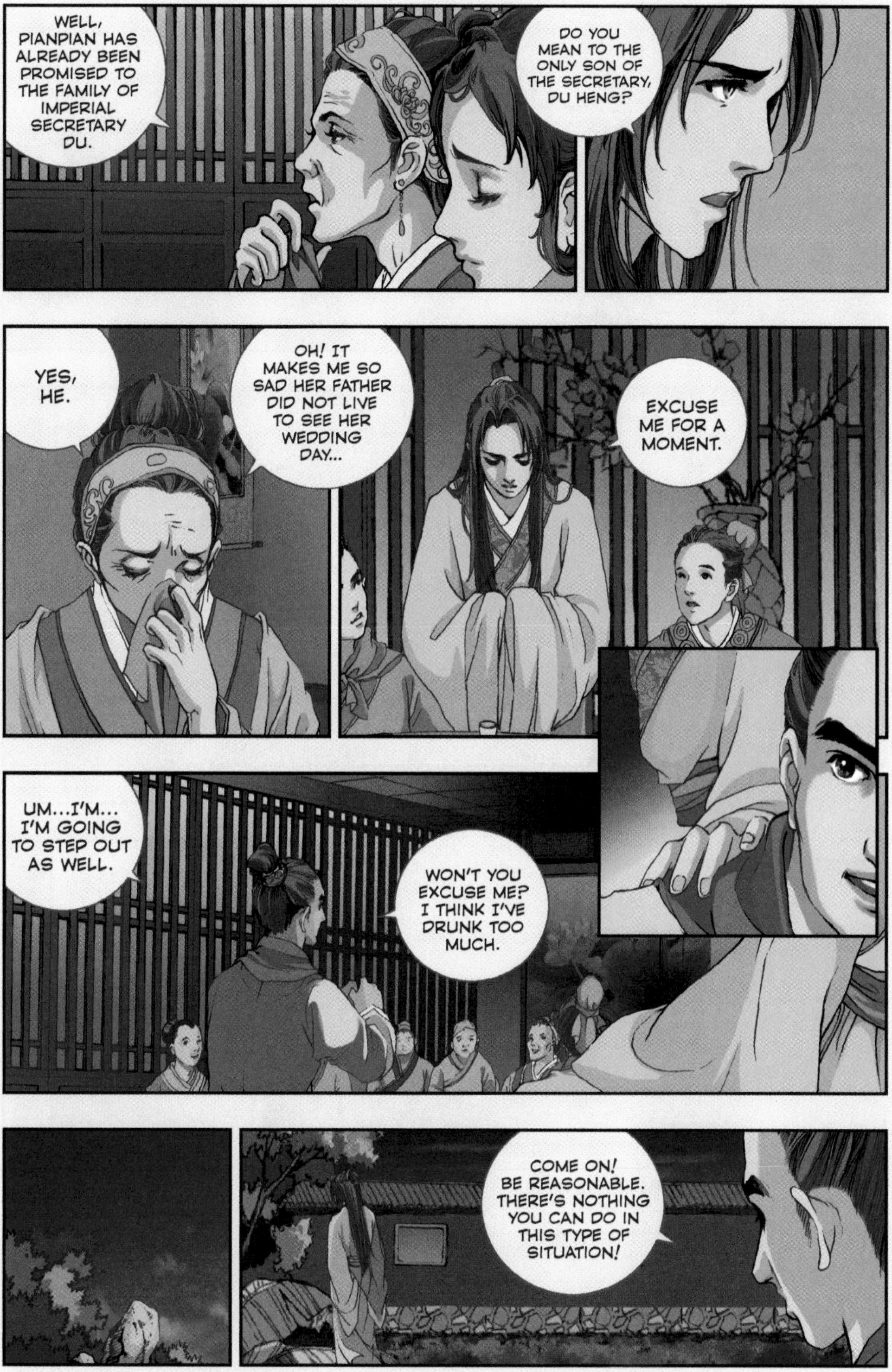
WELL, PIANPIAN HAS ALREADY BEEN PROMISED TO THE FAMILY OF IMPERIAL SECRETARY DU.
DO YOU MEAN TO THE ONLY SON OF THE SECRETARY, DU HENG?
YES, HE.
OH! IT MAKES ME SO SAD HER FATHER DID NOT LIVE TO SEE HER WEDDING DAY...
EXCUSE ME FOR A MOMENT.
UM...I'M... I'M GOING TO STEP OUT AS WELL.
WON'T YOU EXCUSE ME? I THINK I'VE DRUNK TOO MUCH.
COME ON! BE REASONABLE. THERE'S NOTHING YOU CAN DO IN THIS TYPE OF SITUATION!

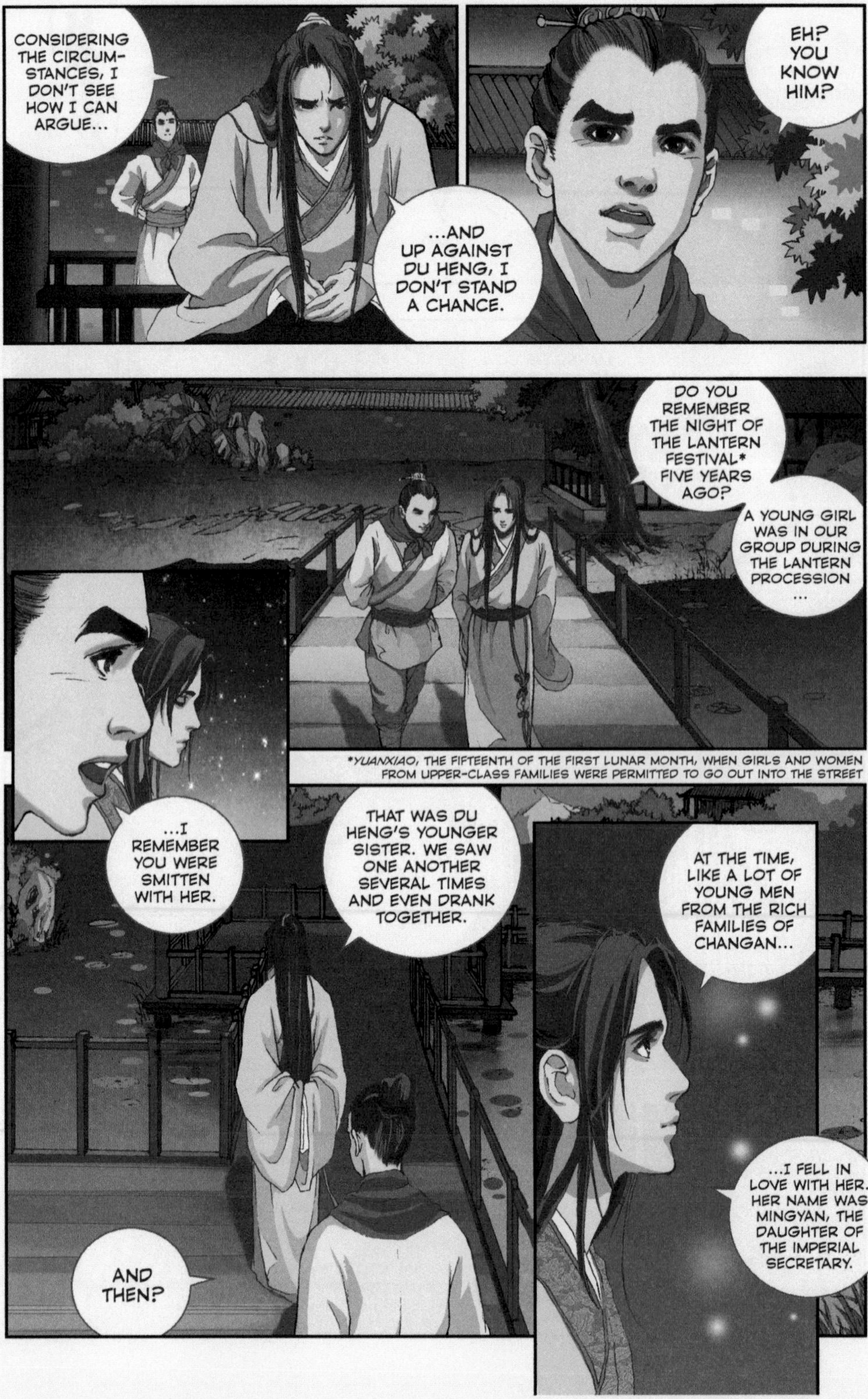
CONSIDERING THE CIRCUMSTANCES, I DON'T SEE HOW I CAN ARGUE...
...AND UP AGAINST DU HENG, I DON'T STAND A CHANCE.
EH? YOU KNOW HIM?
DO YOU REMEMBER THE NIGHT OF THE LANTERN FESTIVAL* FIVE YEARS AGO?
A YOUNG GIRL WAS IN OUR GROUP DURING THE LANTERN PROCESSION ...
...I REMEMBER YOU WERE SMITTEN WITH HER.
THAT WAS DU HENG'S YOUNGER SISTER. WE SAW ONE ANOTHER SEVERAL TIMES AND EVEN DRANK TOGETHER.
AND THEN?
AT THE TIME, LIKE A LOT OF YOUNG MEN FROM THE RICH FAMILIES OF CHANGAN...
...I FELL IN LOVE WITH HER. HER NAME WAS MINGYAN, THE DAUGHTER OF THE IMPERIAL SECRETARY.

**YUANXIAO*, THE FIFTEENTH OF THE FIRST LUNAR MONTH, WHEN GIRLS AND WOMEN FROM UPPER-CLASS FAMILIES WERE PERMITTED TO GO OUT INTO THE STREET

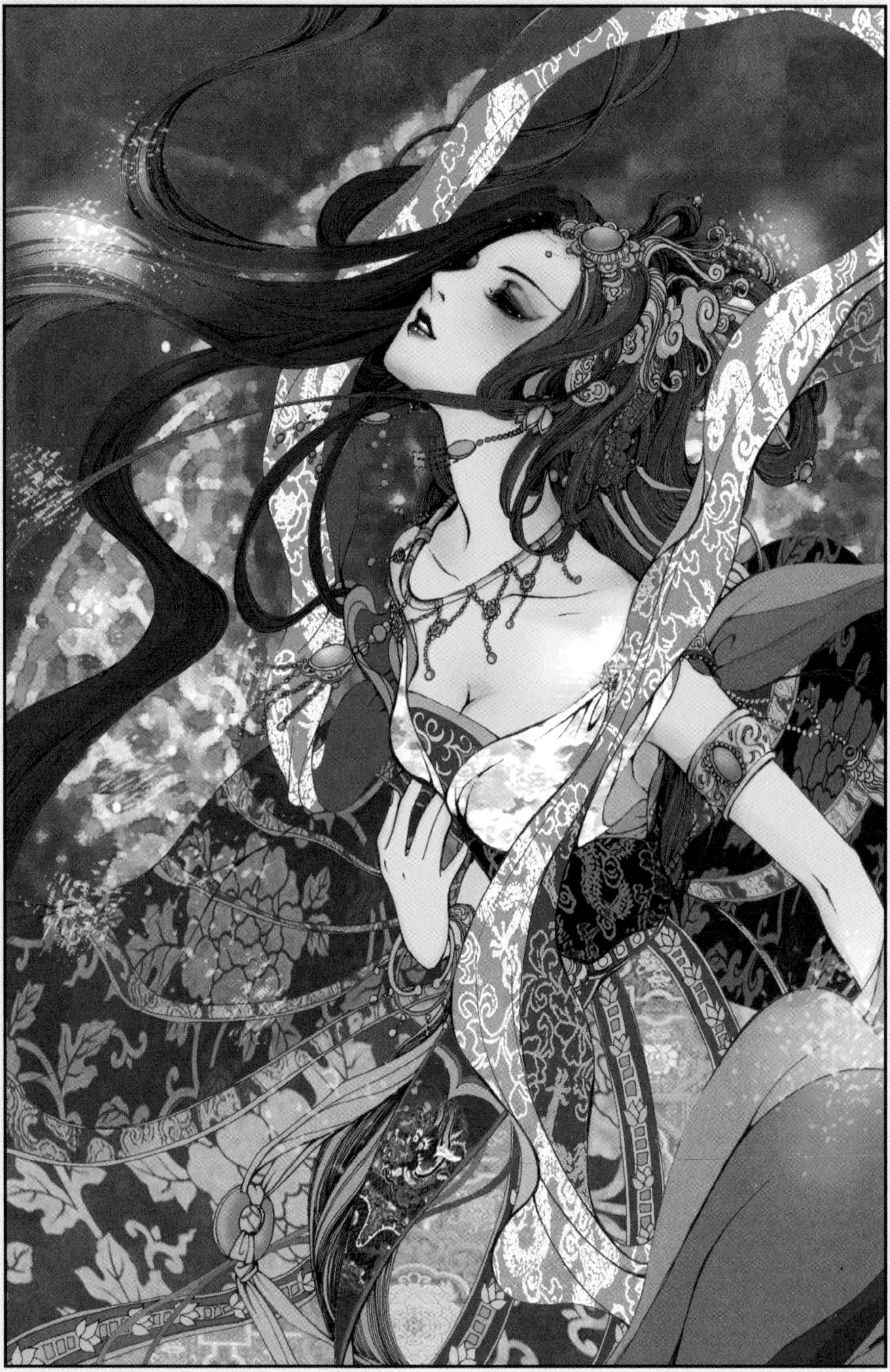

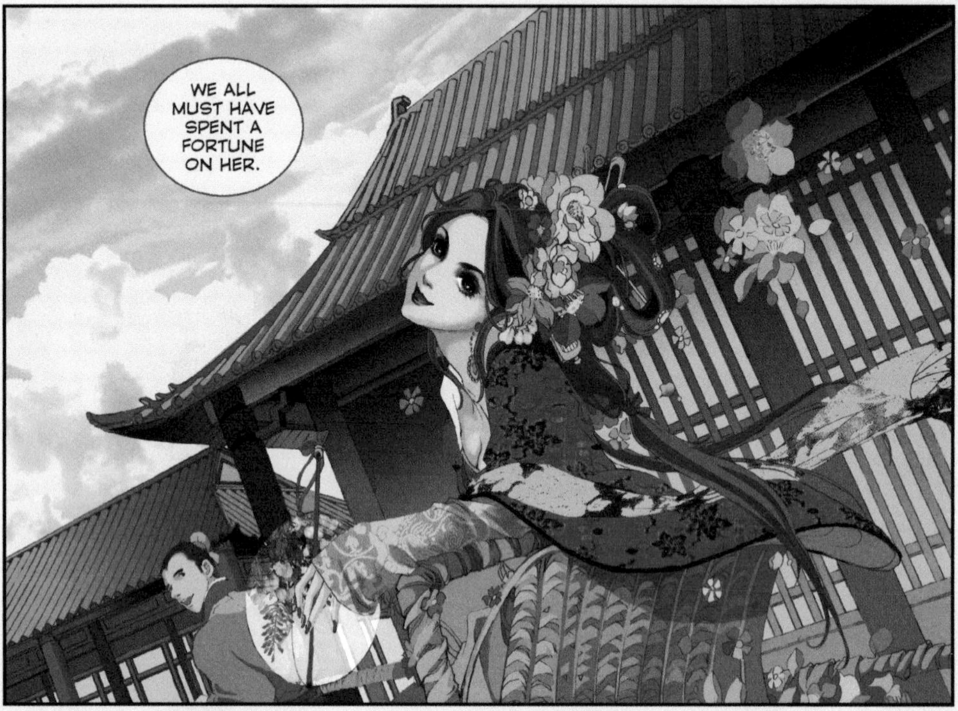
WE ALL MUST HAVE SPENT A FORTUNE ON HER.

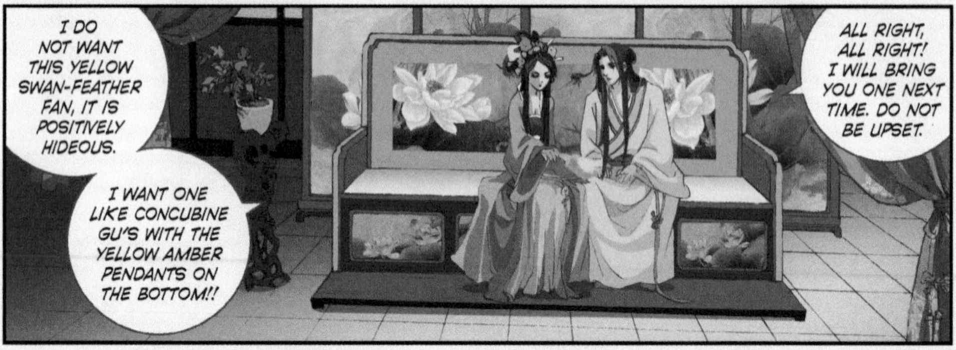
I DO NOT WANT THIS YELLOW SWAN-FEATHER FAN, IT IS POSITIVELY HIDEOUS.
I WANT ONE LIKE CONCUBINE GU'S WITH THE YELLOW AMBER PENDANTS ON THE BOTTOM!!
ALL RIGHT, ALL RIGHT! I WILL BRING YOU ONE NEXT TIME. DO NOT BE UPSET.

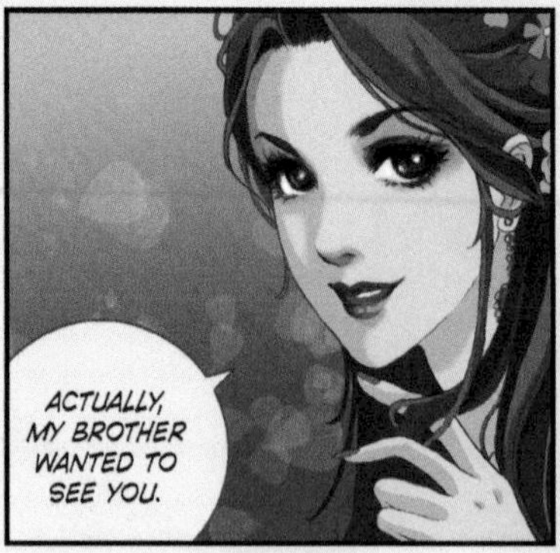
ACTUALLY, MY BROTHER WANTED TO SEE YOU.

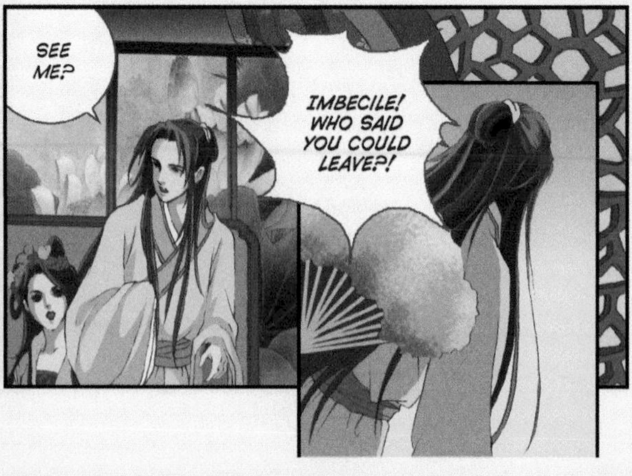
SEE ME?
IMBECILE! WHO SAID YOU COULD LEAVE?!

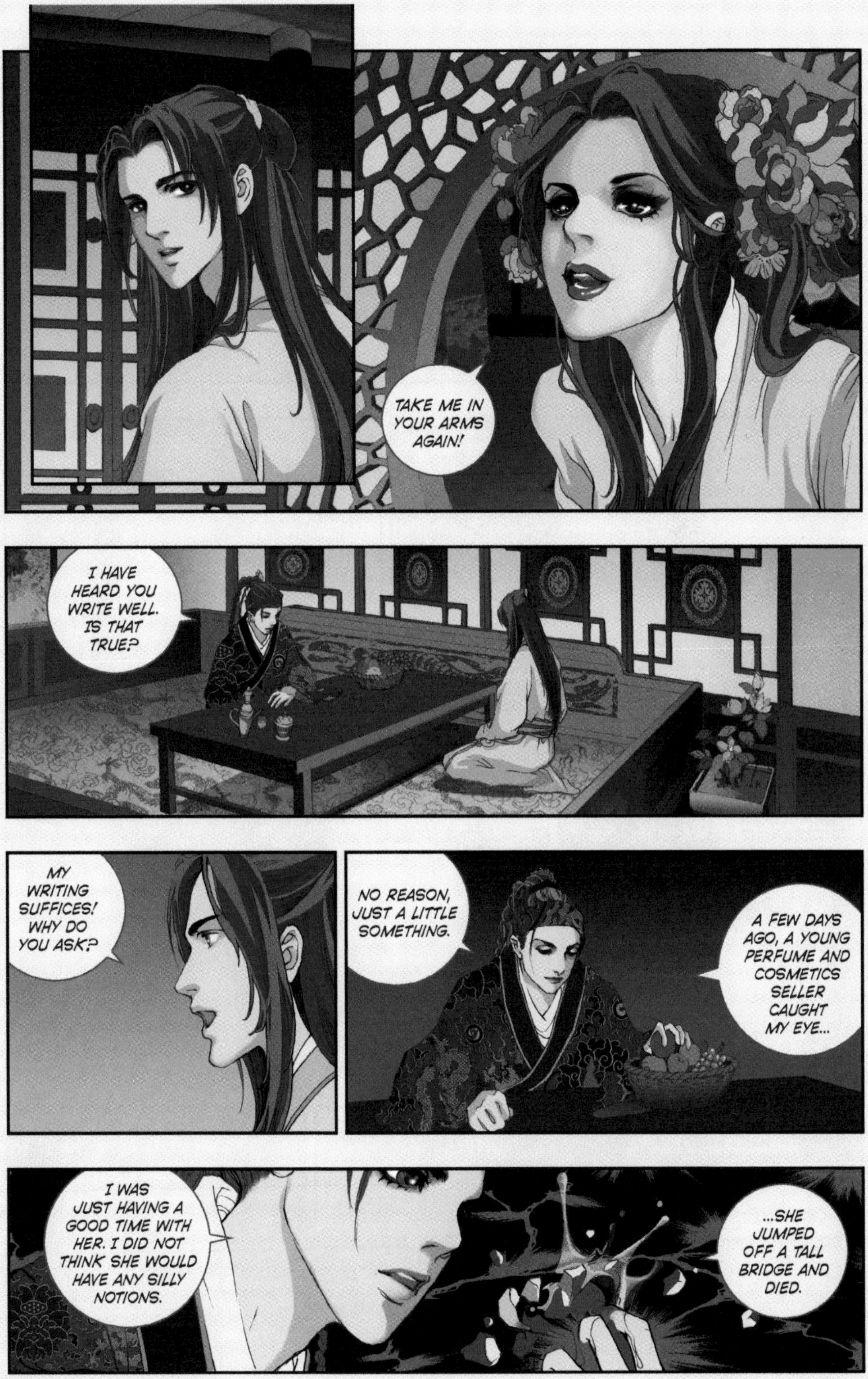
TAKE ME IN YOUR ARMS AGAIN!
I HAVE HEARD YOU WRITE WELL. IS THAT TRUE?
MY WRITING SUFFICES! WHY DO YOU ASK?
NO REASON, JUST A LITTLE SOMETHING.
A FEW DAYS AGO, A YOUNG PERFUME AND COSMETICS SELLER CAUGHT MY EYE...
I WAS JUST HAVING A GOOD TIME WITH HER. I DID NOT THINK SHE WOULD HAVE ANY SILLY NOTIONS.
...SHE JUMPED OFF A TALL BRIDGE AND DIED.

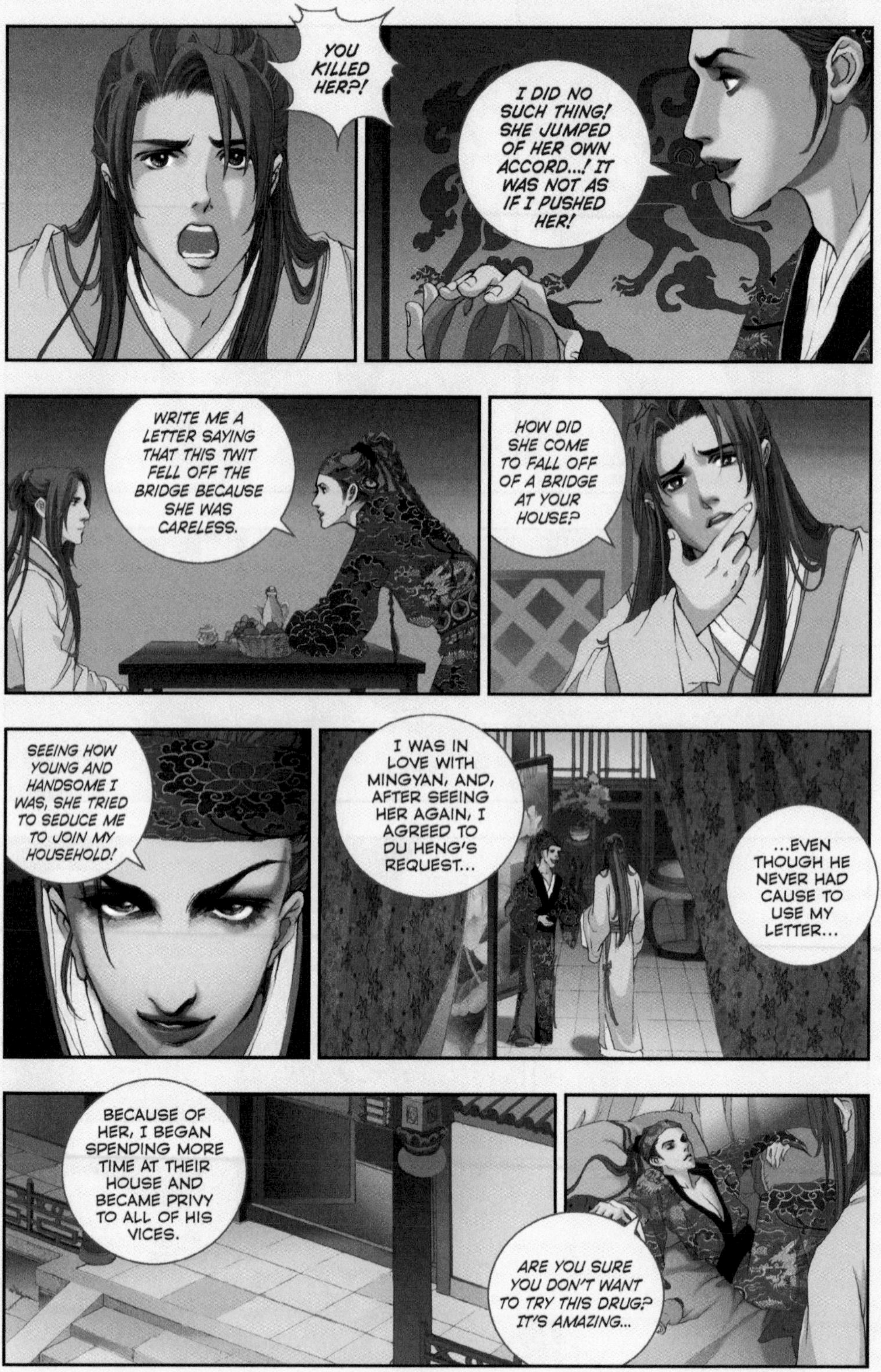

YOU KILLED HER?!
I DID NO SUCH THING! SHE JUMPED OF HER OWN ACCORD...! IT WAS NOT AS IF I PUSHED HER!
WRITE ME A LETTER SAYING THAT THIS TWIT FELL OFF THE BRIDGE BECAUSE SHE WAS CARELESS.
HOW DID SHE COME TO FALL OFF OF A BRIDGE AT YOUR HOUSE?
SEEING HOW YOUNG AND HANDSOME I WAS, SHE TRIED TO SEDUCE ME TO JOIN MY HOUSEHOLD!
I WAS IN LOVE WITH MINGYAN, AND, AFTER SEEING HER AGAIN, I AGREED TO DU HENG'S REQUEST...
...EVEN THOUGH HE NEVER HAD CAUSE TO USE MY LETTER...
BECAUSE OF HER, I BEGAN SPENDING MORE TIME AT THEIR HOUSE AND BECAME PRIVY TO ALL OF HIS VICES.
ARE YOU SURE YOU DON'T WANT TO TRY THIS DRUG? IT'S AMAZING...

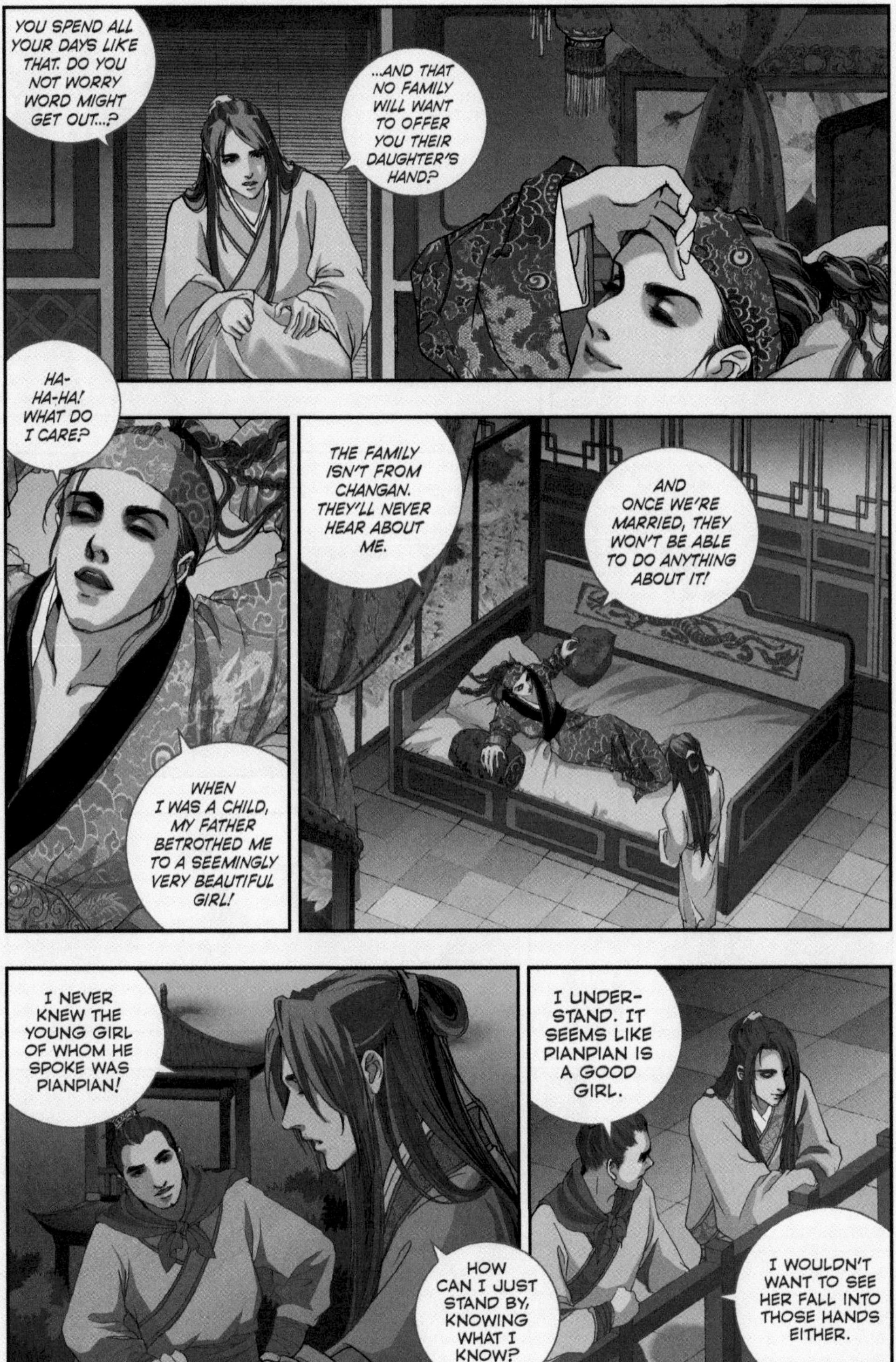
YOU SPEND ALL YOUR DAYS LIKE THAT. DO YOU NOT WORRY WORD MIGHT GET OUT...?
...AND THAT NO FAMILY WILL WANT TO OFFER YOU THEIR DAUGHTER'S HAND?
HA-HA-HA! WHAT DO I CARE?
WHEN I WAS A CHILD, MY FATHER BETROTHED ME TO A SEEMINGLY VERY BEAUTIFUL GIRL!
THE FAMILY ISN'T FROM CHANGAN. THEY'LL NEVER HEAR ABOUT ME.
AND ONCE WE'RE MARRIED, THEY WON'T BE ABLE TO DO ANYTHING ABOUT IT!
I NEVER KNEW THE YOUNG GIRL OF WHOM HE SPOKE WAS PIANPIAN!
HOW CAN I JUST STAND BY, KNOWING WHAT I KNOW?
I UNDER-STAND. IT SEEMS LIKE PIANPIAN IS A GOOD GIRL.
I WOULDN'T WANT TO SEE HER FALL INTO THOSE HANDS EITHER.

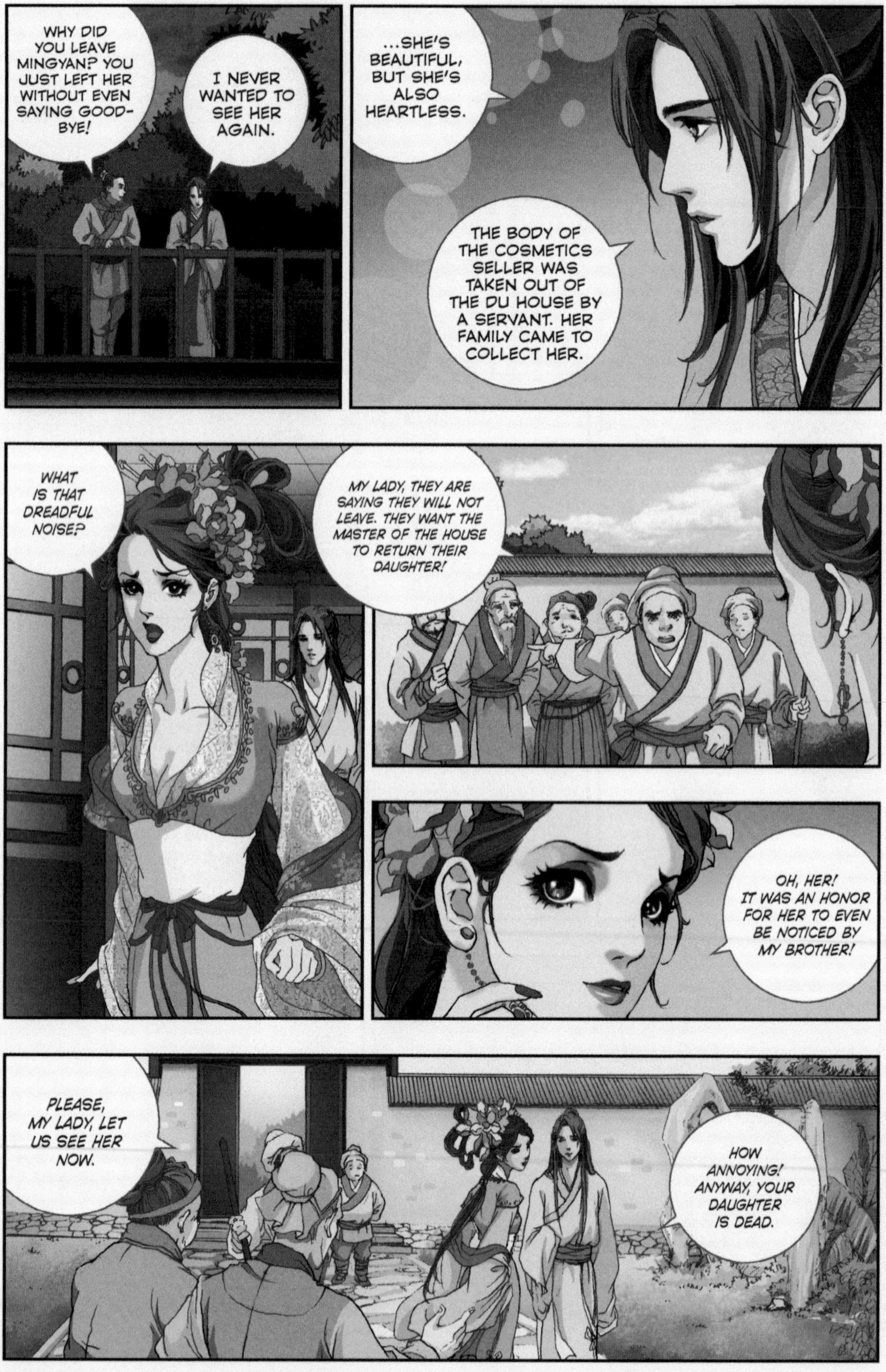
WHY DID YOU LEAVE MINGYAN? YOU JUST LEFT HER WITHOUT EVEN SAYING GOOD-BYE!
I NEVER WANTED TO SEE HER AGAIN.
...SHE'S BEAUTIFUL, BUT SHE'S ALSO HEARTLESS.
THE BODY OF THE COSMETICS SELLER WAS TAKEN OUT OF THE DU HOUSE BY A SERVANT. HER FAMILY CAME TO COLLECT HER.
WHAT IS THAT DREADFUL NOISE?
MY LADY, THEY ARE SAYING THEY WILL NOT LEAVE. THEY WANT THE MASTER OF THE HOUSE TO RETURN THEIR DAUGHTER!
OH, HER! IT WAS AN HONOR FOR HER TO EVEN BE NOTICED BY MY BROTHER!
PLEASE, MY LADY, LET US SEE HER NOW.
HOW ANNOYING! ANYWAY, YOUR DAUGHTER IS DEAD.

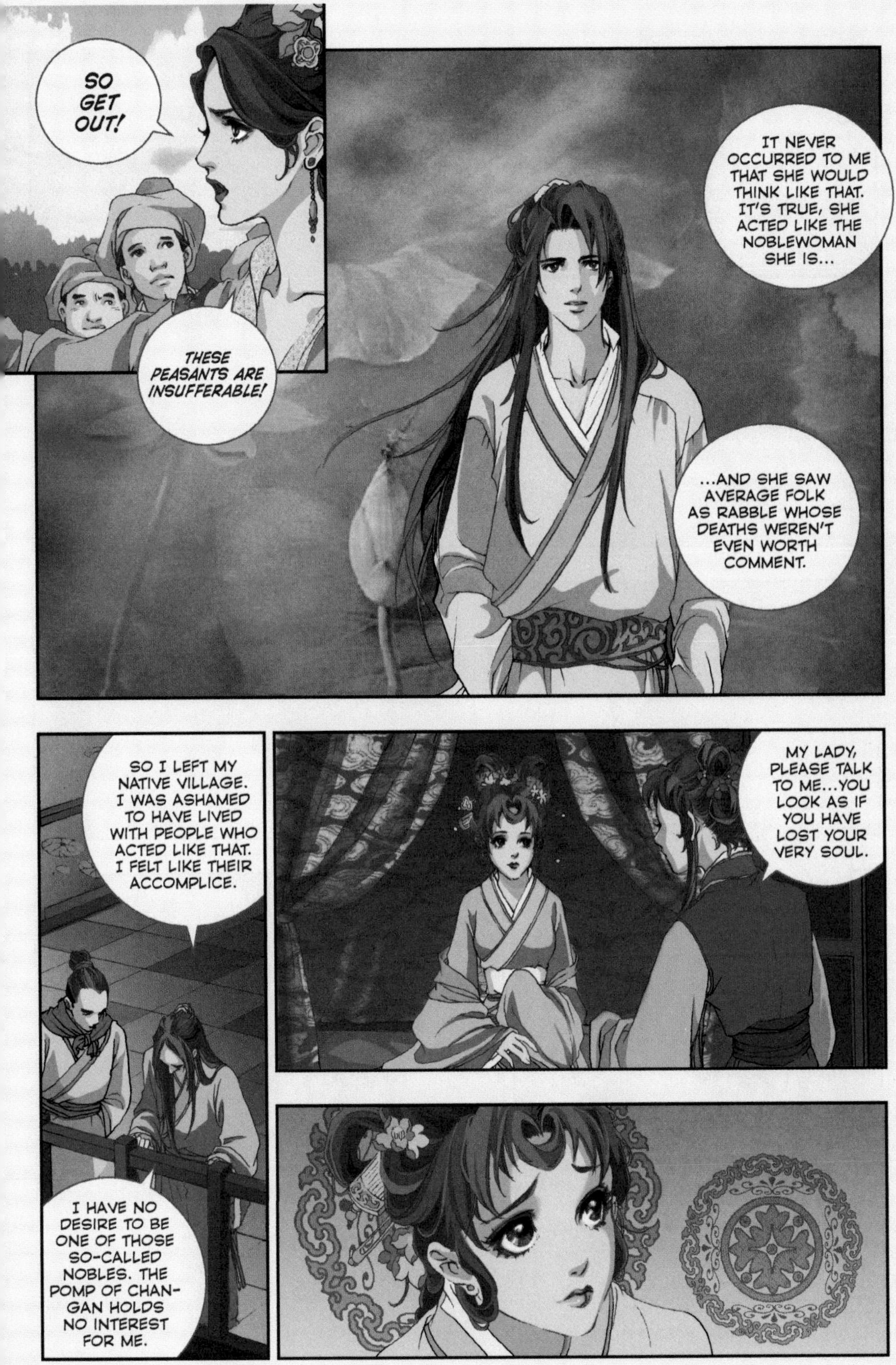
SO GET OUT!
THESE PEASANTS ARE INSUFFERABLE!
IT NEVER OCCURRED TO ME THAT SHE WOULD THINK LIKE THAT. IT'S TRUE, SHE ACTED LIKE THE NOBLEWOMAN SHE IS...
...AND SHE SAW AVERAGE FOLK AS RABBLE WHOSE DEATHS WEREN'T EVEN WORTH COMMENT.
SO I LEFT MY NATIVE VILLAGE. I WAS ASHAMED TO HAVE LIVED WITH PEOPLE WHO ACTED LIKE THAT. I FELT LIKE THEIR ACCOMPLICE.
I HAVE NO DESIRE TO BE ONE OF THOSE SO-CALLED NOBLES. THE POMP OF CHANG-AN HOLDS NO INTEREST FOR ME.
MY LADY, PLEASE TALK TO ME...YOU LOOK AS IF YOU HAVE LOST YOUR VERY SOUL.

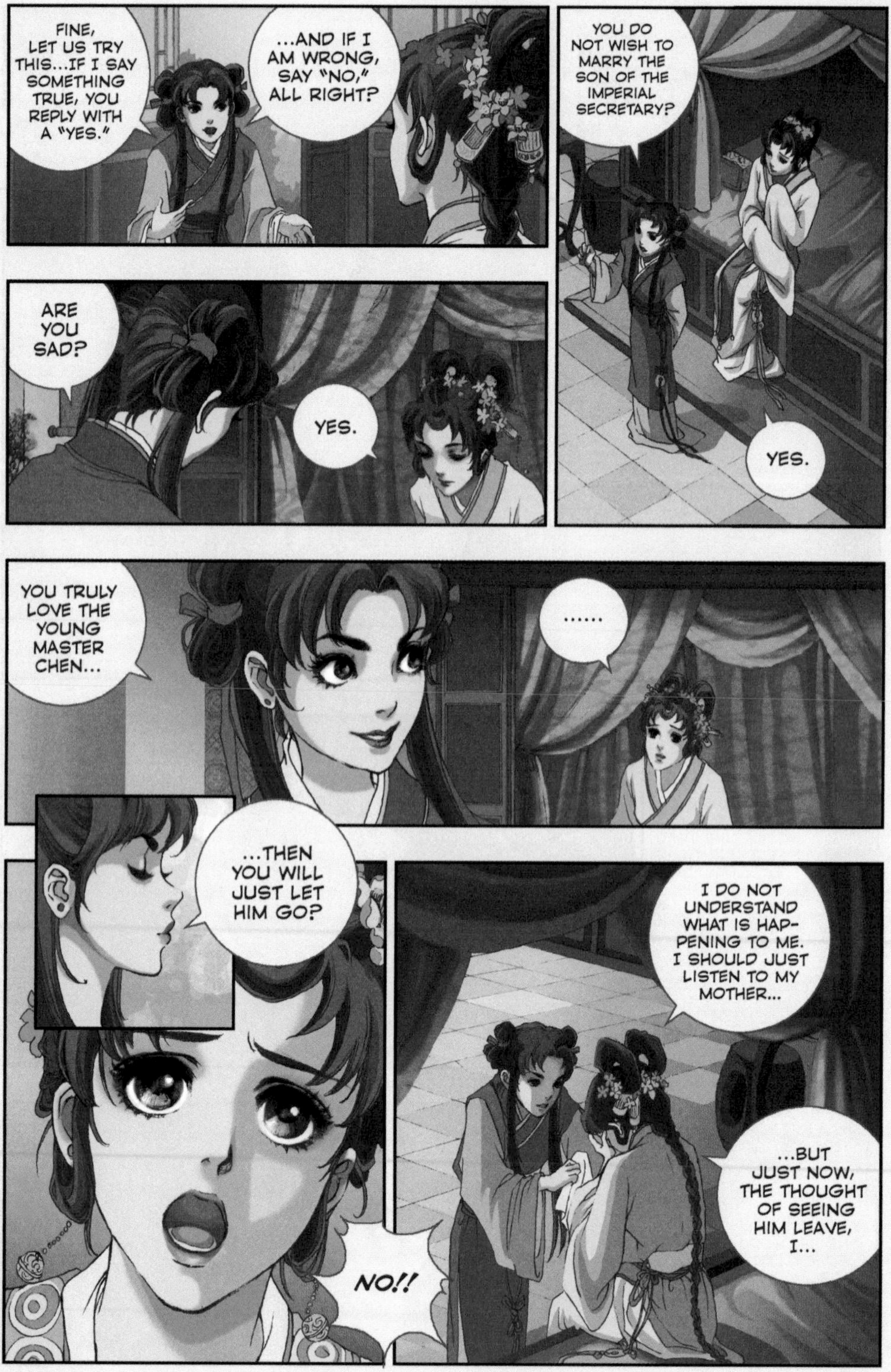
FINE, LET US TRY THIS...IF I SAY SOMETHING TRUE, YOU REPLY WITH A "YES."
...AND IF I AM WRONG, SAY "NO," ALL RIGHT?
YOU DO NOT WISH TO MARRY THE SON OF THE IMPERIAL SECRETARY?
ARE YOU SAD?
YES.
YES.
YOU TRULY LOVE THE YOUNG MASTER CHEN...
......
...THEN YOU WILL JUST LET HIM GO?
NO!!
I DO NOT UNDERSTAND WHAT IS HAP-PENING TO ME. I SHOULD JUST LISTEN TO MY MOTHER...
...BUT JUST NOW, THE THOUGHT OF SEEING HIM LEAVE, I...

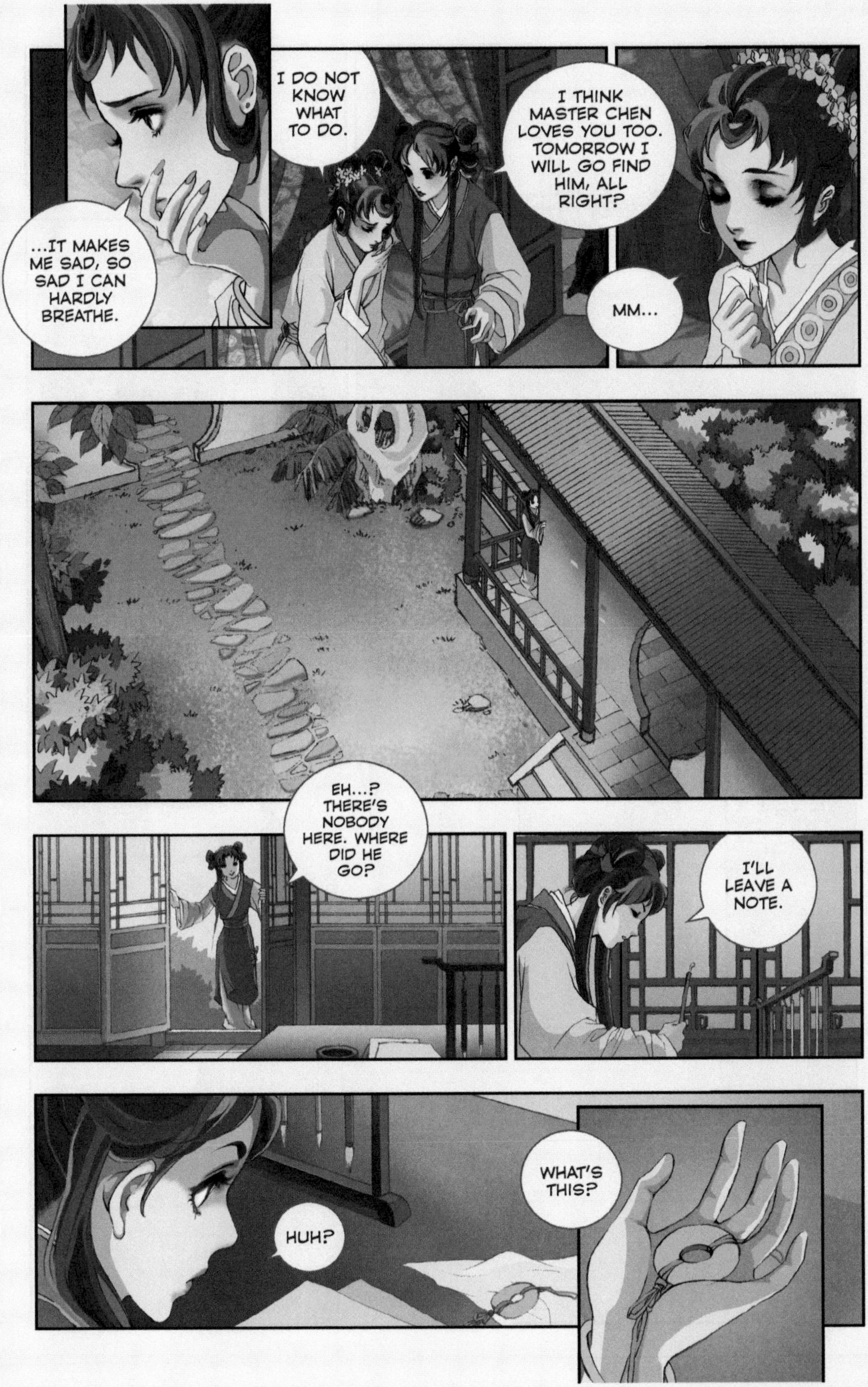
...IT MAKES ME SAD, SO SAD I CAN HARDLY BREATHE.
I DO NOT KNOW WHAT TO DO.
I THINK MASTER CHEN LOVES YOU TOO. TOMORROW I WILL GO FIND HIM, ALL RIGHT?
MM...
EH...? THERE'S NOBODY HERE. WHERE DID HE GO?
I'LL LEAVE A NOTE.
HUH?
WHAT'S THIS?

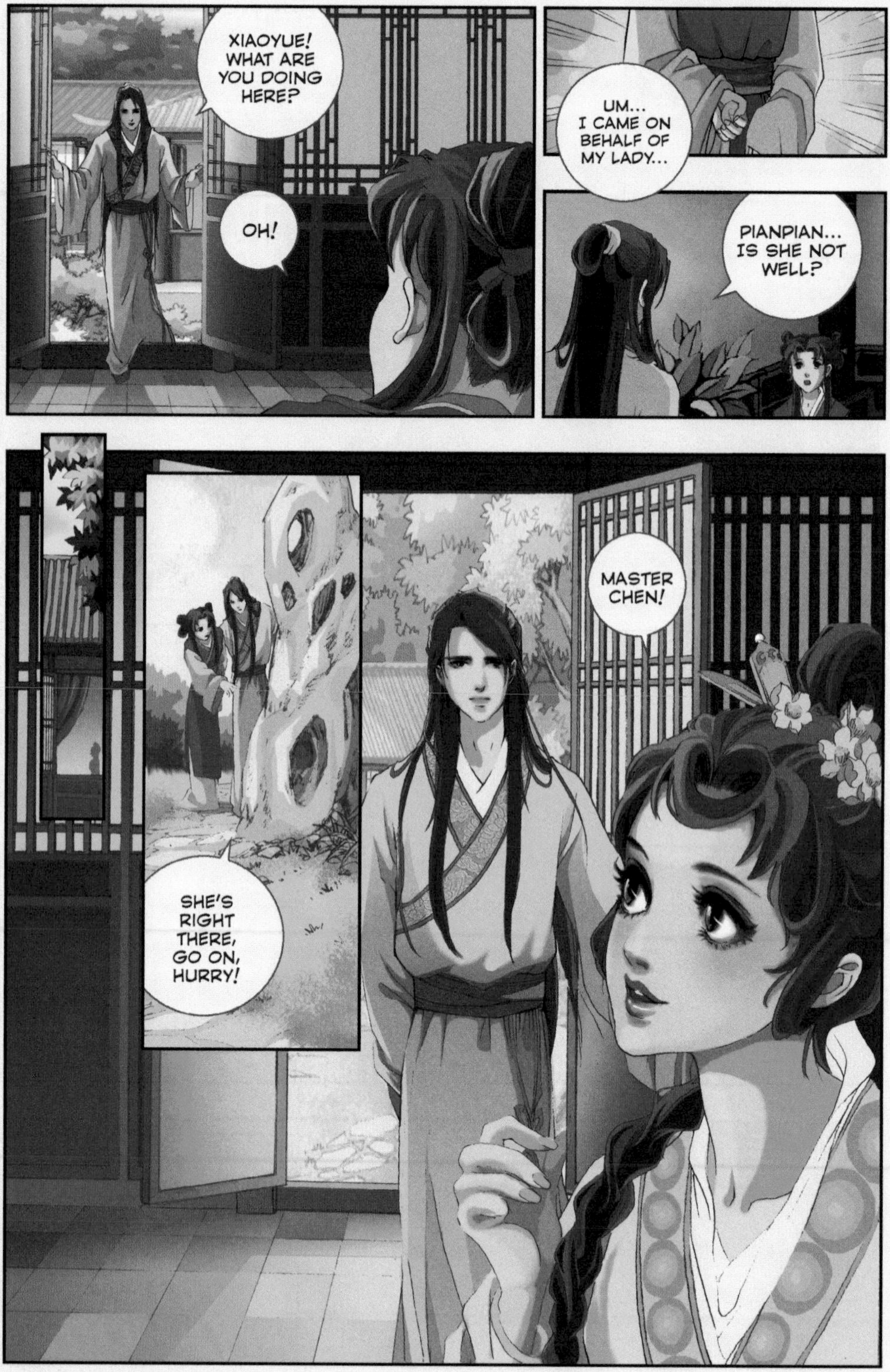
XIAOYUE! WHAT ARE YOU DOING HERE?
OH!
UM... I CAME ON BEHALF OF MY LADY...
PIANPIAN... IS SHE NOT WELL?
SHE'S RIGHT THERE, GO ON, HURRY!
MASTER CHEN!

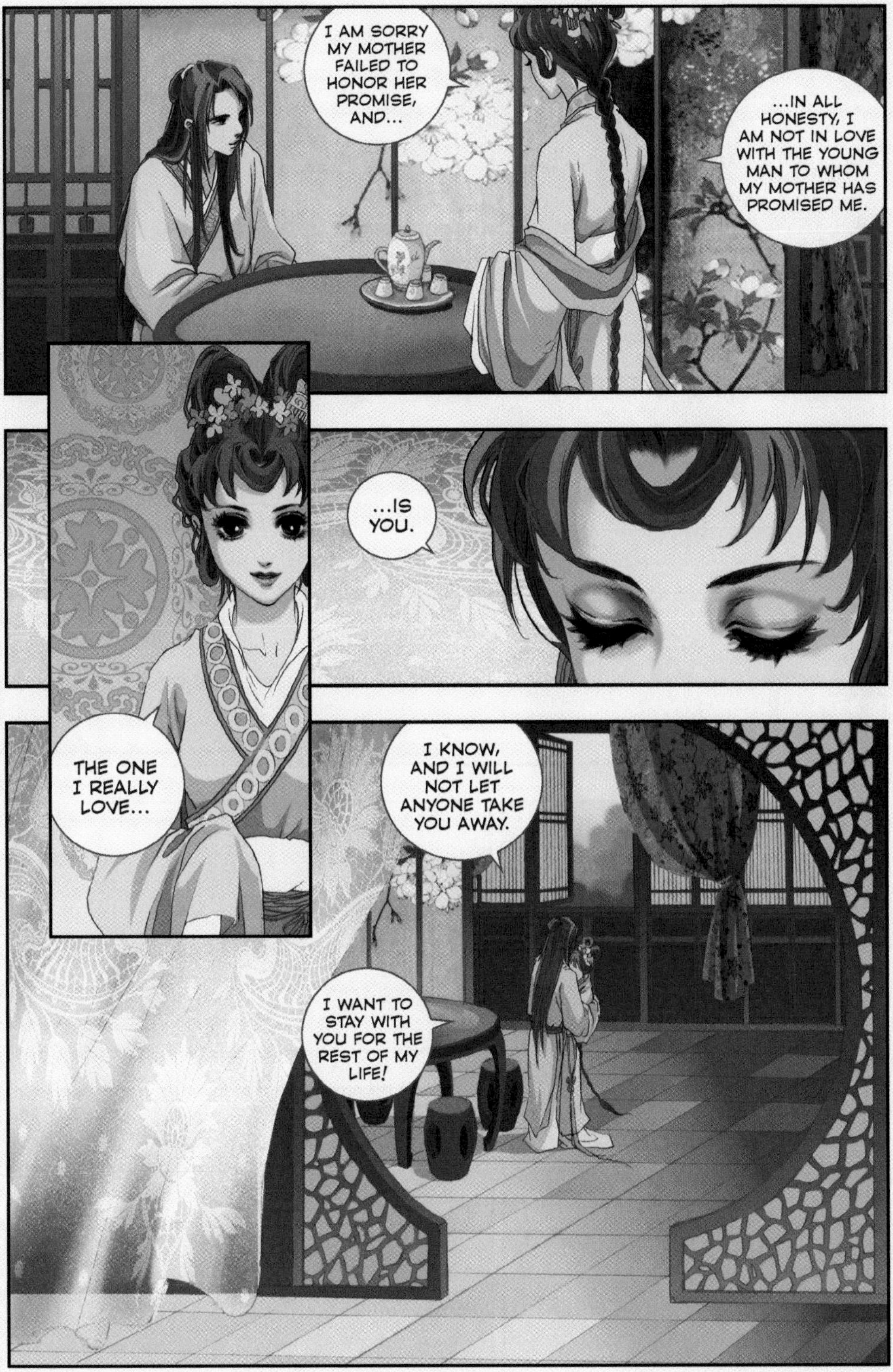
I AM SORRY MY MOTHER FAILED TO HONOR HER PROMISE, AND...
...IN ALL HONESTY, I AM NOT IN LOVE WITH THE YOUNG MAN TO WHOM MY MOTHER HAS PROMISED ME.
THE ONE I REALLY LOVE...
...IS YOU.
I KNOW, AND I WILL NOT LET ANYONE TAKE YOU AWAY.
I WANT TO STAY WITH YOU FOR THE REST OF MY LIFE!

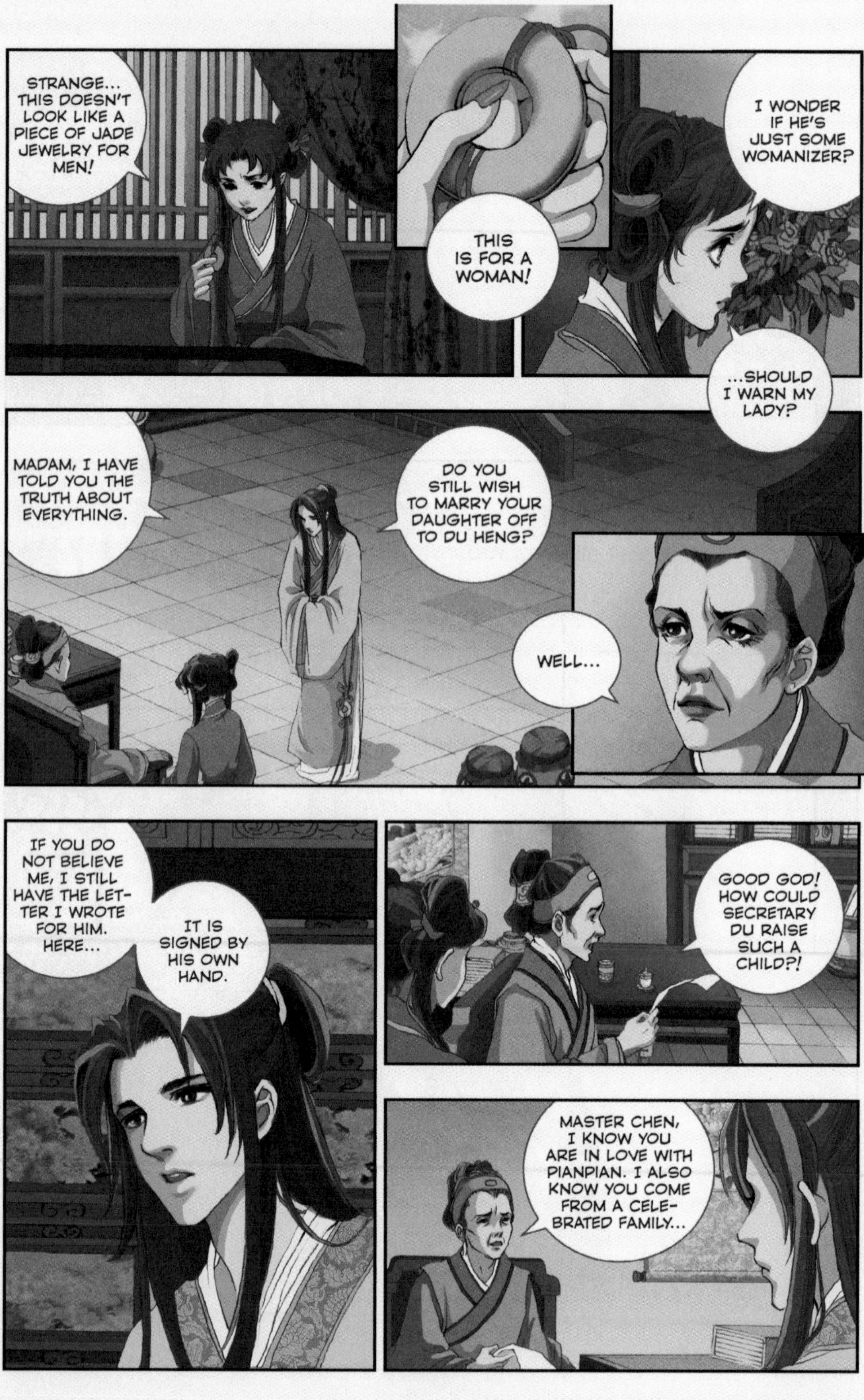
STRANGE... THIS DOESN'T LOOK LIKE A PIECE OF JADE JEWELRY FOR MEN!
THIS IS FOR A WOMAN!
I WONDER IF HE'S JUST SOME WOMANIZER?
...SHOULD I WARN MY LADY?
MADAM, I HAVE TOLD YOU THE TRUTH ABOUT EVERYTHING.
DO YOU STILL WISH TO MARRY YOUR DAUGHTER OFF TO DU HENG?
WELL...
IF YOU DO NOT BELIEVE ME, I STILL HAVE THE LET-TER I WROTE FOR HIM. HERE...
IT IS SIGNED BY HIS OWN HAND.
GOOD GOD! HOW COULD SECRETARY DU RAISE SUCH A CHILD?!
MASTER CHEN, I KNOW YOU ARE IN LOVE WITH PIANPIAN. I ALSO KNOW YOU COME FROM A CELE-BRATED FAMILY...

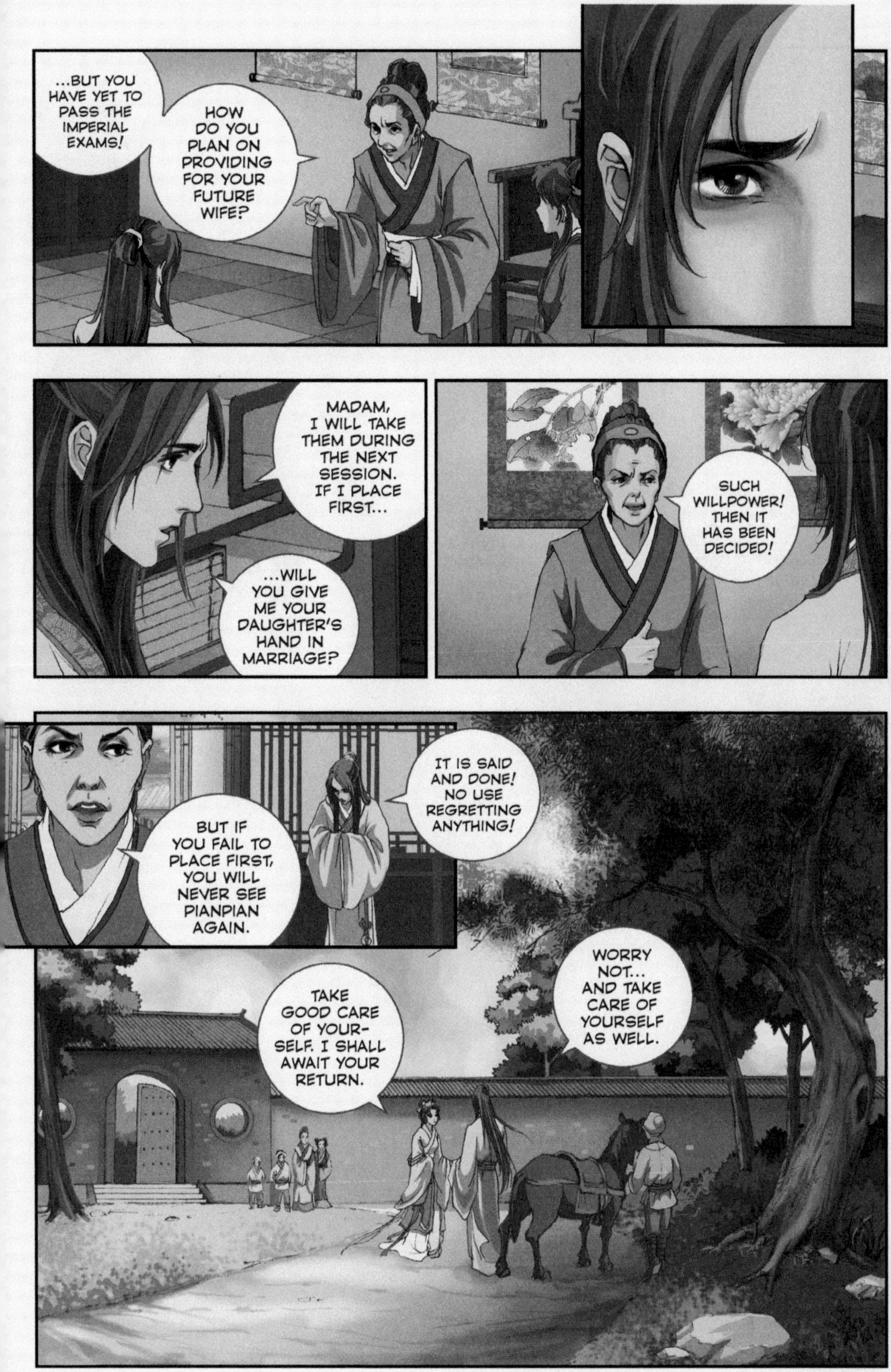
...BUT YOU HAVE YET TO PASS THE IMPERIAL EXAMS!
HOW DO YOU PLAN ON PROVIDING FOR YOUR FUTURE WIFE?
MADAM, I WILL TAKE THEM DURING THE NEXT SESSION. IF I PLACE FIRST...
...WILL YOU GIVE ME YOUR DAUGHTER'S HAND IN MARRIAGE?
SUCH WILLPOWER! THEN IT HAS BEEN DECIDED!
BUT IF YOU FAIL TO PLACE FIRST, YOU WILL NEVER SEE PIANPIAN AGAIN.
IT IS SAID AND DONE! NO USE REGRETTING ANYTHING!
TAKE GOOD CARE OF YOUR-SELF. I SHALL AWAIT YOUR RETURN.
WORRY NOT... AND TAKE CARE OF YOURSELF AS WELL.

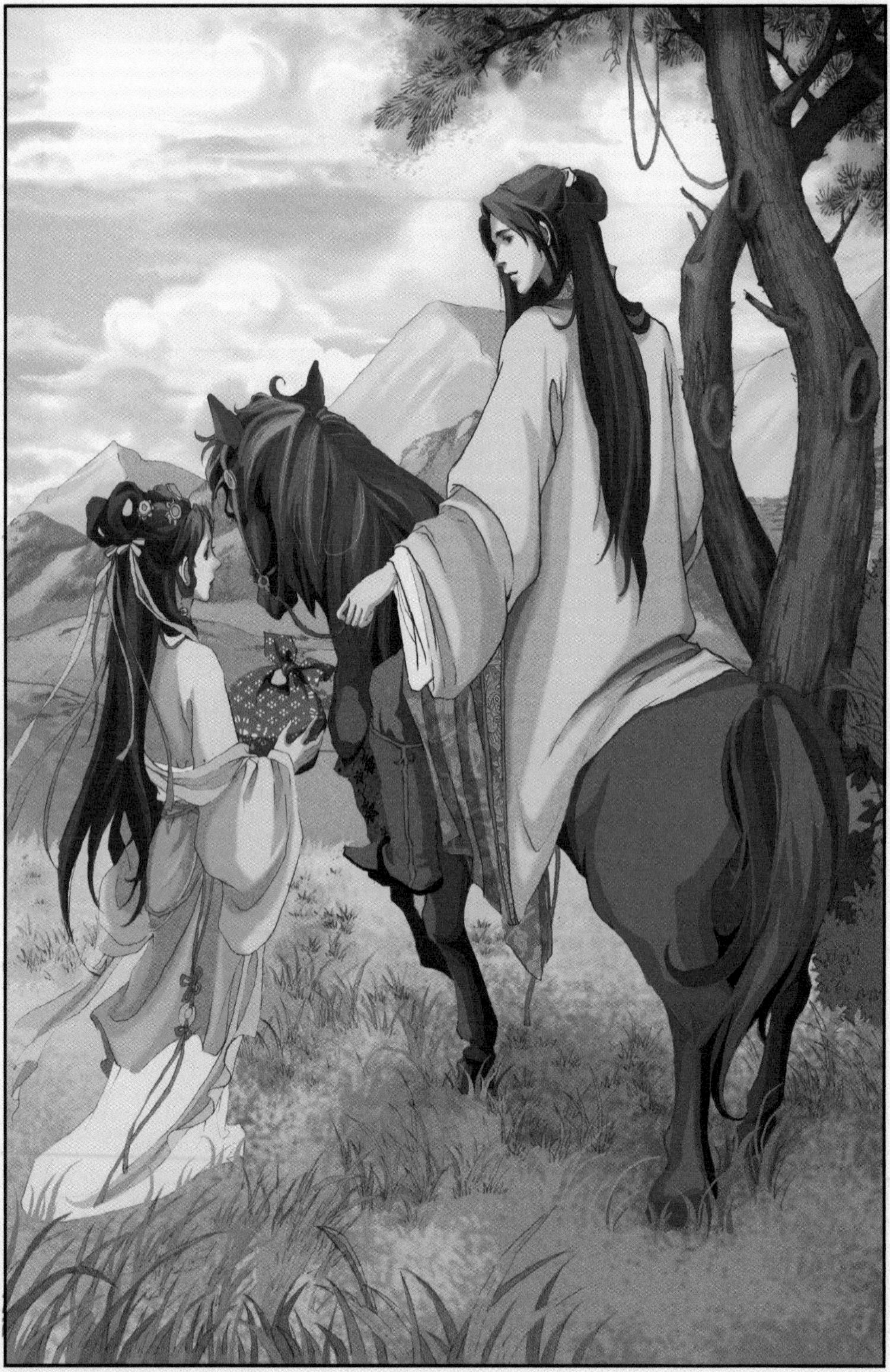

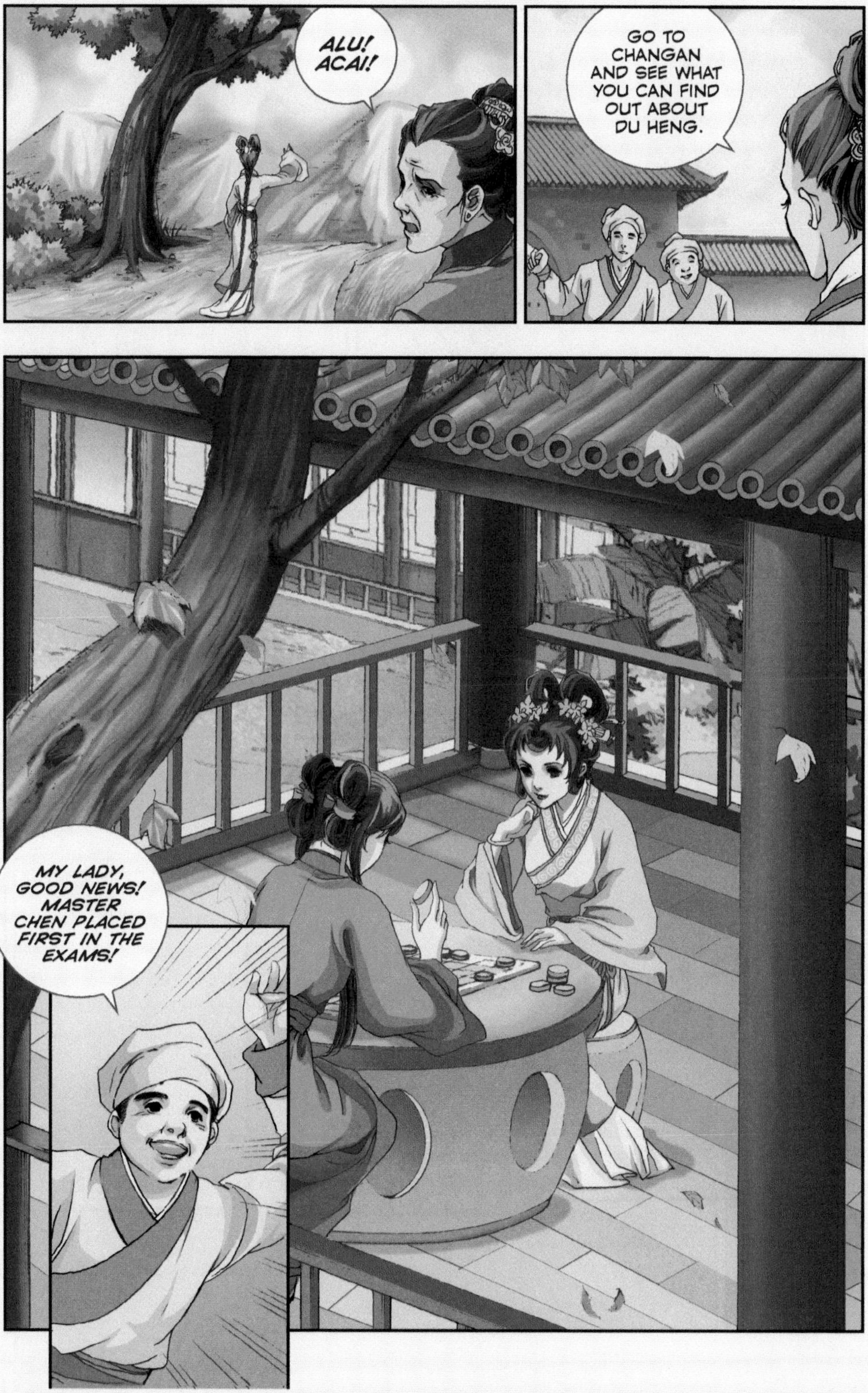
ALU! ACAI!
GO TO CHANGAN AND SEE WHAT YOU CAN FIND OUT ABOUT DU HENG.
MY LADY, GOOD NEWS! MASTER CHEN PLACED FIRST IN THE EXAMS!

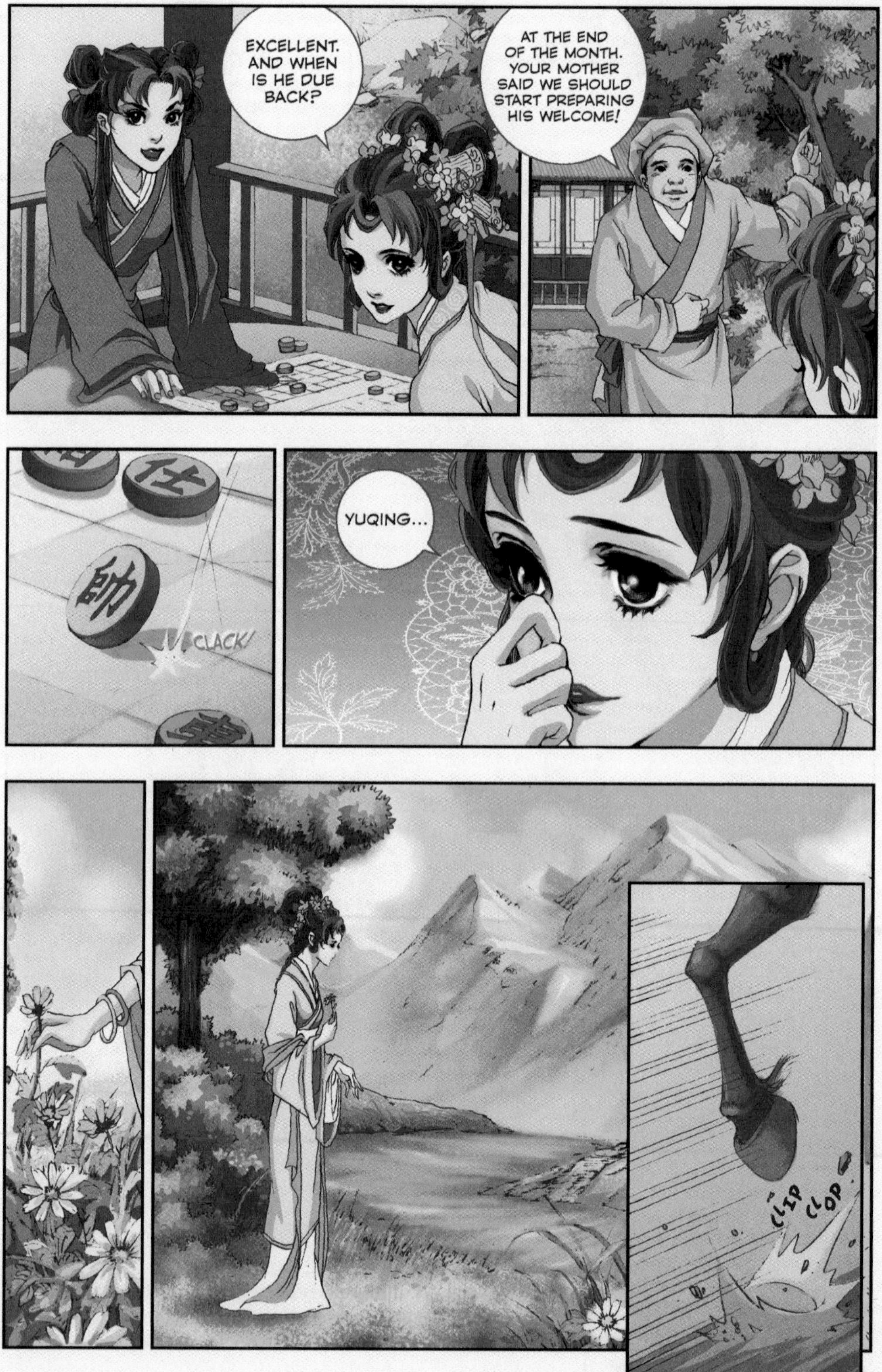
EXCELLENT. AND WHEN IS HE DUE BACK?
AT THE END OF THE MONTH. YOUR MOTHER SAID WE SHOULD START PREPARING HIS WELCOME!
CLACK!
YUQING...
CLIP CLOP

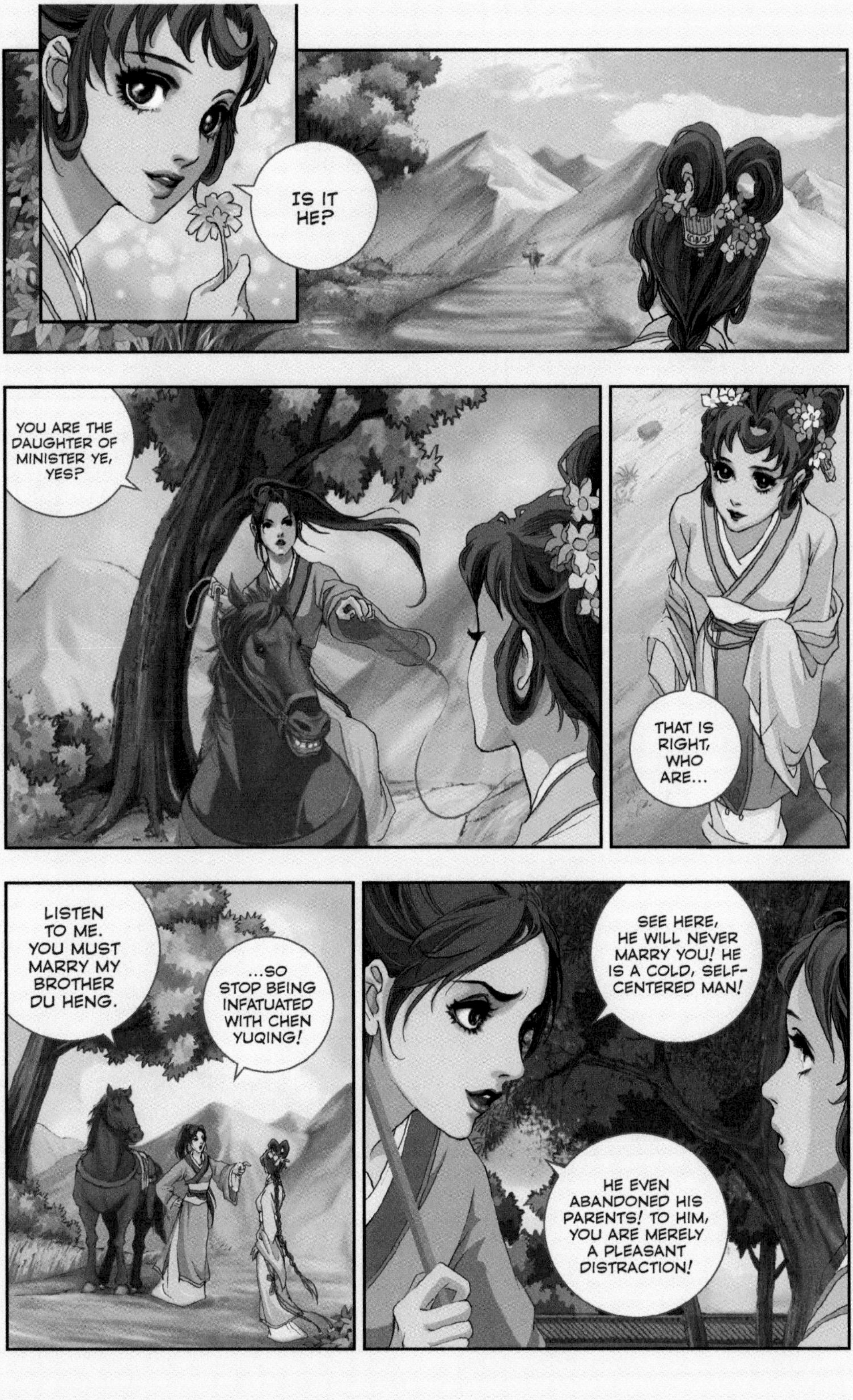
IS IT HE?
YOU ARE THE DAUGHTER OF MINISTER YE, YES?
THAT IS RIGHT, WHO ARE...
LISTEN TO ME. YOU MUST MARRY MY BROTHER DU HENG.
...SO STOP BEING INFATUATED WITH CHEN YUQING!
SEE HERE, HE WILL NEVER MARRY YOU! HE IS A COLD, SELF-CENTERED MAN!
HE EVEN ABANDONED HIS PARENTS! TO HIM, YOU ARE MERELY A PLEASANT DISTRACTION!

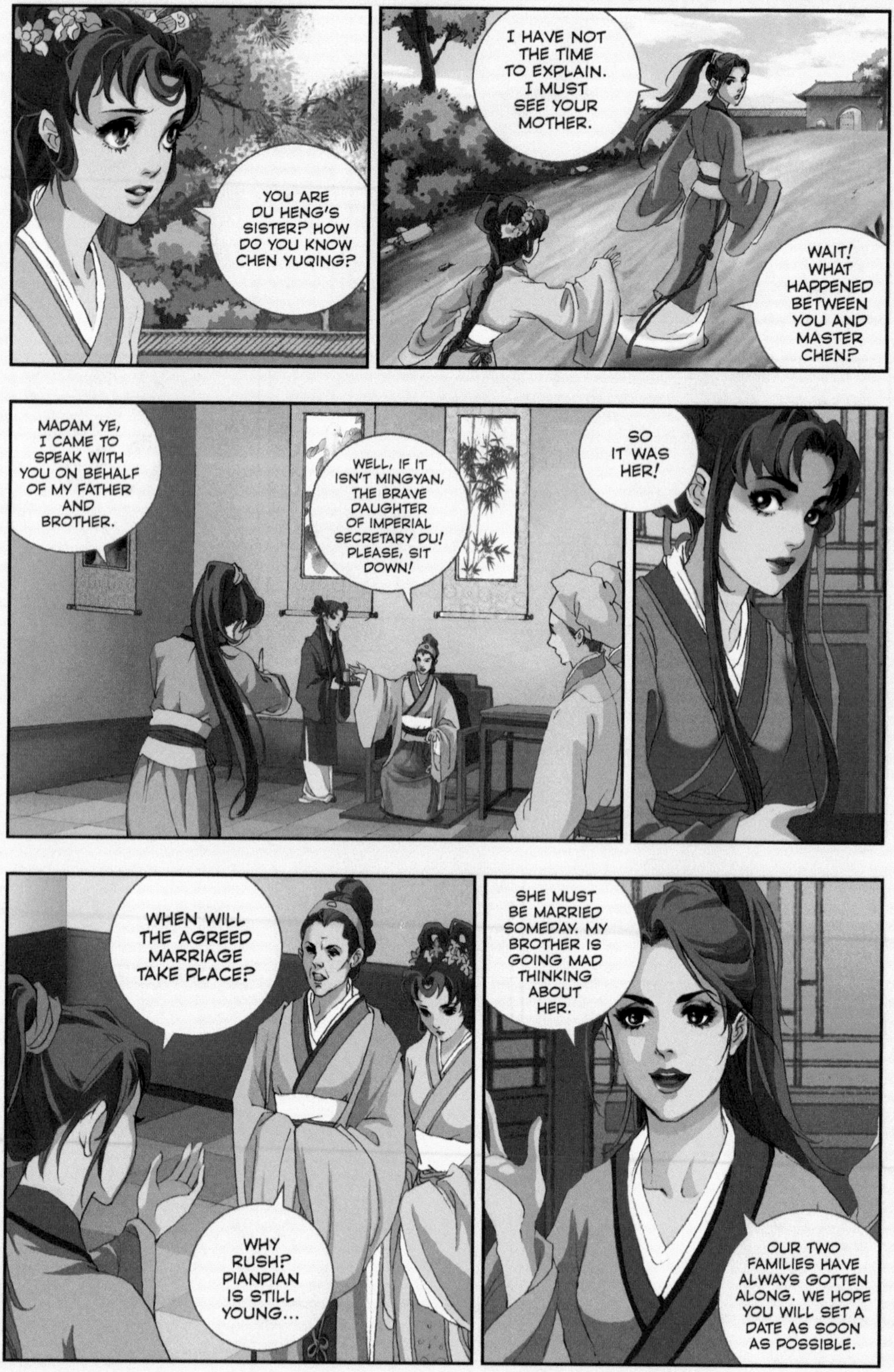
YOU ARE DU HENG'S SISTER? HOW DO YOU KNOW CHEN YUQING?
I HAVE NOT THE TIME TO EXPLAIN. I MUST SEE YOUR MOTHER.
WAIT! WHAT HAPPENED BETWEEN YOU AND MASTER CHEN?
MADAM YE, I CAME TO SPEAK WITH YOU ON BEHALF OF MY FATHER AND BROTHER.
WELL, IF IT ISN'T MINGYAN, THE BRAVE DAUGHTER OF IMPERIAL SECRETARY DU! PLEASE, SIT DOWN!
SO IT WAS HER!
WHEN WILL THE AGREED MARRIAGE TAKE PLACE?
WHY RUSH? PIANPIAN IS STILL YOUNG...
SHE MUST BE MARRIED SOMEDAY. MY BROTHER IS GOING MAD THINKING ABOUT HER.
OUR TWO FAMILIES HAVE ALWAYS GOTTEN ALONG. WE HOPE YOU WILL SET A DATE AS SOON AS POSSIBLE.

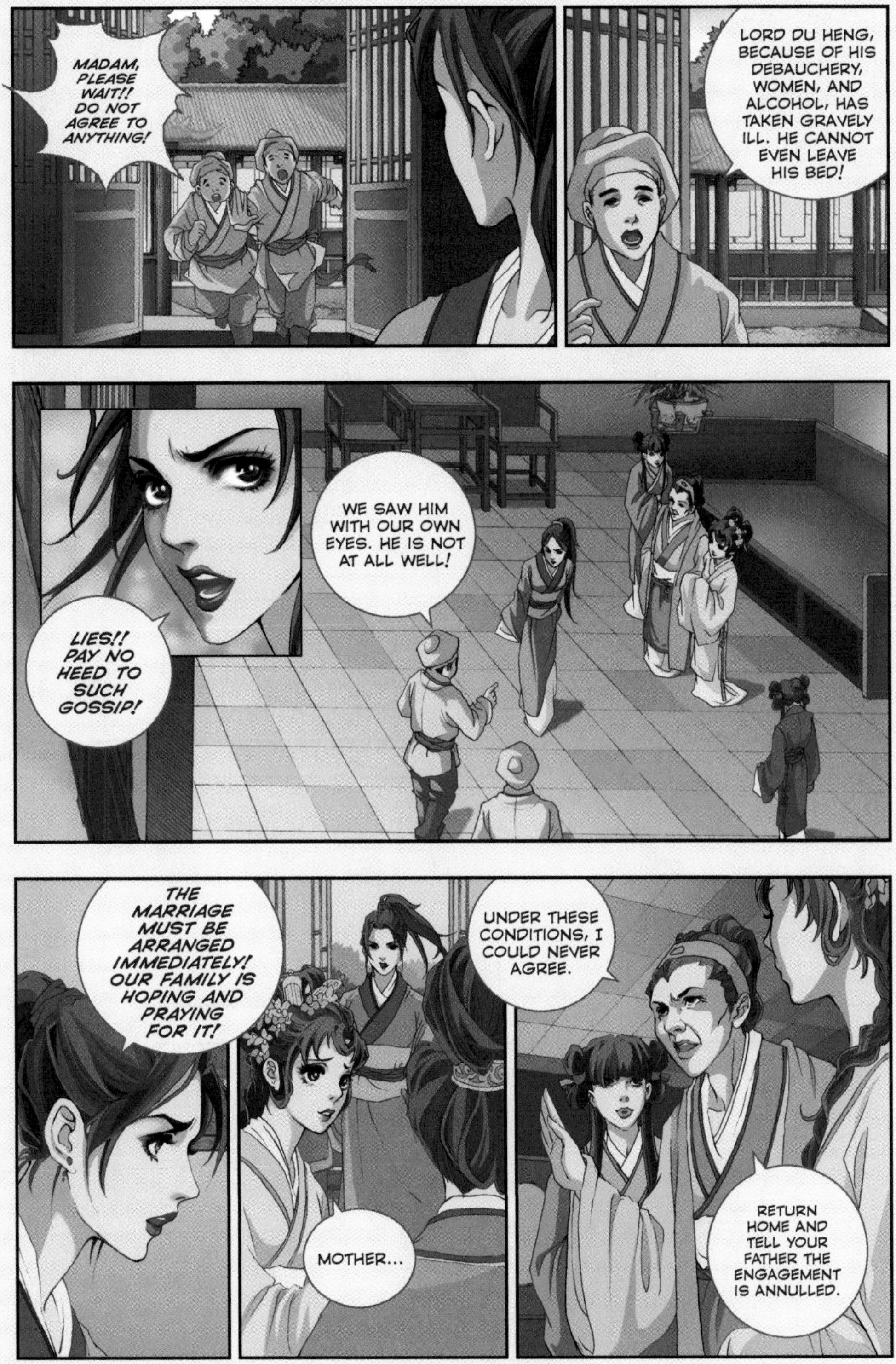
MADAM, PLEASE WAIT!! DO NOT AGREE TO ANYTHING!
LORD DU HENG, BECAUSE OF HIS DEBAUCHERY, WOMEN, AND ALCOHOL, HAS TAKEN GRAVELY ILL. HE CANNOT EVEN LEAVE HIS BED!
WE SAW HIM WITH OUR OWN EYES. HE IS NOT AT ALL WELL!
LIES!! PAY NO HEED TO SUCH GOSSIP!
THE MARRIAGE MUST BE ARRANGED IMMEDIATELY! OUR FAMILY IS HOPING AND PRAYING FOR IT!
MOTHER...
UNDER THESE CONDITIONS, I COULD NEVER AGREE.
RETURN HOME AND TELL YOUR FATHER THE ENGAGEMENT IS ANNULLED.

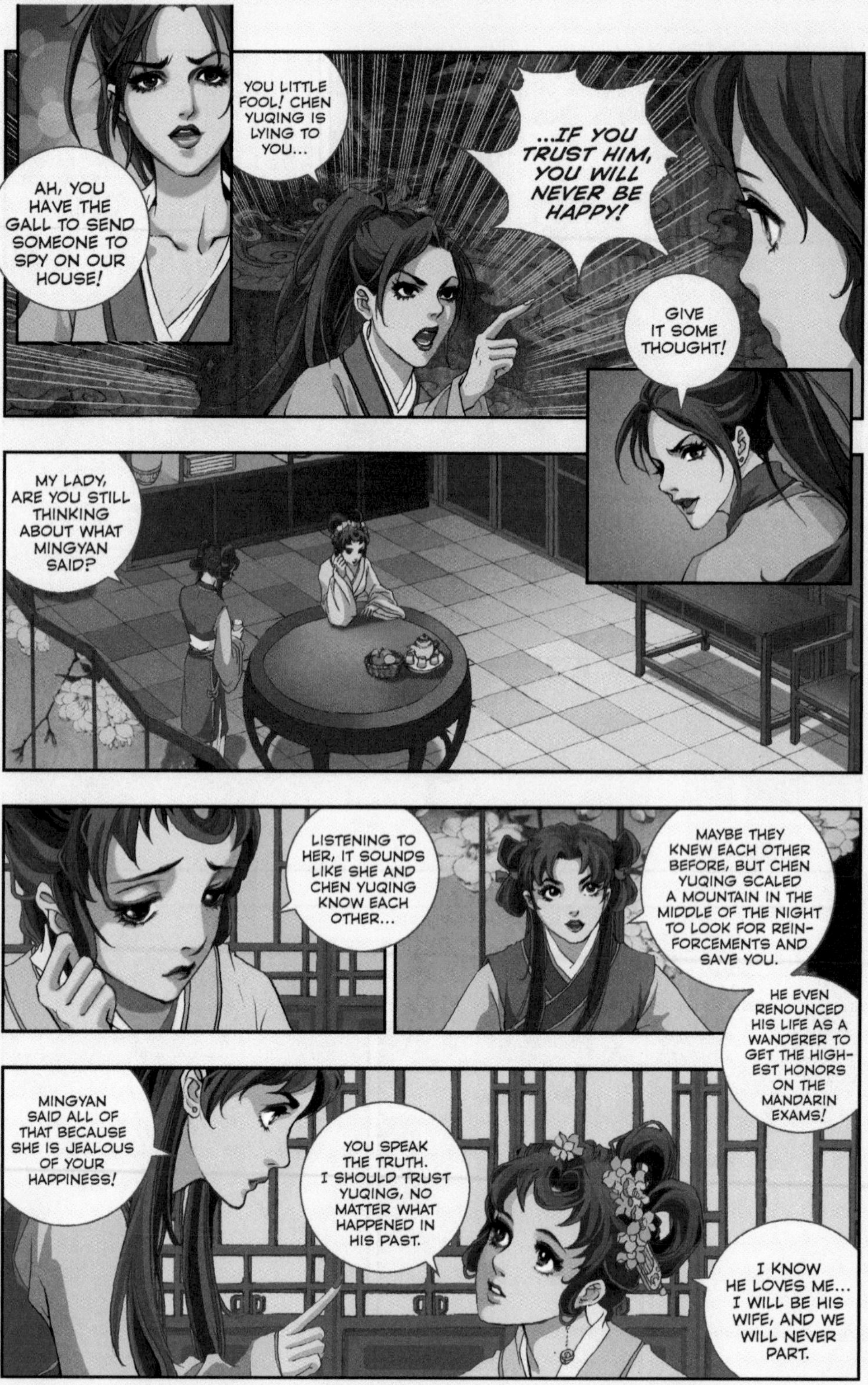

AH, YOU HAVE THE GALL TO SEND SOMEONE TO SPY ON OUR HOUSE!
YOU LITTLE FOOL! CHEN YUQING IS LYING TO YOU...
...IF YOU TRUST HIM, YOU WILL NEVER BE HAPPY!
GIVE IT SOME THOUGHT!
MY LADY, ARE YOU STILL THINKING ABOUT WHAT MINGYAN SAID?
LISTENING TO HER, IT SOUNDS LIKE SHE AND CHEN YUQING KNOW EACH OTHER...
MAYBE THEY KNEW EACH OTHER BEFORE, BUT CHEN YUQING SCALED A MOUNTAIN IN THE MIDDLE OF THE NIGHT TO LOOK FOR REIN-FORCEMENTS AND SAVE YOU.
HE EVEN RENOUNCED HIS LIFE AS A WANDERER TO GET THE HIGH-EST HONORS ON THE MANDARIN EXAMS!
MINGYAN SAID ALL OF THAT BECAUSE SHE IS JEALOUS OF YOUR HAPPINESS!
YOU SPEAK THE TRUTH. I SHOULD TRUST YUQING, NO MATTER WHAT HAPPENED IN HIS PAST.
I KNOW HE LOVES ME... I WILL BE HIS WIFE, AND WE WILL NEVER PART.

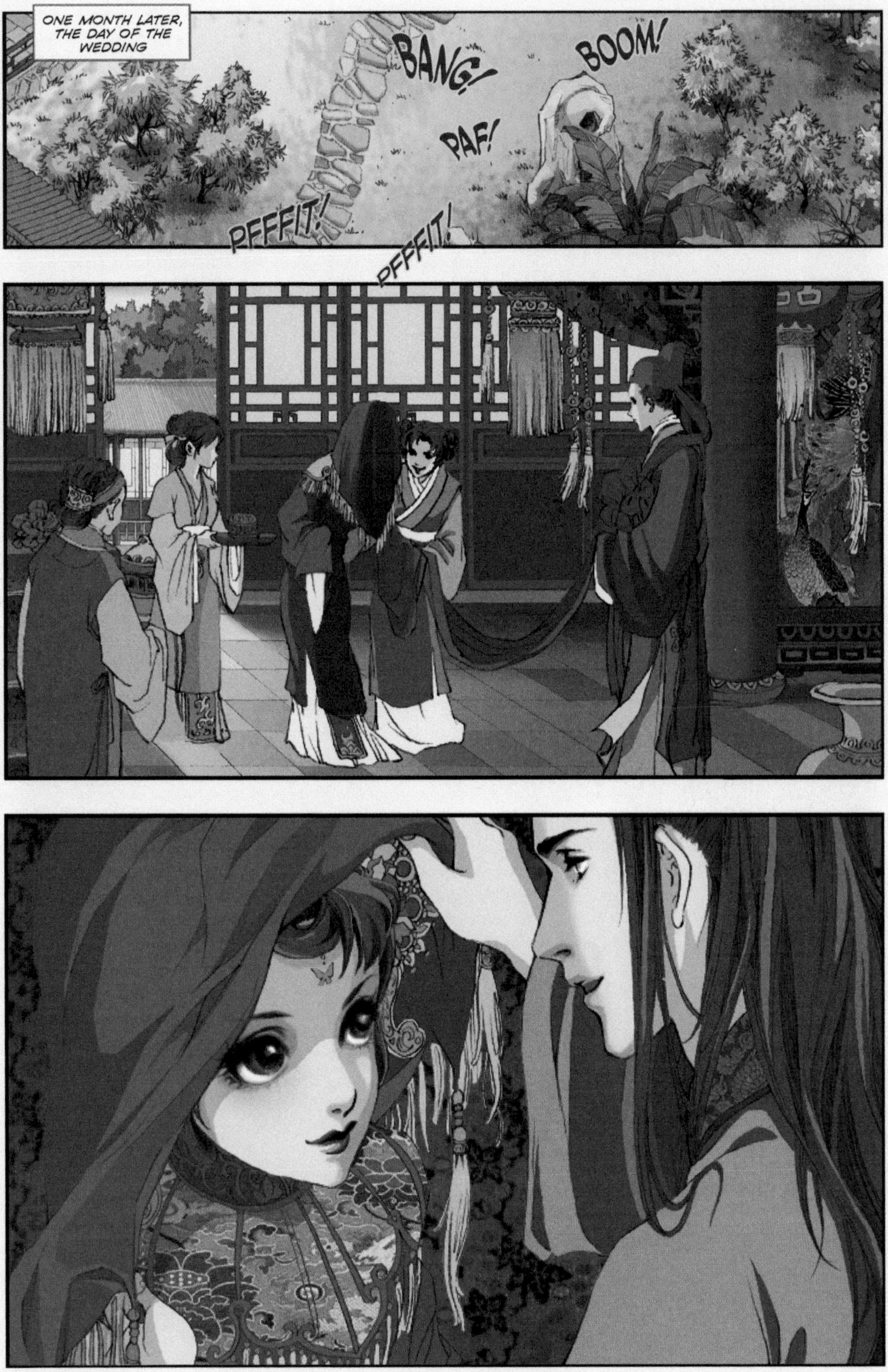
ONE MONTH LATER, THE DAY OF THE WEDDING
BANG!
BOOM!
PAF!
PFFFIT!
PFFFIT!

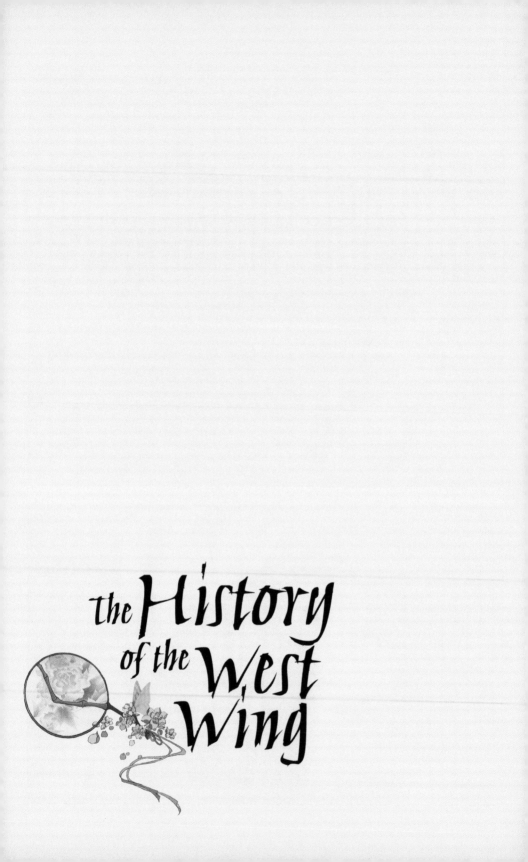

the History
of the West
Wing

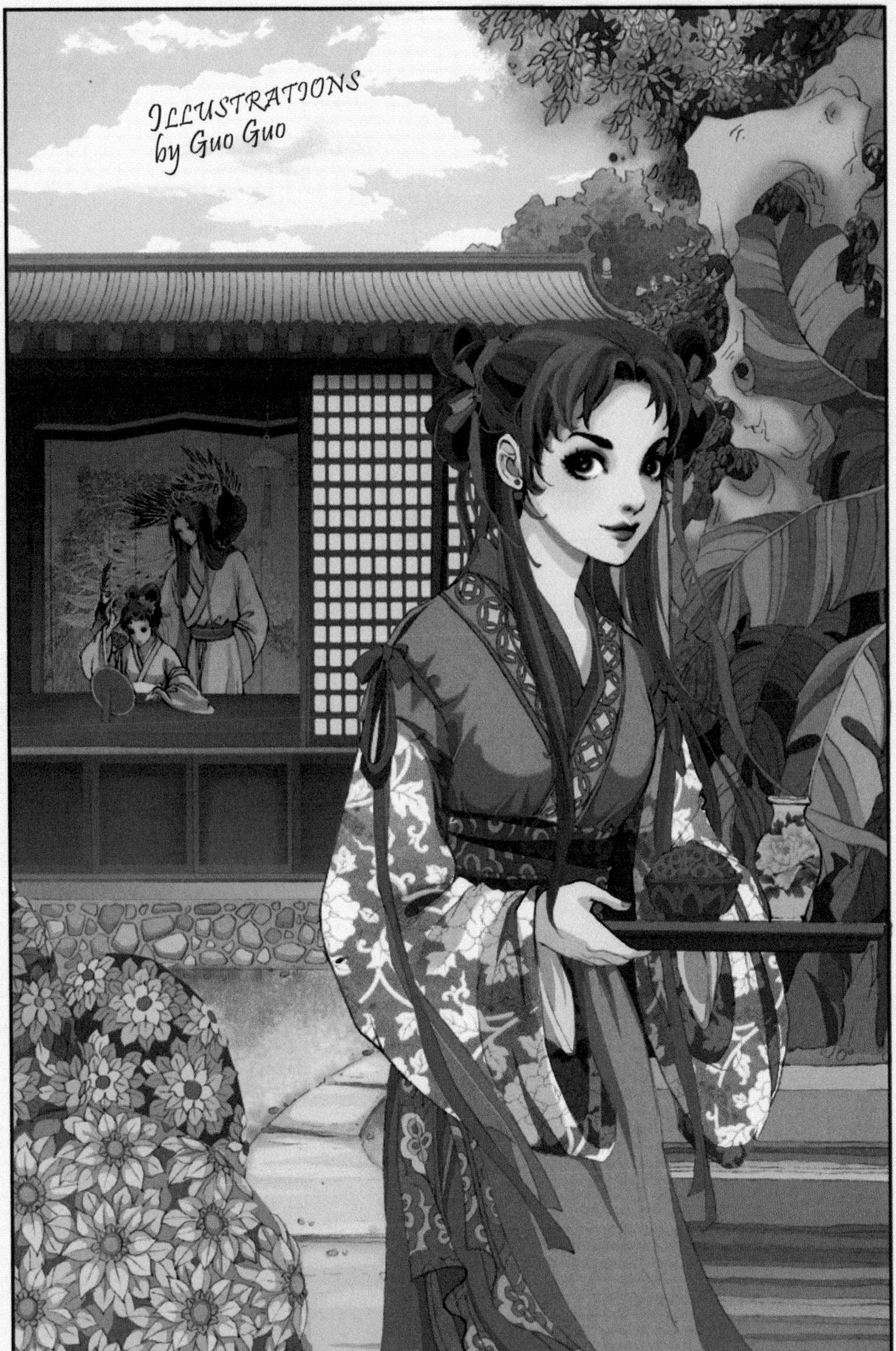
ILLUSTRATIONS
by Guo Guo

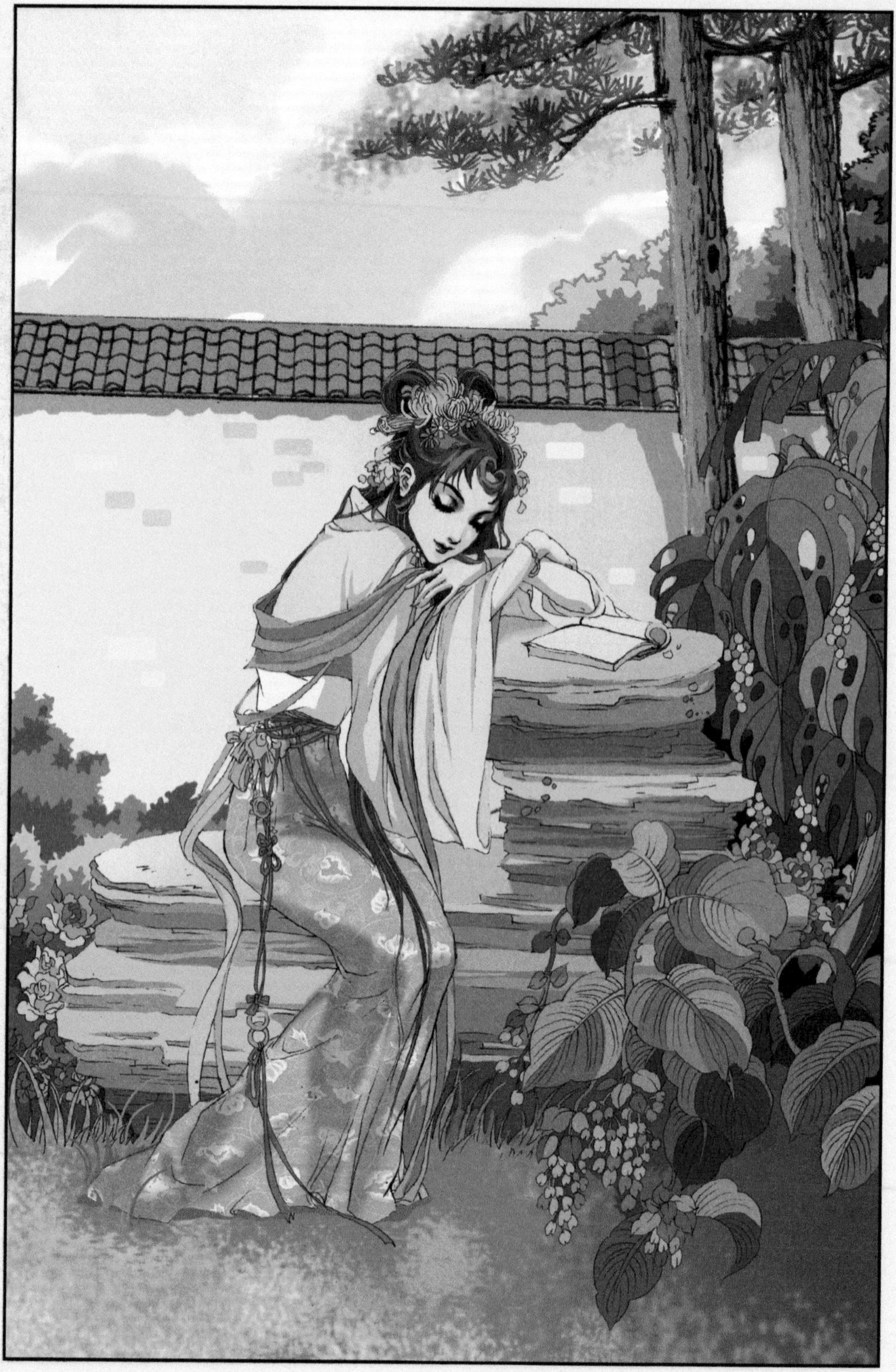

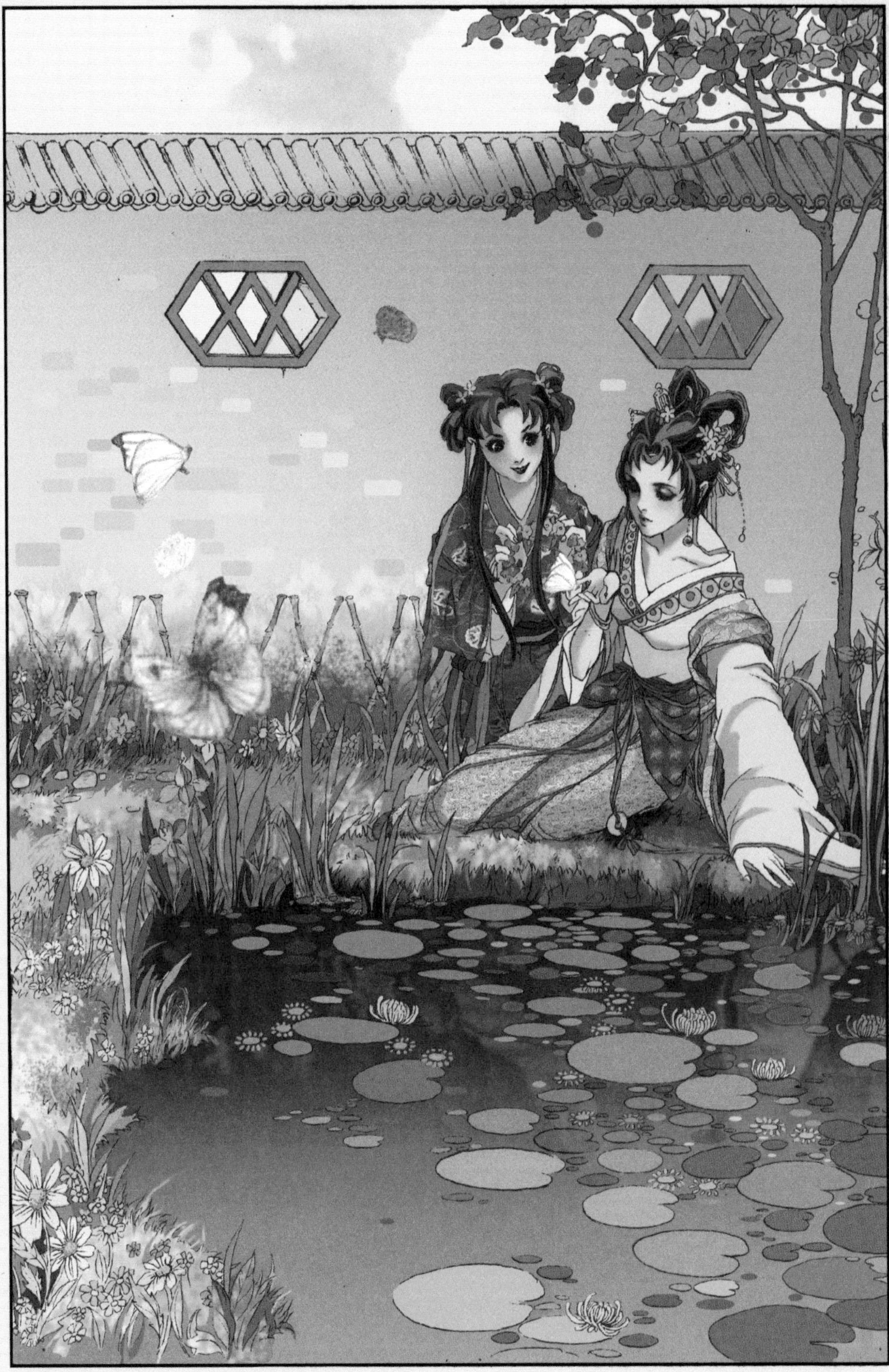

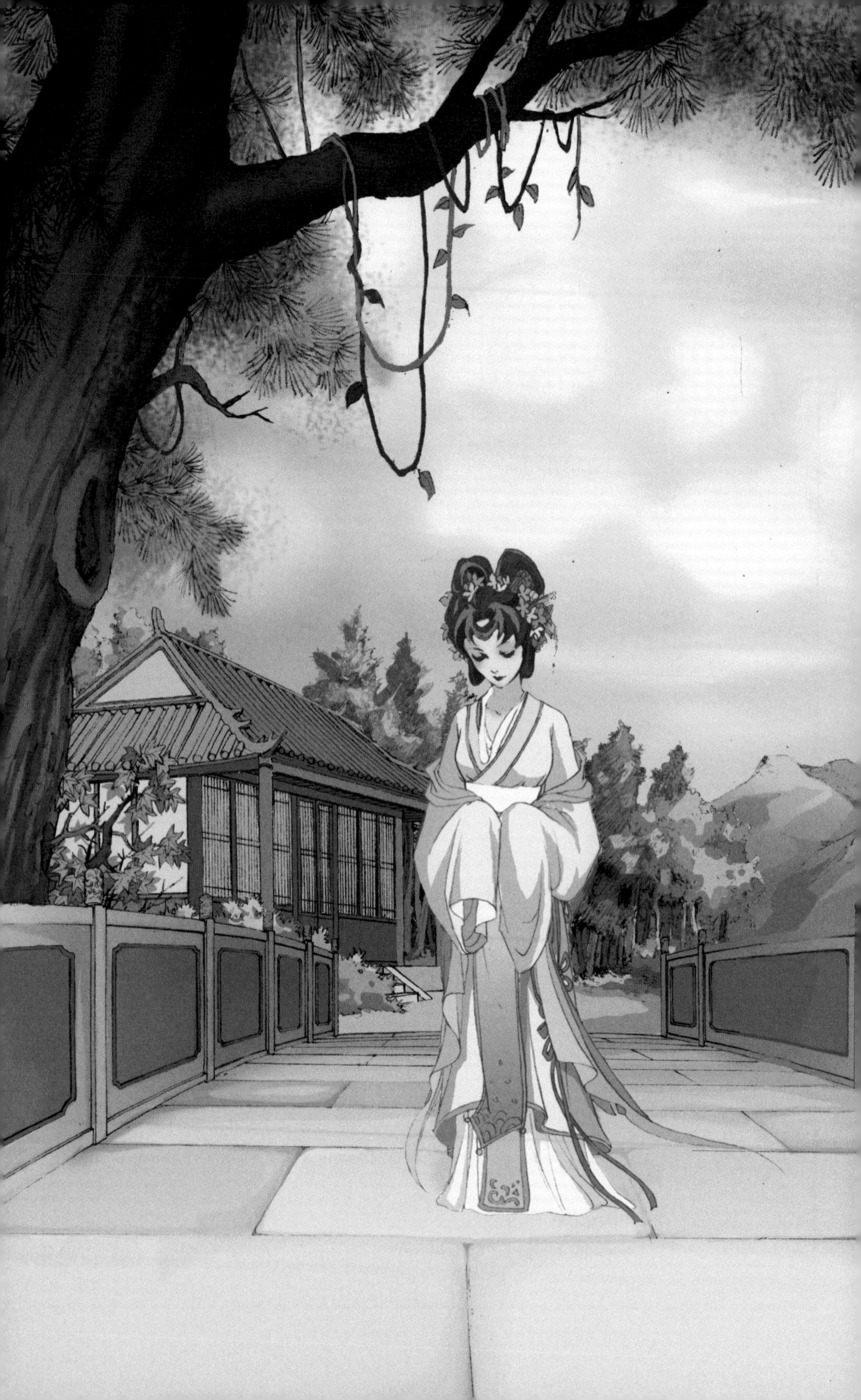

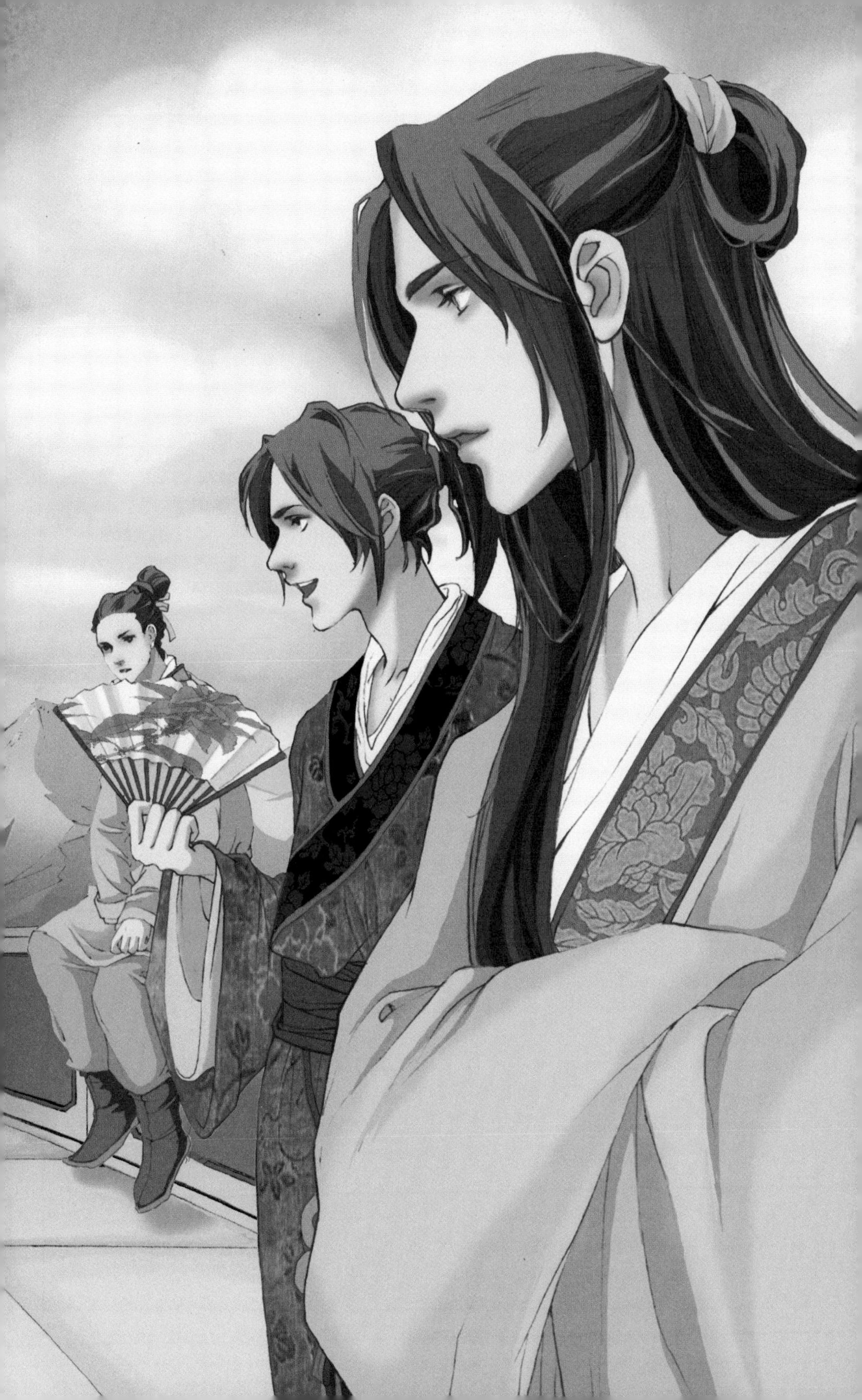

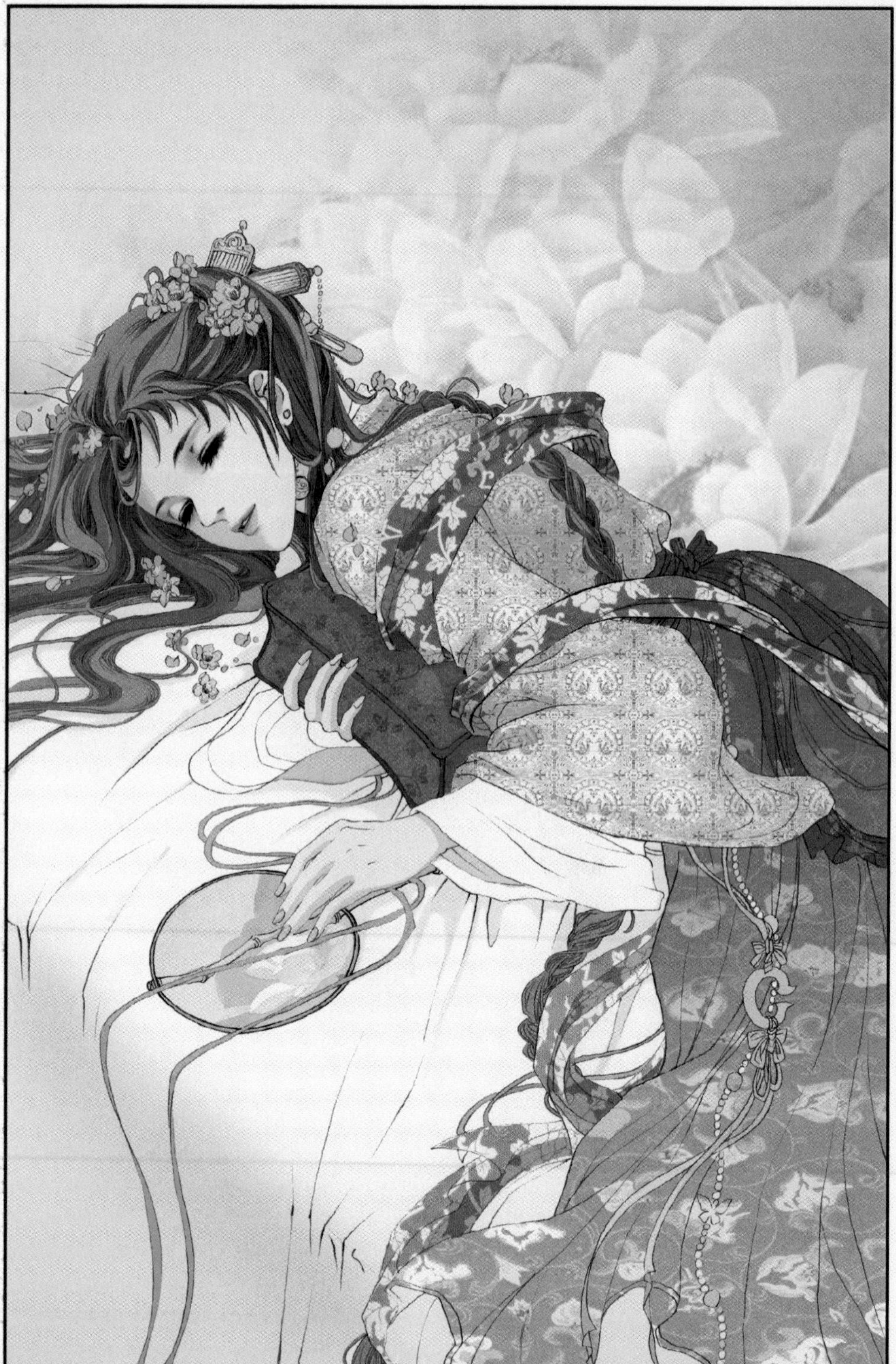

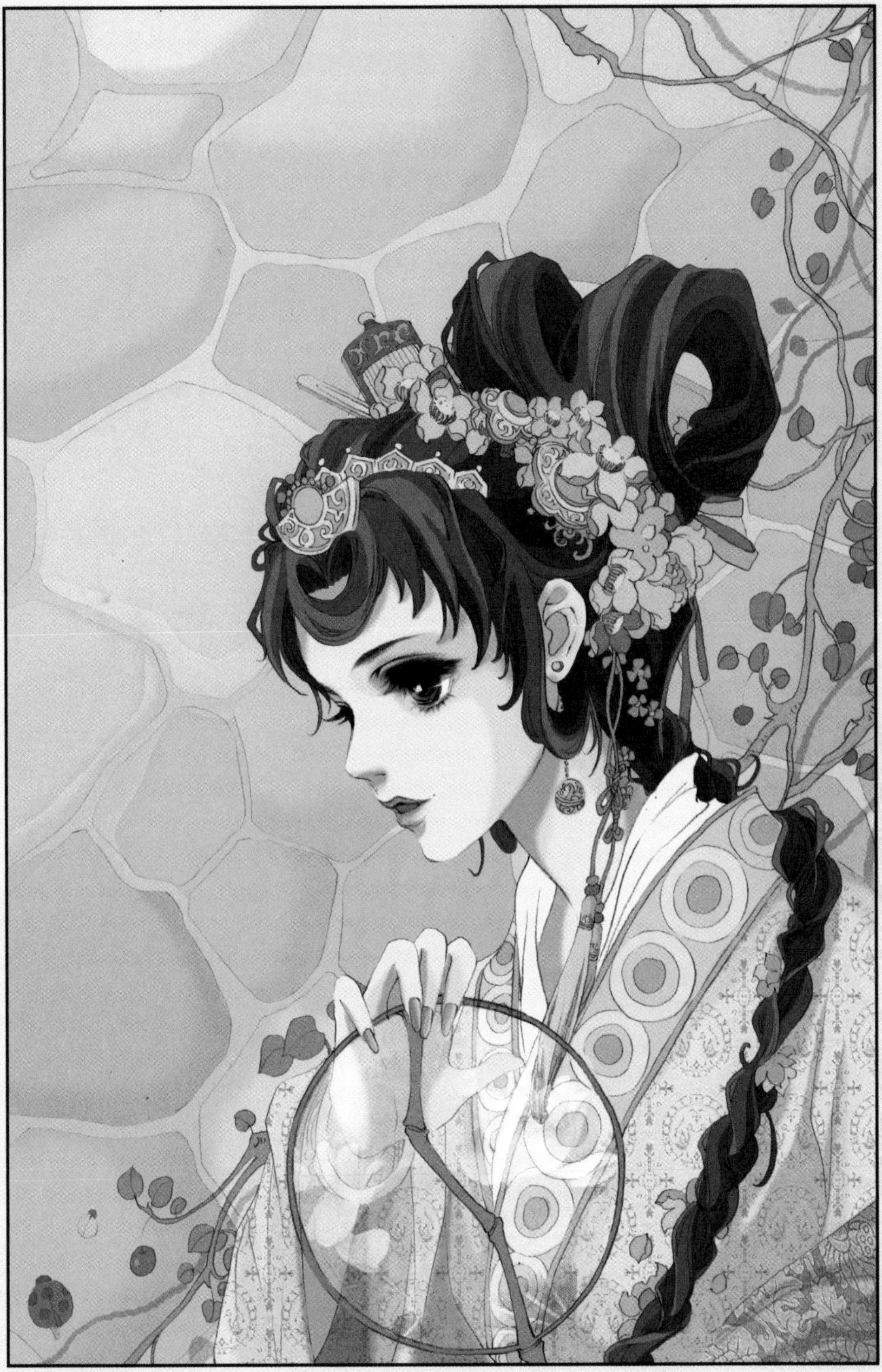

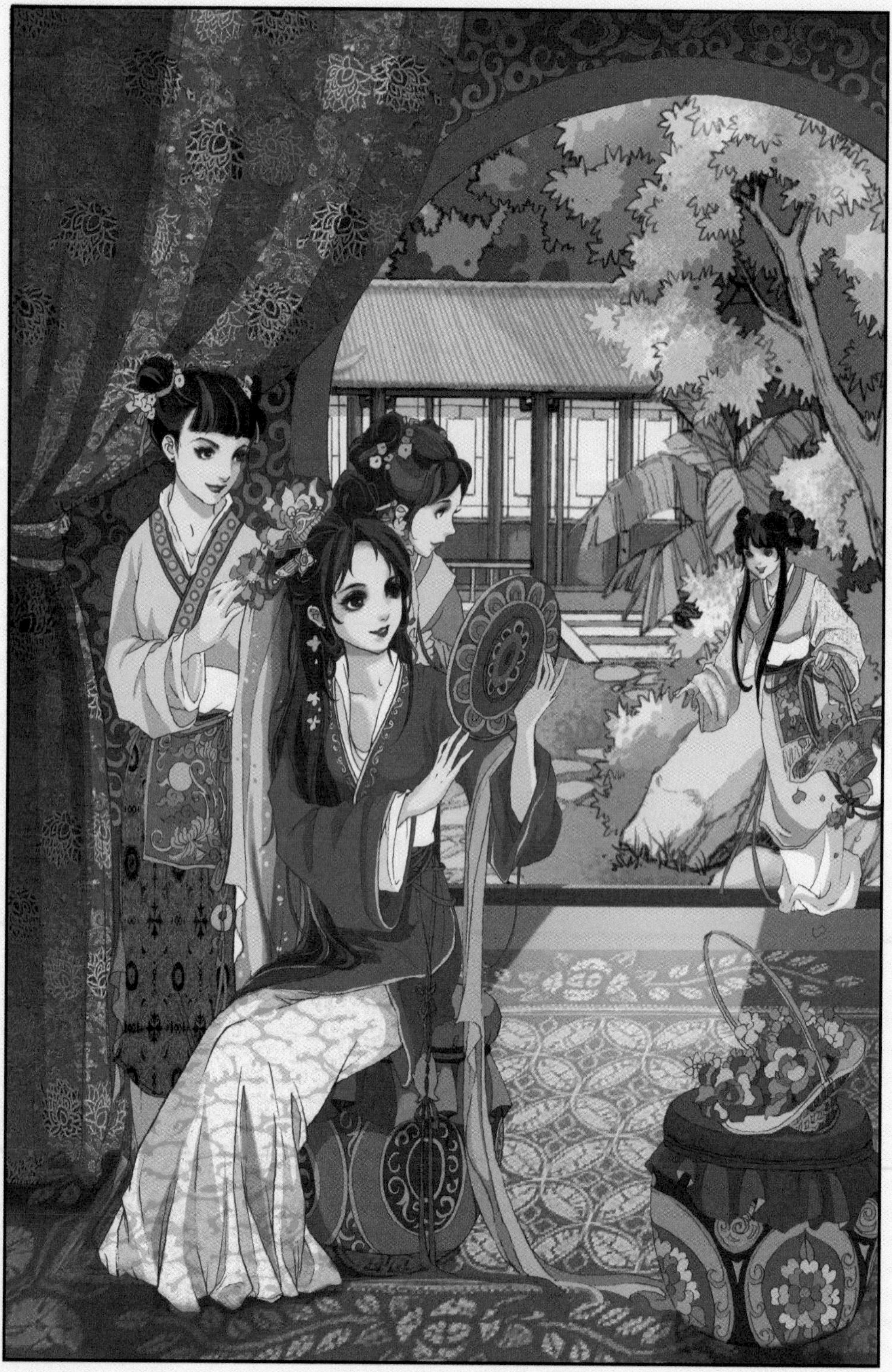

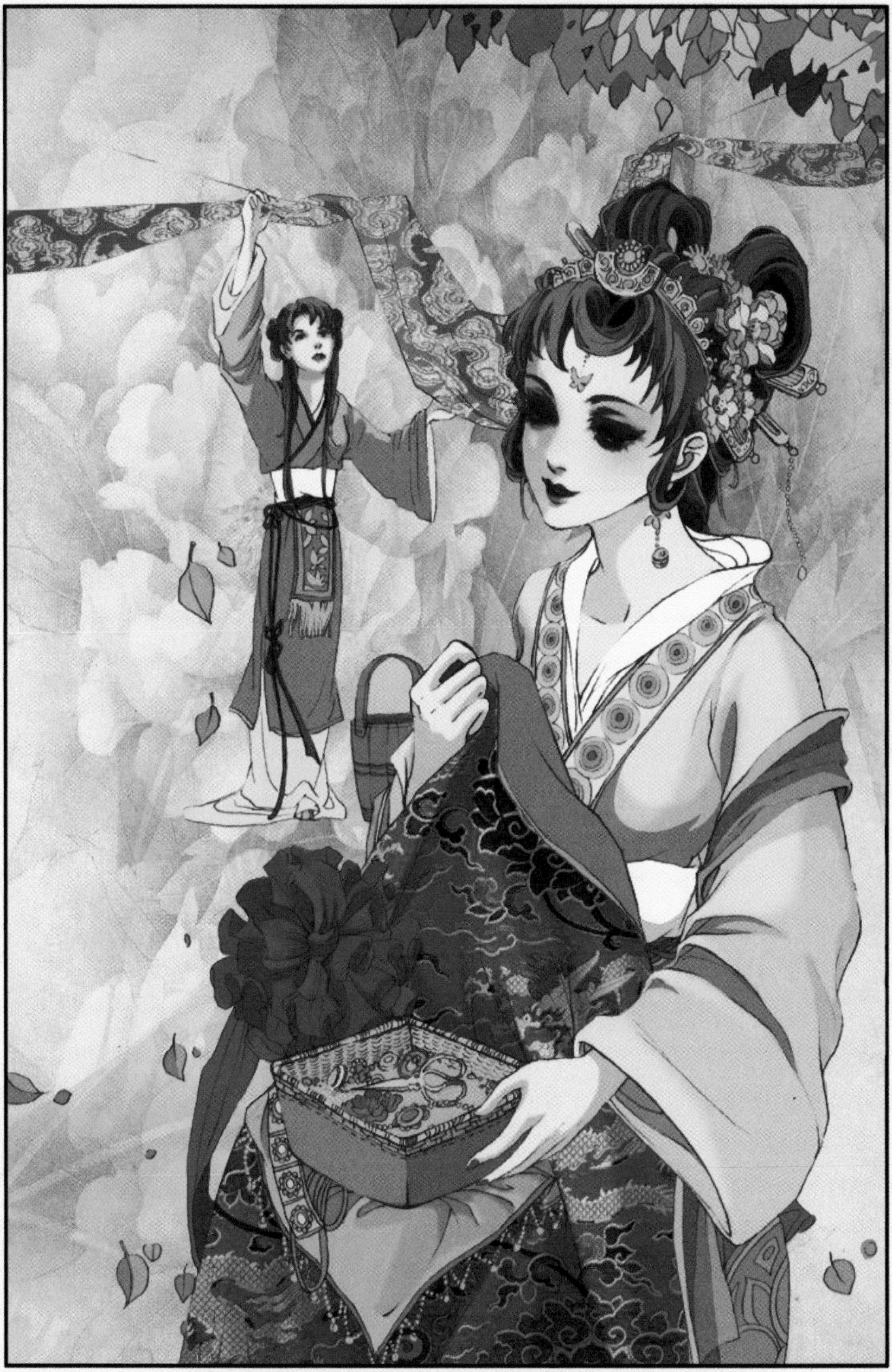

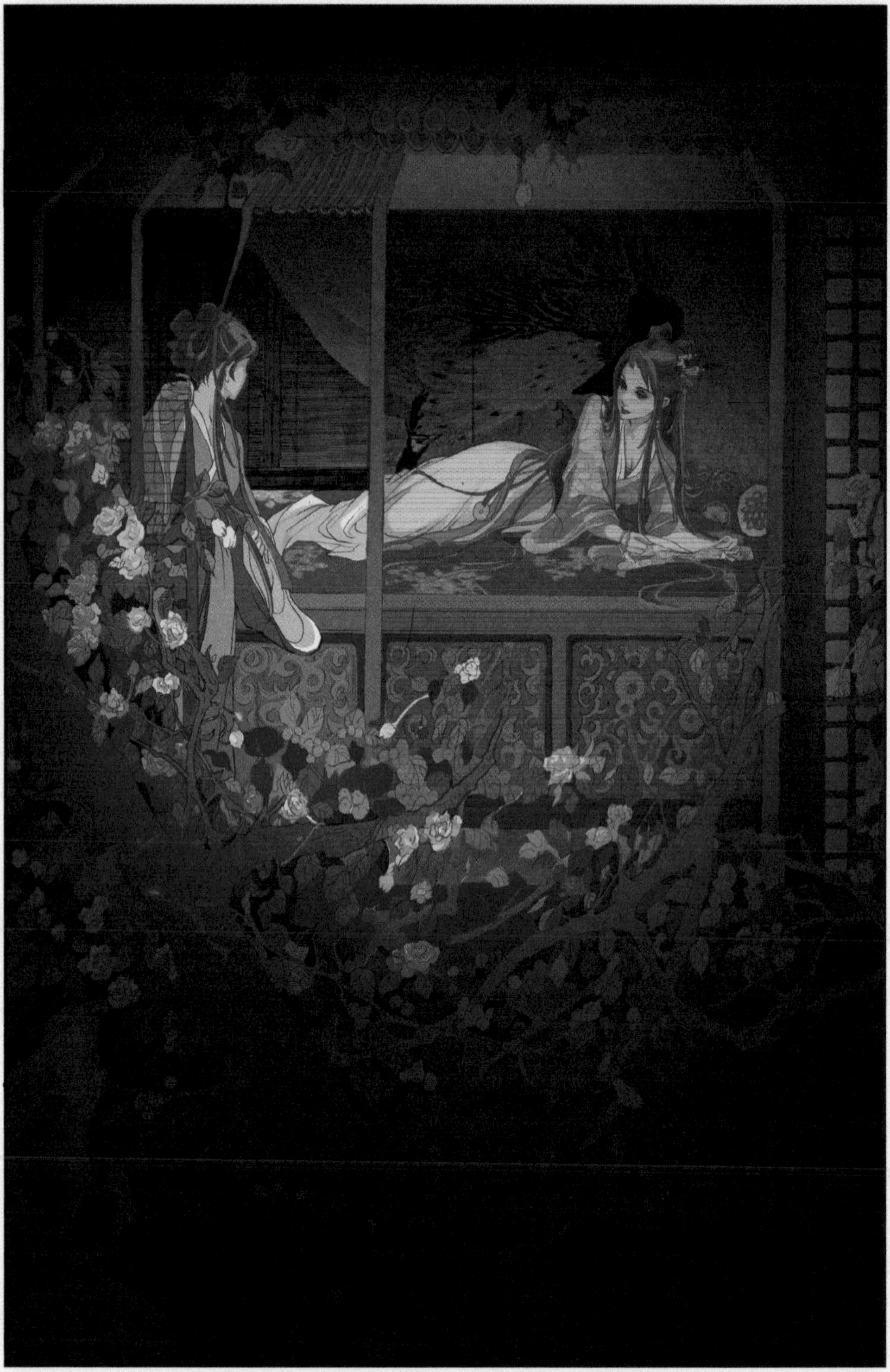

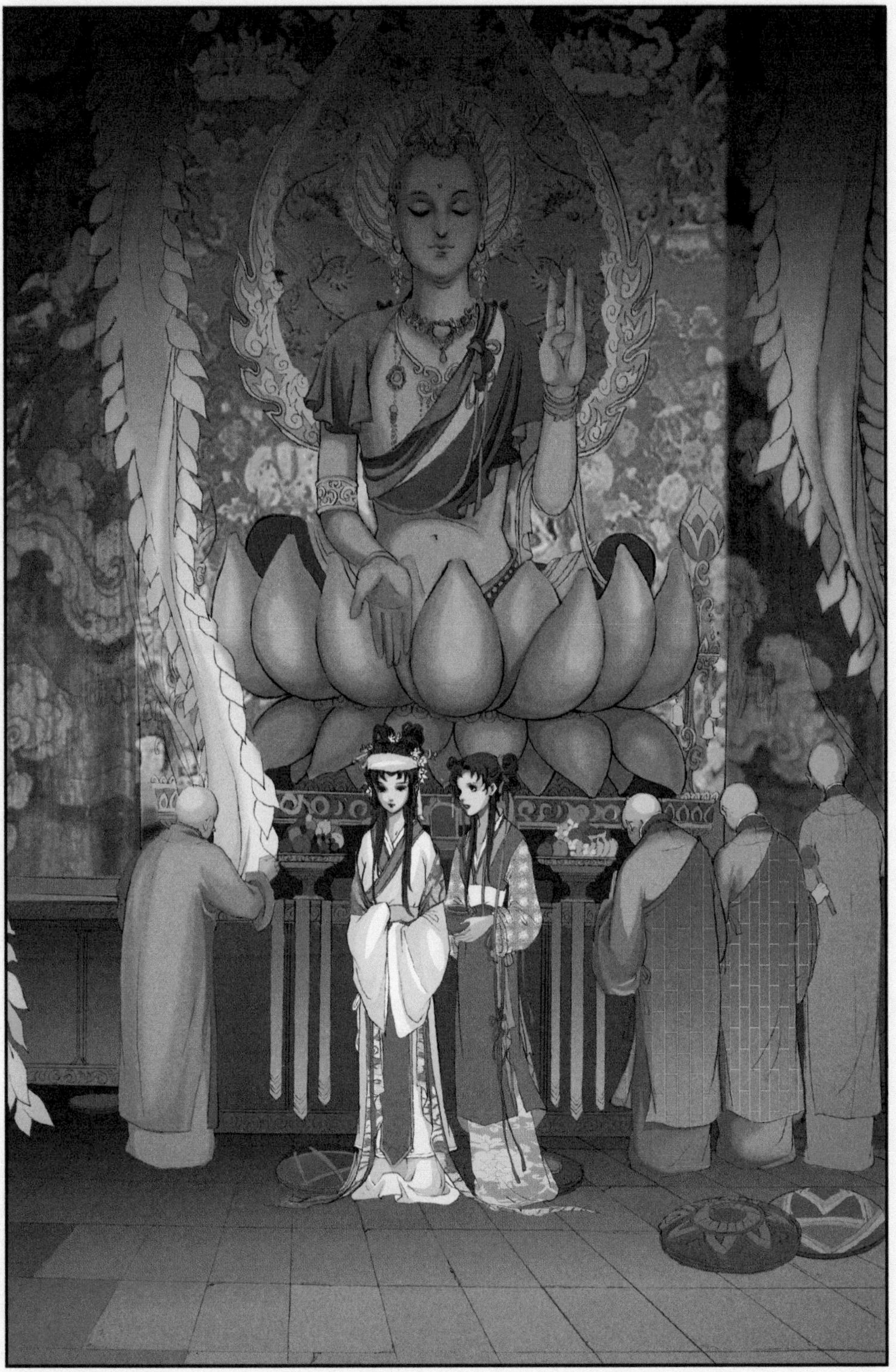

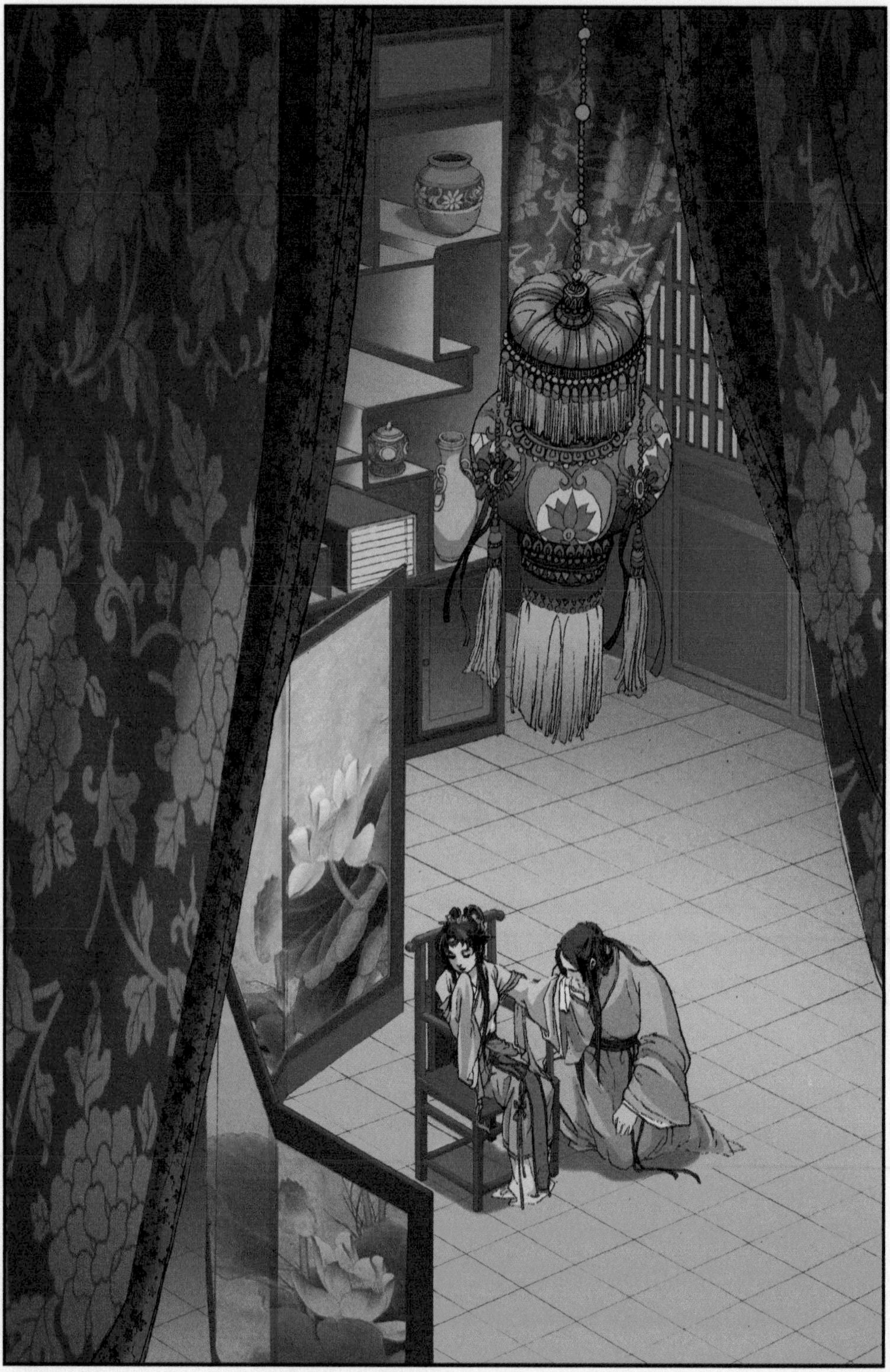

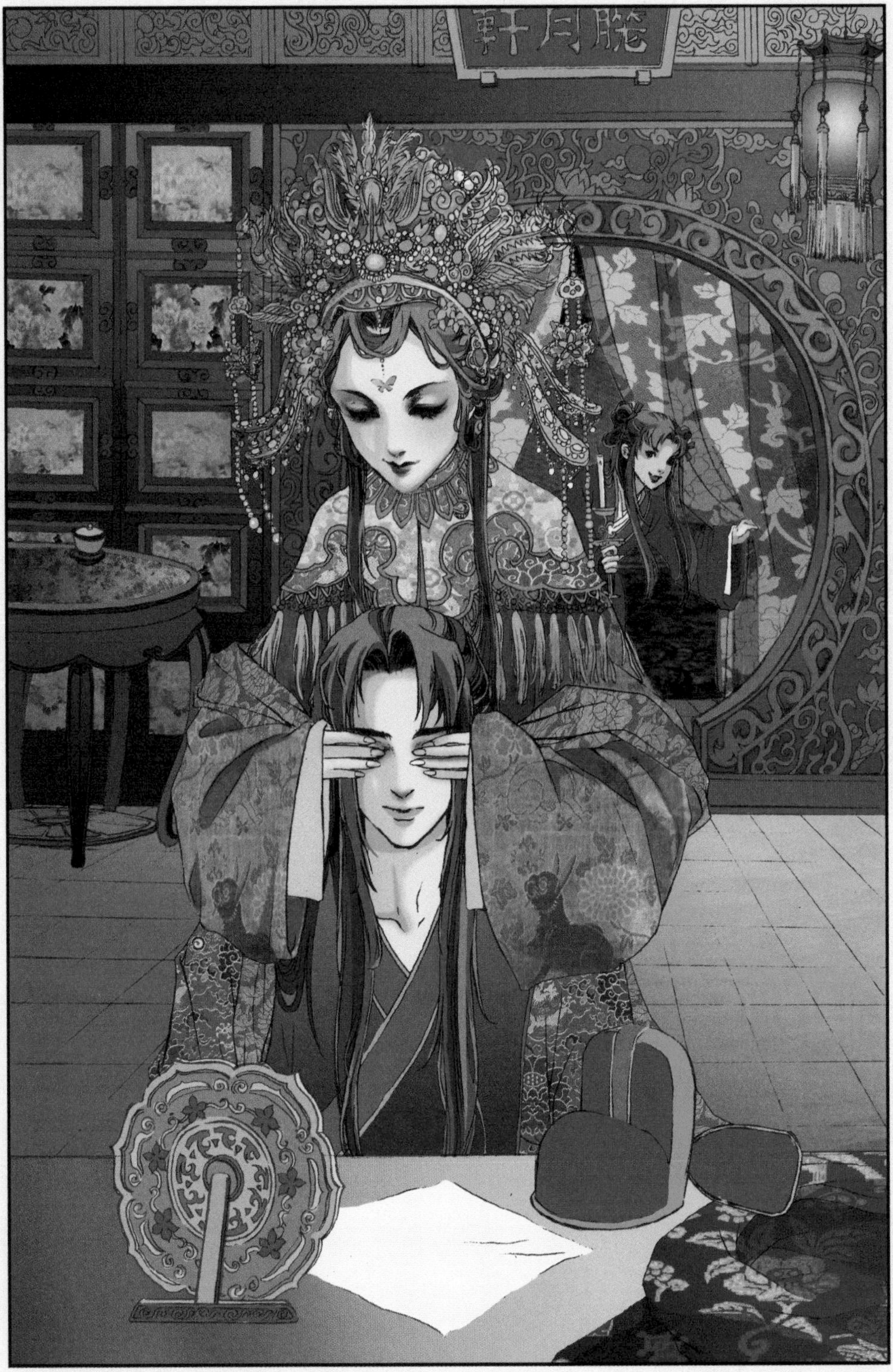
胧月軒

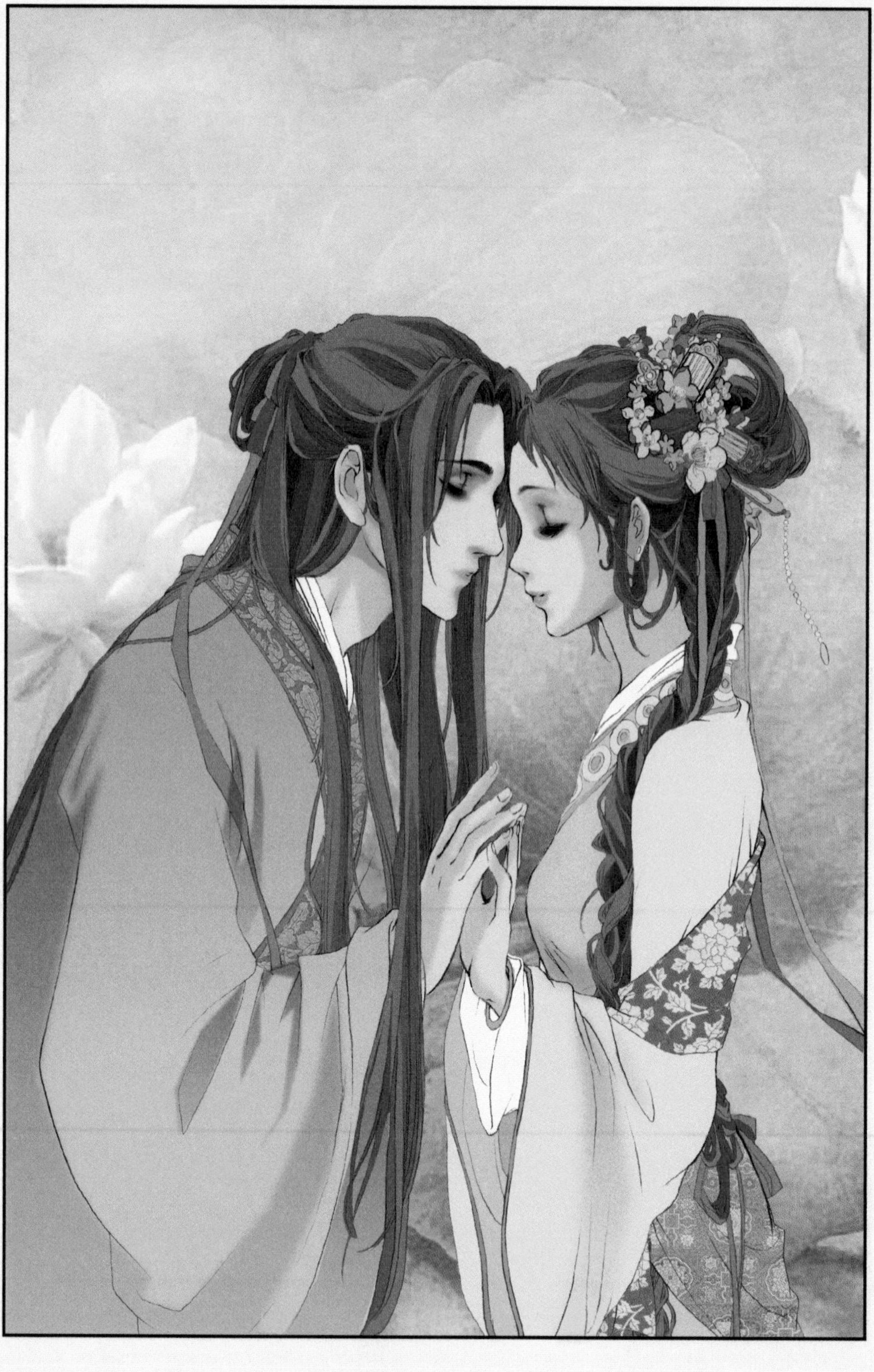

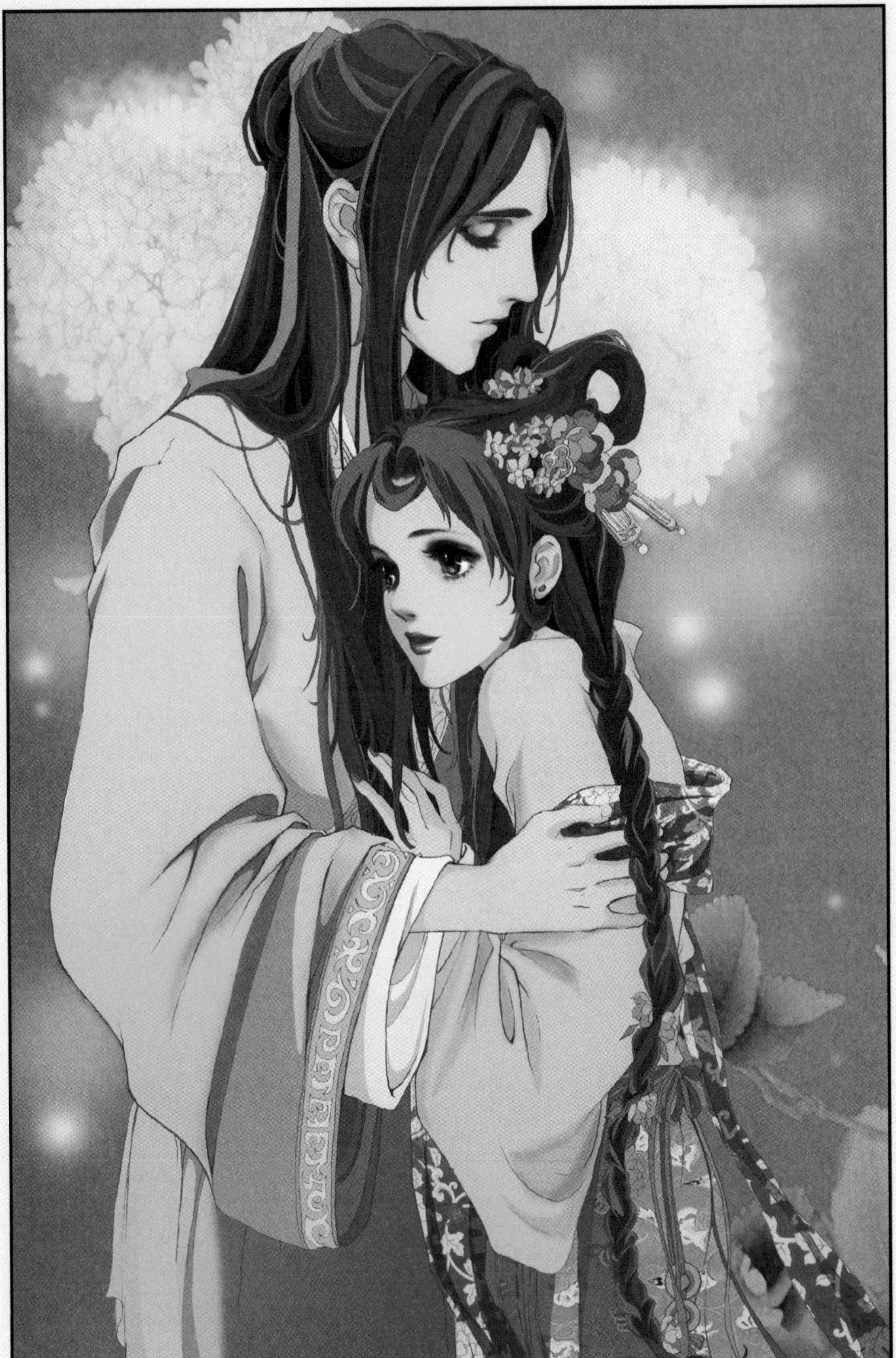

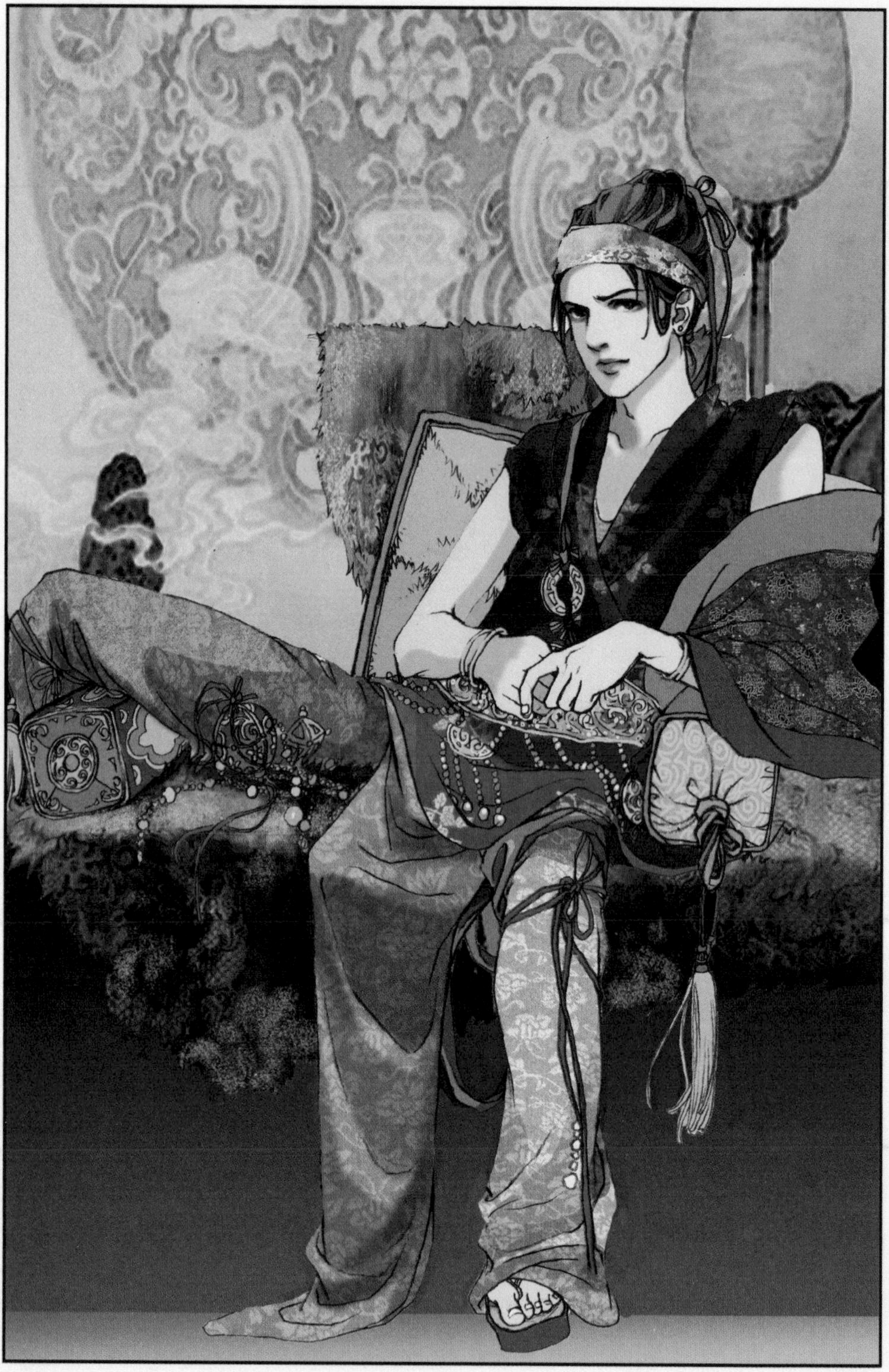

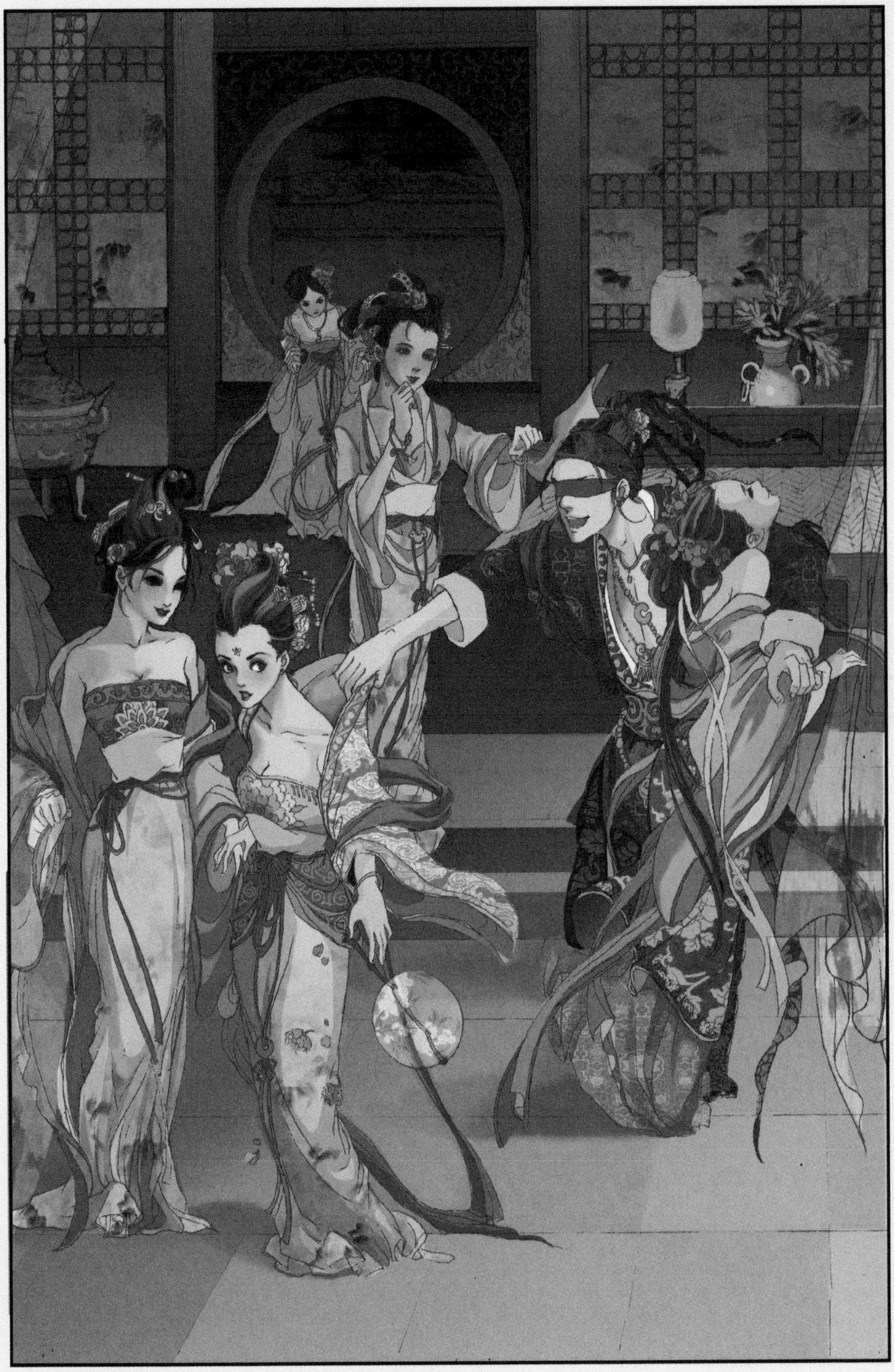

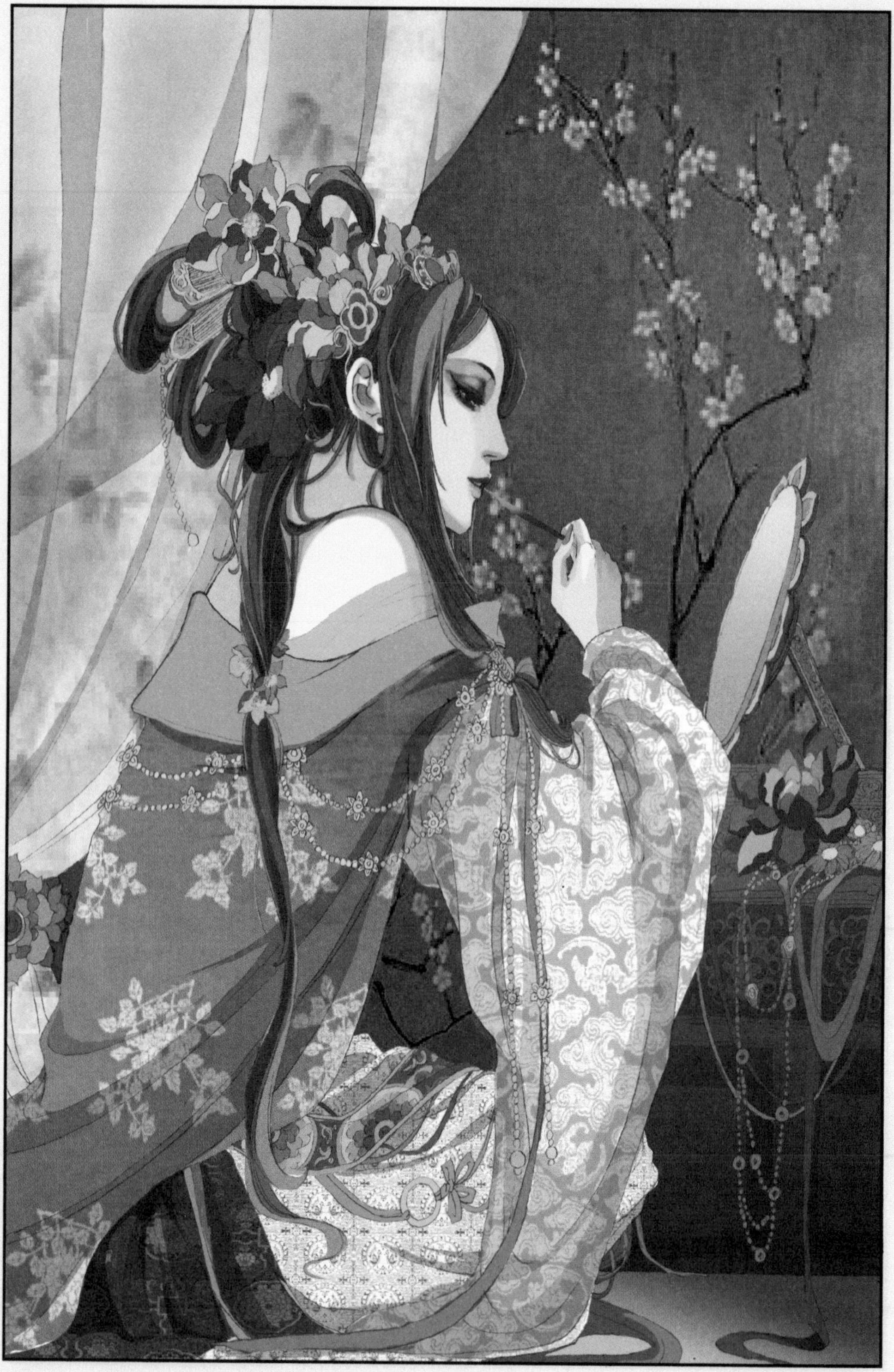

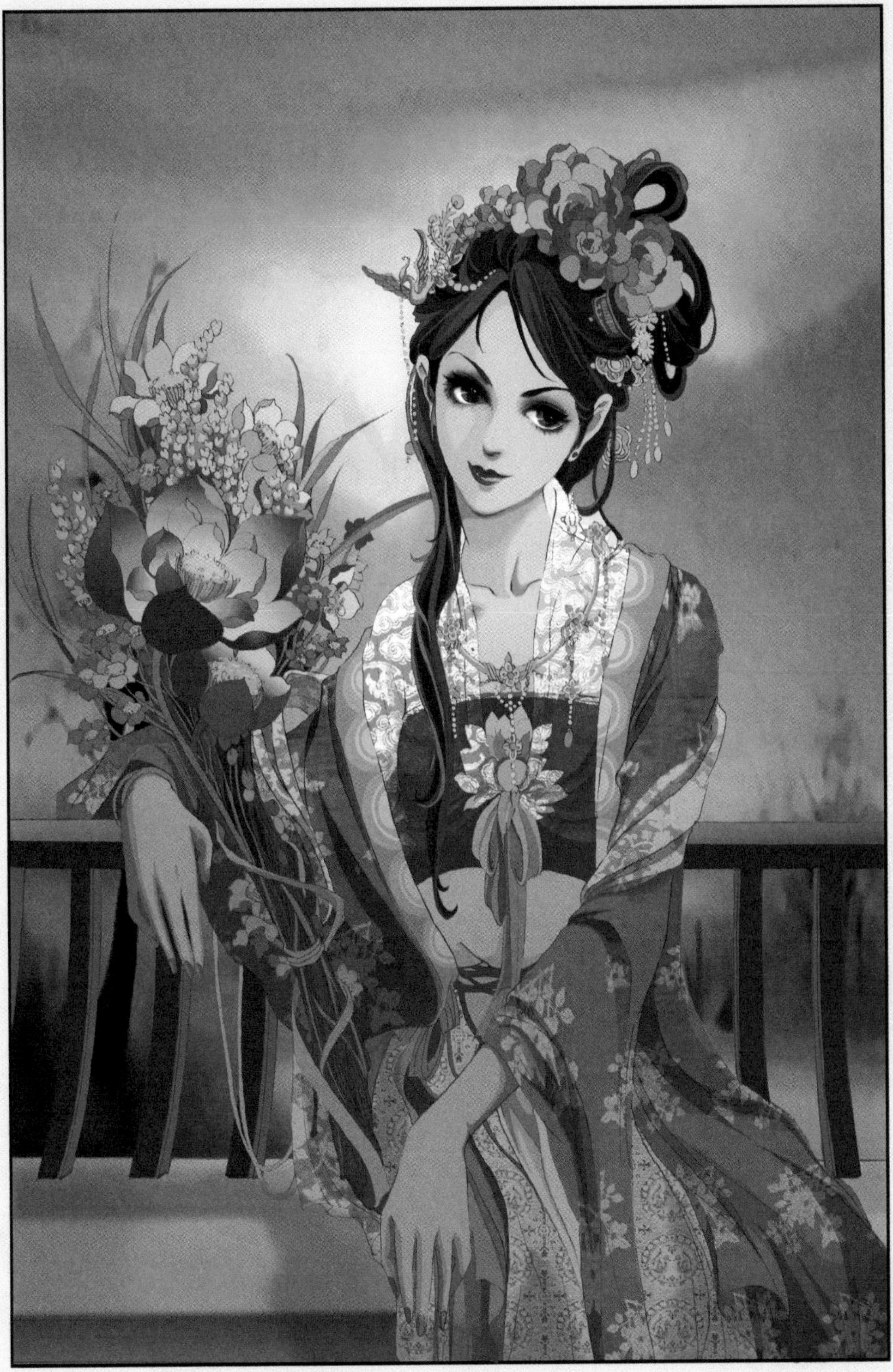

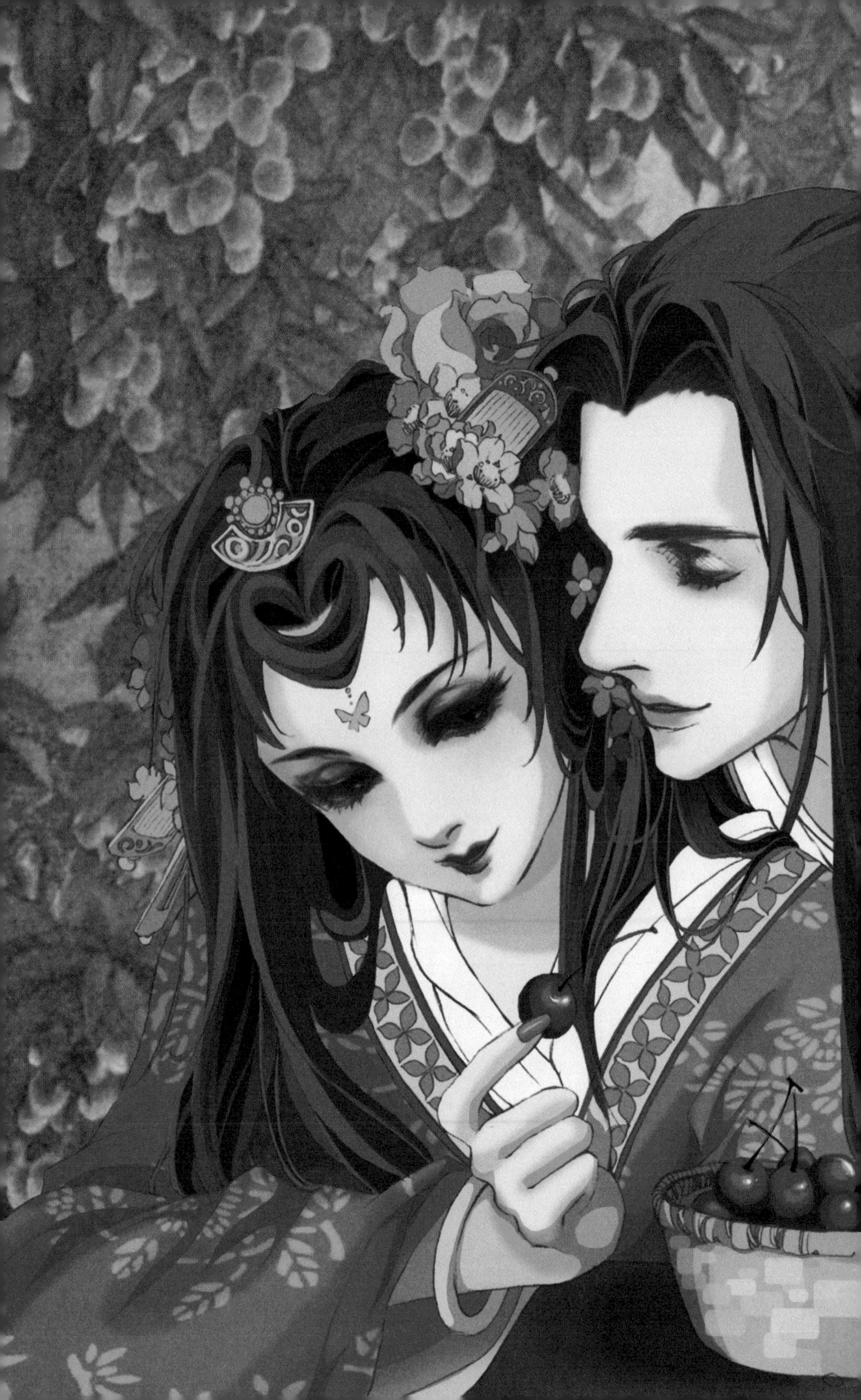

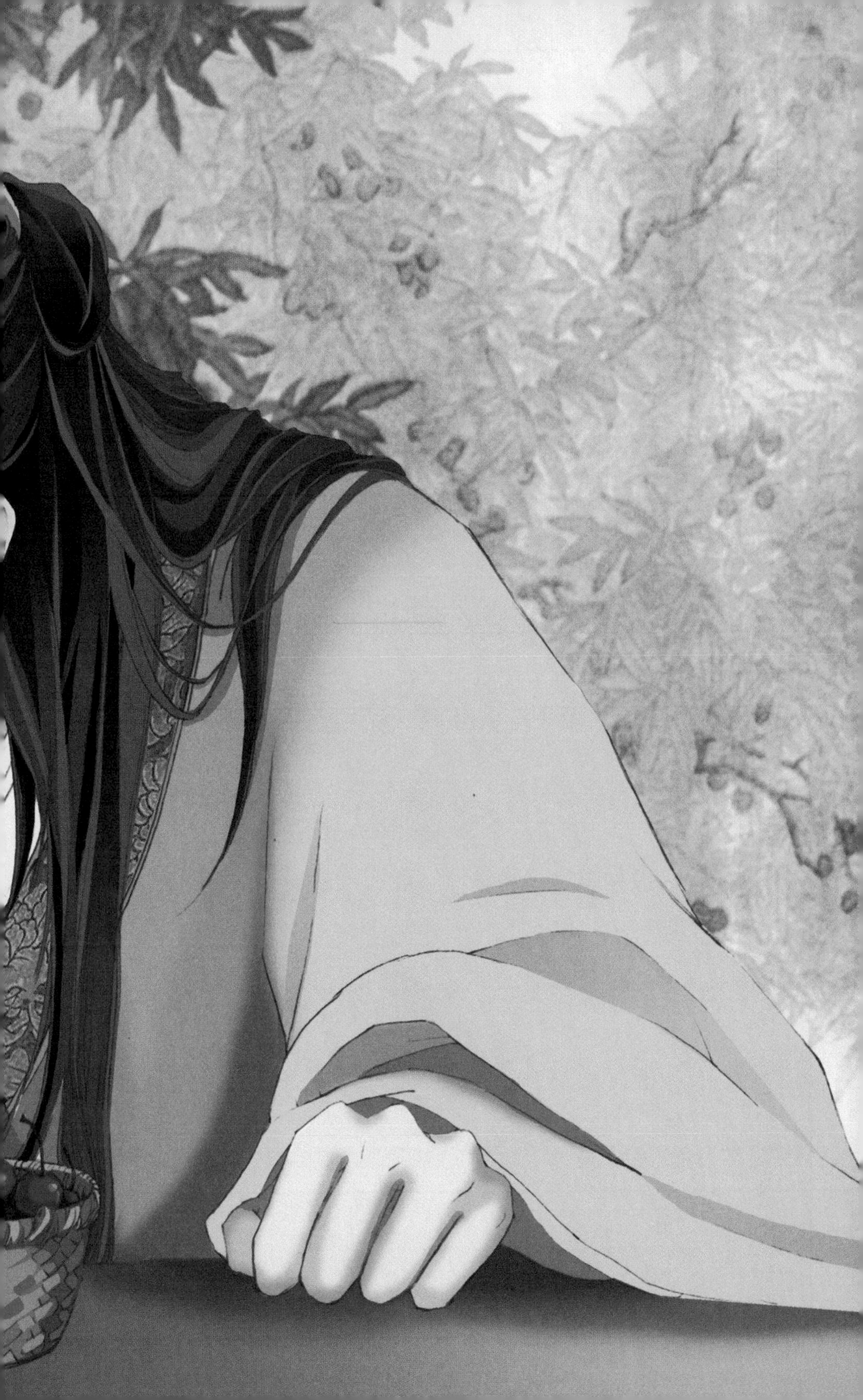

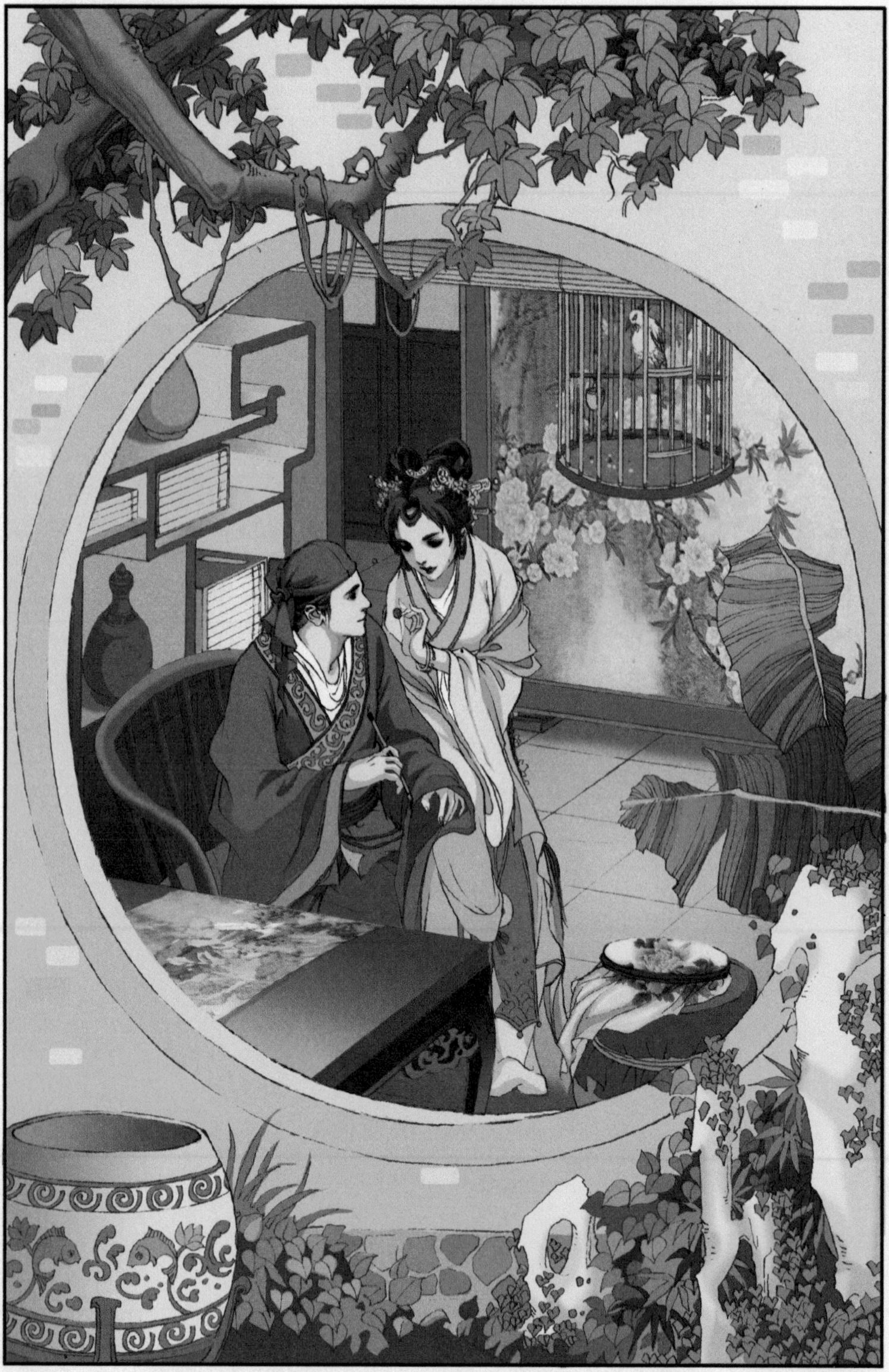

The History of the West Wing

SUN Jiayu

In 1980, SUN Jiayu entered the world of manhua. During that decade of the genre's renewal, he participated in a number of editorial projects. But it wasn't until 1992 that he created his first series, "The Seventy-Two Changes," followed two years later by "The Story of the Ancient Chinese Sages." Since 2000, he has produced more than ten comic book series with the Jing Ding Company studio, all published on the Chinese mainland.

Guo Guo

This young Chinese artist (real name: GUO Chaoxu) has a diploma from the University of Shanghai (majoring in costume design). This is her first graphic novel, which displays her exquisite mastery of art and especially color.

GuoGuo

The History of the West Wing

SUN Jiayu
Guo Guo

Translation: J. Gustave McBride   ◆   Lettering: Terri Delgado

Le Pavillon de l'Aile Ouest © XIAO PAN – Guo Guo – SUN Jiayu – 2007. All rights reserved.

English translation © 2009 by Hachette Book Group, Inc.

The characters and events in this book are fictitious. Any similarity to real persons, living or dead, is coincidental and not intended by the author.

Yen Press
Hachette Book Group
237 Park Avenue, New York, NY 10017

Visit our Web sites at www.HachetteBookGroup.com and www.YenPress.com.

Yen Press is an imprint of Hachette Book Group, Inc. The Yen Press name and logo are trademarks of Hachette Book Group, Inc.

First Yen Press Edition: May 2009

ISBN: 978-0-7595-2992-2

10 9 8 7 6 5 4 3 2 1

WOR

Printed in the United States of America